Santo Domingo:
Revolt of the Damned

Santo Domingo:
Revolt of the Damned

BY DAN KURZMAN

G. P. Putnam's Sons   New York

PRINTED IN THE UNITED STATES OF AMERICA

VAN REES PRESS • NEW YORK

To Cal and Pat

CONTENTS

Introduction

THE Dominican Republic, embracing part of a Caribbean
island and some 3.5 million people, is one of the smallest
countries in the world. But it has also become one of the most
important, with the crisis that exploded there in April 1965
having echoed throughout the globe with shattering force. Indeed, the smallness of the nation, in accentuating the massive-
ness of the American power that was brought to bear on it,
amplified the fears of a world wary of massive power in an age
of nuclear bombs and colonial liberation.

It was perhaps logical that the Dominican Republic should
have brought to a head the intensifying conflicts and contradic-
tions between American policy and Latin-American psychology
on the one hand, and among various aspects of American policy
on the other. For in that small country, many of Latin America's most serious economic, social, and political problems have
long simmered in concentrated form. In few hemispheric nations has a larger percentage of the population been economically worse off; in few has a smaller proportion received some
education, or been divided into classes more rigidly immobile;
and in few has dictatorship been as cruel and monolithic as that
which has brutalized the Dominicans.

9

When dictator Rafael Trujillo was assassinated in 1961, all the accumulated frustration and misery of the Dominican people, denied an outlet for decades by one of the most infamous police systems in history, suddenly sought expression. It was converted for a time, with the help of the Kennedy Administration, into a source of peaceful revolutionary energy released through democratic channels. But with the blocking of these channels in October 1963, when Juan Bosch, the nation's first freely elected President in more than 30 years, was ousted in a military coup after serving only seven months in office, the revolutionary pressures inevitably found the violent outlet of April 1965.

And therein lies a lesson to ponder. Revolution in Latin America, economic, social, and political, cannot be prevented or halted. The only question is whether it will be peaceful and democratic or violent and possibly Communist. Since violence can produce political revolution overnight, and since communism can spur social and economic revolution with maximum speed, in however distorted a context, this kind of revolution is likely to grow in appeal as the patience of people steeped for centuries in feudalism and oppression wears thin.

It is therefore in the interest of the United States to foster peaceful revolution, as envisaged by President Kennedy when he announced the Alliance for Progress, with all the stops pulled out. This means that, if necessary, the United States must intervene in individual Latin-American countries, but on the side of the revolutionaries against the status quo militarists and oligarchs. If Washington feels itself free to send troops into a nation to make sure the Communists don't take over, qualms about exerting maximum diplomatic and economic pressures on those who would create conditions favorable to Communist advances hardly seem justified.

In fact, only peaceful intervention of this type, it appears, can render less likely the violence that might again invite the armed brand of intervention that has taken place in the Dominican Republic at untold cost to American prestige in the hemisphere and the world.

In the event of such violence, however, two questions arise. First, should the United States intervene with armed force at all, particularly when the Communist role in the revolution is far from clear? And second, once such intervention is regarded as advisable, what should be the U. S. role in the revolution?

In the case of the Dominican Republic, it is difficult to judge whether the armed intervention was justified since the Johnson Administration insists it had undisclosable information—the information made public has not been convincing—that the Communists were seriously threatening to take over the country. What is clear, however, is that the United States tried to stop not just the Communists but the revolution itself.

This is the central conclusion that emerges from the details of the Dominican revolution as presented in this book. Aside from an account of these details, treated fully are the historical and psychological influences that produced both the revolution and the effort to thwart it.

But this book is intended as more than a report of past and current events. It is a study of tragically frustrated people on all sides, of cruel dictators and idealistic democrats, of bumbling, well-meaning diplomats and hungry peasants, of individuals seeking the same destiny, yet finding themselves at cross-purposes with each other. It is, fundamentally, the story of frightened men.

Most of the material presented in this book was obtained directly from conversations and experiences in the Dominican Republic. As a correspondent for *The Washington Post,* I visited the country several times in 1962, before, during and after the presidential election of Juan Bosch. I returned in 1963 following the coup d'état that ousted Bosch from office. And I went back again immediately after the 1965 revolution broke out.

I would like to thank the many people representing all sides in the crisis who gave me information that has been fitted into the mosaic of this book. In particular, I wish to thank some of my colleagues—Murrey Marder of *The Washington Post,* Leslie Whitten of Hearst Newspapers, Georgie Ann Geyer of the *Chicago Daily News,* John T. Skelly of the *Latin American Times,* and others.

DAN KURZMAN

Washington, D.C.

Santo Domingo:
Revolt of the Damned

CHAPTER 1

The Stick and the Stones

SOMEWHERE in cinematic China, William Holden was about to respond to a declaration of love by an inscrutable Oriental beauty when suddenly the lights went out.

"Darken the ship," boomed the vessel's loudspeaker. "The movie will continue down in the mess hall."

Immediately the marines and sailors who had been watching the film from wooden benches on deck made their way in the dark into the body of the LST.

The order lent weight to the feeling that this was to be no routine cruise. Shortly before, at about 6:50 on that warm evening of April 28, 1965, we had received our first hint when a signal was flashed to "close the coast, prepare to land."

The skipper of the LST, Lt. Commander James Robert Allingham, informed the 22 reporters and photographers aboard that this was the first time since the Cuban missile crisis in 1962 that he had received orders to flash such a signal. And almost before Bill Holden was given another chance to heed the advances of the Chinese damsel, the news came through over the radio that President Johnson had announced that over 400 marines had landed in the Dominican Republic to save the lives of Americans and other foreigners.

15

The newsmen aboard had all been stranded for two or three days in San Juan, Puerto Rico, trying to find some way to get into the Dominican Republic, where the airports had been closed since the civil war had started on April 24. Only that morning, with reports drifting in from Santo Domingo that the rebels supporting the return of exiled constitutional President Juan Bosch had surrendered, I had planned to return to Washington immediately, as suggested by my *Washington Post* editors. Indeed, I had not expected to be away for more than two or three days, figuring that the Dominican crisis, like most Latin-American coups and counter-coups, would be settled one way or the other within that period. My optimism was perhaps reflected in the fact that I left my car in a two-hour parking zone in downtown Washington.

But late in the afternoon of April 28, a naval officer phoned me at my hotel, as he did other correspondents, and said that I should be aboard the USS *Wood County* within an hour if I wanted to go to the Dominican Republic, adding, however, that there was no guarantee that the reporters would get ashore. As this LST was one of two that had arrived in San Juan from Santo Domingo that morning loaded with refugees, I assumed that the idea was to try to get us ashore while the vessel was picking up another batch of evacuees.

Actually, even before the naval officer called me I had begun to suspect that the reports of a rebel surrender may have been exaggerated. I had spoken that day, for one thing, to Lt. Colonel Manuel Rodríguez Negrón, the pilot of a DC-3 that had, with four crewmen, deserted the rightist anti-Boschists and flown to San Juan. Rodríguez Negrón, a stocky man with a thick, black moustache, said when I met him on arrival that anti-Bosch planes were "slaughtering the people," but that the situation at San Isidro Air Base, the rightist stronghold, was desperate. "There's no electricity, almost no food or gasoline. It will have to give up after a few days."

Shortly afterward, I spoke by telephone with an American

Embassy official in Santo Domingo who told me that the forces supporting Bosch were no longer under the control of his moderate, left-of-center Dominican Revolutionary Party (PRD), but were now being led by Communists. Then, on receiving the naval invitation, I telephoned Bosch at his home and asked him if he had any information about what was happening in Santo Domingo.

"I have just talked by phone with my military commanders," he said, "and they assured me that they still have control of the capital and that 10,000 men are still fighting with us and stopping Wessin's tanks from coming over Duarte Bridge. They say they will fight to the last man if necessary."

After checking this appraisal with the latest news reports from Santo Domingo, which indicated that the anti-Bosch forces led by General Elias Wessin y Wessin had only to mop up scattered Boschist remnants, I tended to regard Bosch's report as a wishful effort to buoy up a lost cause. Even so, his report, together with that of Negrón and the U. S. Embassy official, appeared to indicate that a chaotic situation might be developing. That evening, aboard the rocking LST, I learned I had erred indeed in leaving my car in a two-hour parking zone.

Late in the morning of April 29, the distant gray Dominican shore came into view, its lines broken by a scattering of U. S. naval vessels anchored in the vicinity. When our LST had come within about 30 yards of the aircraft carrier *Boxer,* a highline was set up connecting the two vessels and the reporters were transferred to the *Boxer* one by one in a chair that bobbed across the Caribbean waves. We were immediately led into a large stateroom where naval and marine officers confirmed to us over coffee that the mission of the marines was to protect Americans and other foreigners. The task force leader, Captain James A. Dare, added:

"As far as I know we don't intend to leave here until the establishment of a non-Communist government in the Dominican Republic is assured."

Thus were we offered our first indication that the United States had embarked on a tragic venture that was to produce over 100 American casualties, including some 25 dead, contribute to the death and wounding of over 2,000 Dominicans, shake the structure of hemispheric relations, and color the attitude of the whole world toward this country.

No one can say for certain that the Dominican Communists would or would not have come to power in the chaos that engulfed Santo Domingo on April 27 and 28. No one, in fact, can say for certain whether the Communists would come out on top in any popular revolution, since Communists inevitably try to exploit all revolutions, whoever starts them, and in most cases are more militant and better trained than non-Communist revolutionaries. If communism had been an organized force at the time of the American revolution, the Reds would certainly have tried to help George Washington in his struggle against the British.

Whether the Communist threat in Santo Domingo was great enough to justify so drastic a step as the sending of U. S. troops may be open to question in view of the lack of unity, numerical strength, and quality leadership among the Dominican Communists. But an argument, at least, can be made for their dispatch on the grounds that it is better to be safe than sorry. And while it would seem logical that since the U. S. government went so far as to offer unchecked lists of Communists to the press as evidence that they controlled the revolution it would have little other evidence of a more substantial nature in its files, one cannot dismiss the explanation of Thomas C. Mann, Undersecretary of State for Economic Affairs, that "the kind of proof the public demands involves breaking up your intelligence sources."

In any event, the original reason given for the landings—the need to protect American and other foreign nationals during a period of chaos—is hard to refute. Chaos did exist, and foreigners were threatened and without protection, though this has often been the case in many other countries where the United States has not considered sending troops; and though one might find puzzling the dispatch of one serviceman per ten Santo Domingans to assure such protection.

It is therefore fruitless to ponder the wisdom of the U. S. decision to dispatch troops under the circumstances that existed at the time of the decision. What can be challenged is, first, the U. S. role in creating these circumstances, and second, the U. S. policy which the troops, once ashore, were ordered to follow. On both counts, American officials appear to have committed their worst blunders since the Bay of Pigs, blunders that contributed enormously to the Communist cause that was meant to be contained by American actions.

First of all, prior to the revolt, the American Embassy seemed to have collected little information of the gathering storm. It appeared to realize neither the extent to which the Dominican people desired constitutionalism after experiencing over 30 years of terroristic rule under assassinated dictator Rafael Trujillo, nor the extent to which the followers of Juan Bosch had made inroads in the army since Bosch was ousted from office by the military in September 1963 after serving for seven months as one of the first freely elected presidents in Dominican history.

According to leaders of Bosch's Dominican Revolutionary Party, U. S. Embassy officials, particularly Ambassador W. Tapley Bennett, Jr., had seldom contacted them or showed much sympathy for their constitutional cause, despite the fact that the party had won an overwhelming majority of votes in the 1963 election that shot Bosch to power. U. S. officials denied that their contacts with and interest in the PRD had been unsubstantial. But some of these same officials agreed that they were caught by surprise, even lacking adequate information on the backgrounds of some of the top rebel leaders. When the rebellion broke out, Bennett was visiting his mother in Georgia, and 11 of the 13 of the U. S. military mission were in Panama for a routine conference.

Moreover, the Embassy apparently failed to evaluate correctly the little intelligence it did receive. Officials told me they did have some reports of a pending Boschist move, in fact that it was to have been made shortly before it actually was. But, they argued, they receive a constant stream of reports about planned coups and revolutions and this was simply one of them.

When the revolt broke out the United States viewed it with grave misgivings, even before the Communists began to show their hand. It spurned Bosch, the elected leader of the people, and thereby encouraged Wessin to resist the constitutional movement. No U. S. official even contacted Bosch before American troops landed. Yet, only a year and a half before, the United States, under President Kennedy, had publicly deplored Bosch's overthrow as a bitter blow to democracy in Latin America. It had cut off diplomatic and economic relations with the succeeding government for months. Now Bosch was an undesirable man and those who had deposed him were about to become U. S. allies in a joint effort to frustrate his return.

As the war gained momentum, the United States had another chance to foster peace. On September 28, the rebel leaders, including Colonel Francisco Caamaño Deñó, voluntarily came to the American Embassy and, feeling they had lost the war, asked Ambassador Bennett to help mediate the conflict. They were ready, they said, to agree to Wessin's terms—the establishment of a military junta to be followed in several months by a free election. But Bennett said he had no authority to mediate. The rebel leaders walked out in a rage, and some of them, including Caamaño, decided to fight "to the last man." Miraculously, the "beaten" rebel forces, propelled in part, ironically enough, by the words of Ambassador Bennett, pushed back the enemy and were winning when the first U. S. troops landed the next day.

Once Bennett called for U. S. armed intervention, the Administration gave the order to land marines without first consulting the Organization of American States, many of whose members regard intervention by one country in the affairs of another, for whatever reason, as the worst crime a fellow member could commit. This neglect has threatened to split the OAS and undo all the efforts made by U. S. Administrations in the last few decades to obliterate the long-held popular Latin-American image of an "imperialistic" United States dedicated to "gunboat diplomacy."

Then, as soon as American troops started to pour into Santo Domingo, the United States, at least on the surface, appeared to justify the fears of Latin-American countries trying to promote political democracy in the hemisphere. It officially declared itself neutral in the Dominican dispute. Unofficially, however, it strongly backed the junta set up by the Wessin forces in every possible way, using the junta's request for U. S. help, in fact, as a "legal" excuse for the landings.

Instead of peacefully soliciting the cooperation of rebel leaders in creating an International Safety Zone, marines, helped by junta troops, stormed into rebel-held territory by force. U. S. troops also drove through rebel territory to form a corridor from Santo Domingo to San Isidro Air Base about ten miles away, thereby splitting the rebel forces in two. But the U. S. forces were inactive, even helpful to the junta, when its troops began taking over the rebel-held area in the northern industrial sector of the city. At the same time, junta troops, at least in the first several weeks, could cross into the International Safety Zone at will, while rebel forces were denied such freedom.

No less aggravating to the rebels was the employment by the United States of McCarthyite techniques to justify the dispatch of an enormous American force, which included 22,000 troops and 8,000 sailors manning some 40 ships, to Santo Domingo. Instead of simply pointing to the Communist danger inherent in chaos, it issued lists of people it branded as Communists without checking them—the lists had to be periodically changed as reporters punched holes in them—or offering evidence that the accused persons "controlled," or even participated in, the revolution as charged by the Administration. This policy presented the Communist bloc with highly potent propaganda fuel for use in countries where McCarthyism is still remembered as one of the more odious aspects of recent American history.

As a result of U. S. policy both before and after American troops landed, varying degrees of anti-Americanism have taken root among people who, psychologically crippled by decades, indeed centuries, of political oppression, feel that the United States cheated them of a freedom that had at long last been within their grasp. The Dominicans had learned the meaning of freedom for the first time during the seven months that Juan Bosch ruled as constitutional president in 1963. But they had only fully appreciated what it meant when Bosch was ousted, to be replaced by a military-influenced civilian junta. Finally they had the opportunity to get Bosch back, and they were thwarted.

If the U. S. forces had stepped in to crush only what Washington considered a Communist threat, many Dominicans ask, why did these troops not bring Bosch back to guarantee that the revolution, which was rooted in the same principles as the American revolution, would have democratic leadership instead of trying to put down the revolt itself in partnership with the hated militarists? The answer, these Dominicans conclude, whatever the true American logic may be, is that the Johnson Administration is distrustful of the political democracy and social reform that had been so meticulously nurtured by the Kennedy regime, and would prefer to see a rightist authoritarian government in power.

The irony is that if Washington committed important blunders in the Dominican crisis, it acted with the best of intentions, having been stampeded into unfortunate decisions by a panicky, ill-informed Embassy. Its action did not represent any new policy based on "gunboat diplomacy." It sent troops into the Dominican Republic not as a routine matter, but in a situation which it saw, rightly or wrongly, as desperate, and did so with

great reluctance and misgivings. It did so because it thought
it had no choice.

United States policy is still fundamentally geared to the pro-
motion of political democracy and social reform, contrary to
America's policy only a few years ago. It can be argued that
the Johnson Administration's tactics in achieving such aims are
too sluggish and unimaginative, and even foolish, but tactics
should be distinguished from strategy and goals. The decision
not to support the return of Bosch to his homeland despite the
fact that he was the popularly elected constitutional President
may seem deplorable to many democrats. But however questionable the Administration's logic, it was rooted, not in the
old disdain for Latin democratic development, but in a conditioned fear that perhaps the Communists could use him. Despite
their good intentions, and for all the progress they have made
in recent years in the fashioning of a new, progressive hemispheric policy, U. S. officials are still prone to view right-wing
military cliques, however undesirable, as a more certain bul-
wark against communism than the democratic governments they
wish to develop.

Diplomats and politicians simply don't like to gamble, especially since Cuba, where communism and the Caribbean are
concerned. And they view democracy, unless backed up by the
traditional militarists with experience in handling Communists—even though these militarists might sometimes deal with
them—as a gamble. This underscores the heart of the U. S.
dilemma. Can it trust democracy to stand up to communism if
the army no longer has ultimate control of national policy?

Whatever the answer, it is clear that the United States wishes
to promote democracy in Latin America to the degree it can
without taking what it considers a gamble. Whether it would
really be taking the gamble it thinks it would is another issue.
Many observers believe that the alternative is a much greater
gamble, since U. S. support for right-wing groups, even for
tactical purposes, simply breeds more and more Communists

among people losing faith in democracy. But this view does
not bring into question the enlightened intentions of U. S.
hemispheric policy, only the psychology directing its implemen-
tation.

However, good intentions don't necessarily make for good
policy—or good friends. In Santo Domingo, where U. S. troops
were concentrated, I seldom found either deep bitterness or
unrestrained glee among the people, whether from the pro-
Bosch or anti-Bosch communities, but usually a conditional
hostility. On the veranda of his room in the American-protected
Hotel Embajador, a young Dominican politician who fled to
the hotel after rebel extremists threatened his life said: "As a
man who selfishly wants to live, I am glad the American
troops are here. But as a nationalist, I deplore their presence."

A waiter in a small dingy coffee house that recently reopened
in the rebel-controlled Ciudad Nueva in downtown Santo
Domingo said from behind the counter as I sipped a cup of
strong Latin coffee: "If the troops hadn't come Wessin would
probably have taken over the whole city. But why do you have
to take sides against us?"

A businessman told me amid the comfort of his sprawling,
garden-surrounded home as we sat by a large open window
watching marines stroll by: "We now have a split image of you
Americans. On the one hand, you are generous, peace-loving
people who understand freedom. And on the other, you are
people with rifles and steel helmets and grenades—symbols of
force."

These three views are typical of the mixed answers one gets
when he tries to discover popular reaction in Santo Domingo
to the U. S. military occupation. Many Dominicans who opposed the Boschists reluctantly supported the U. S. military
presence as a guarantee of their personal safety.

Some rebels as well were not overly unhappy about the troop
landings since they were uncertain that they could defeat Wessin's superior military force, though many claimed that without

U. S. interference they could have beaten Wessin. In any event, it was not the fact that American troops landed that greatly disturbed the constitutionalists. Rather, they were disturbed by what for a long time was America's clear identification with the enemy side, the side of the traditional militarists and oligarchs that had throughout history suppressed the great majority of people.

However, their feeling appeared to be less one of anger than of disillusionment. For most of the rebels I met maintained that they had always admired the United States for its democratic system, and could not understand why it opposed the rebel demand that constitutionalism, as symbolized by Bosch, be restored in the Dominican Republic.

But whatever tactical considerations may have eased the pain of Dominicans as they watched the uniformed, gun-bearing men of a foreign country give orders in their sovereign homeland, this pain remained, and grew as peace and normalcy gradually set in again. After every incident of death or destruction in which U. S. forces were involved, more and more Dominicans became embittered.

Take, for example, Antonio Jiménez Dajer, who was at home with his three sons, twelve, fourteen, and fifteen, on April 30 when several marines climbed on his roof in search of snipers who were shooting at American forces in the area. Jiménez and his sons lay terror-stricken on a mattress in his bedroom during the fire fight when the father got up to answer the telephone in the next room. Suddenly an explosion rocked the house. Jiménez rushed back to the bedroom and saw his sons lying dead or dying on the blood-drenched mattress. A grenade had accidentally fallen into the room through an open window while a marine was climbing to the roof.

"Oh my God, my God," the grieving father cried as marines, some of them in tears, patted him on the back trying to console him. "Why did this have to happen?"

This same question is being asked by Evelyn Gómez, a beautiful twenty-year-old Dominican girl I met as she ran weeping from her apartment after marines seeking snipers yelled at her from bushes across the street to leave immediately. She made the mistake of locking her door as she dashed out. When she finally returned home after marine bullets had peppered the building—without getting the sniper they suspected was there —she found the door broken open and full of bullet holes. Inside, bullets had defaced the walls. One had damaged a painting of Christ, going right through the heart.

In the first few weeks of occupation, dozens of such incidents occurred daily in Santo Domingo, where no house or shop was outside the periphery of the battlefield. In some cases, particularly along the edges of the international zone, where machine-gun emplacements were set up at many street corners, every apartment in a block of buildings was searched and broken into. When a sniper was thought to have been located, a barrage of fire often destroyed all or part of the structure.

U. S. military leaders, while expressing regret for such action, explained that they had to take measures they considered necessary to protect themselves and the populace in general from sniper fire. Troops were given orders to look for the key before they broke down any door, and compensation was promised for all damage done.

But this did not pacify the rage, calm the fear, or lessen the misery of the Dominican people. Nor was their bitterness diluted by the need to submit to an intensive search, conducted by U. S. troops with guns at the ready, each time they left or entered the International Safety Zone established by the G. I.'s. To the Dominican, whatever side he was on, commands given in a foreign tongue were bringing home with increasing agony the extent of his nation's humiliation—and the U. S. role in it.

Moreover, in view of the difficulty in distinguishing friend from foe, there was little fraternization between the troops and the population so that Dominicans might have learned about the Americans as people rather than as professional soldiers. Occasionally one saw young women of a questionable trade loitering near checkpoints trying to catch the eye of a serviceman. And sometimes the troops waved and smiled at girls as they passed by in trucks, usually to be greeted in kind. Also, many Dominican spectators watched from fenced-off areas as U. S. teams played baseball in their bivouac fields. In one case, when I saw a young, raggedly dressed Dominican boy sleeping on the floor of a U. S.-occupied house next to a marine, an officer explained that the waif was a "mascot," but that this was not for publication in view of the nonfraternization policy. That was about the extent of informal communication.

Actually, anti-Americanism appeared to be considerably stronger in the provinces than in Santo Domingo. For the tragedies that occurred in the capital were highly exaggerated by the time news reached the outlying areas. This was particularly so during the first several weeks of the U. S. occupation when Radio Santo Domingo was in rebel hands, and reported constantly of supposed American-perpetrated rapes, murders, and looting. In other words, the provincial people couldn't see for themselves.

"Things sure have changed in the last couple of weeks," a young blond-haired Peace Corpsman said in one northern town about two weeks after the first marines landed. "Before, we were very popular. Now people won't even talk to us."

The youth was one of several Peace Corps members who had been teaching boys and girls in the area modern farming methods—before the troops arrived. When I, and several other reporters, visited them, they were to a large extent isolated from the Dominican community.

"Our pupils are scared to work with us," the blond youth, who wore a T-shirt and jeans, said. "It isn't considered proper now to associate with Americans."

This revelation was consistent with impressions we received during a 250-mile tour of the lush central region of the country

from Santo Domingo in the south to Santiago in the north.
Whether we stopped off in shanty villages composed of board,
tin-roofed cabins, or in Spanish-colonial towns steeped proudly,
if pathetically, in a past symbolized by brightly painted, once
elegant houses with shutters and balconies, the evidence appeared to indicate overwhelming support for the Boschist forces
led by Caamaño. Almost uniformly, only deprecating comment
could be heard about the opposition junta led by General Antonio Imbert Barreras, who succeeded Wessin as head of the
anti-Bosch forces.

Likewise, as we bumped along narrow, rocky roads that led
through rice-green valleys hemmed in by thickly wooded hills,
workers, professional men, shopkeepers, farmers, and waiters
almost sounded like a single voice on a phonograph record,
with only members of the small upper middle class, mostly businessmen, appearing to dissent.

"Caamaño represents the people because he is the constitutional President."

"The militarists have always exploited the people."

"We expected the Americans to support us, but they turned
against us."

"We are not Communists, because communism is slavery.
We are simply hungry."

Perhaps these sentiments were phrased differently in each
case, but their substance remained constant throughout the
trip, and was occasionally underscored by cries of "Caamaño,
Caamaño" as we passed through villages announcing with large
painted letters spelling PRENSA on our windshield that we represented the press.

Most people didn't seem to know much about Caamaño personally, but they knew he had succeeded Juan Bosch as constitutional President, and this made him, they said, their leader.
Even illiterate ditch diggers we stopped to talk with along the
road, unlike many of their counterparts in other underdeveloped countries, displayed a deep sense of involvement in their

nation's politics. Why did the Constitution mean so much to them?

"Because," answered a gaunt, unshaven man dressed in torn trousers and a dirty blue shirt, "the Constitution will give us freedom and bread."

Stating what appeared to be the minority view in the places we visited, a small-town banker said he was "glad the Americans have come to save the country from communism."

The Peace Corpsmen—all asked to remained unidentified— estimated that 90 percent of the people in their town harbored pro-Caamaño sentiments. They said that only the few relatively wealthy people in the town supported the Imbert regime.

So strongly did most people back the constitutional forces, they said, that many, when the revolution began, commandeered trucks and drove to Santo Domingo in the hope of obtaining arms there and joining the fight against the militarists. In other towns we visited, including Santiago and Salcedo, people we met—sometimes we were encircled by scores at a time—told us similar stories. In Salcedo, some men, when they returned home from Santo Domingo, were jailed for about 24 hours by author- ities loyal to the armed forces. If the people had arms, we were told many times, they would all have stormed into Santo Do- mingo, at least before American troops arrived.

"The United States probably doesn't realize it," said a doctor in Santiago who proclaimed himself anti-Bosch but pro-Con- stitution, "but it has taken on the whole Dominican people— and ironically, after teaching them what constitutional gov- ernment means."

According to the Peace Corpsmen, Dominicans in their town were actually hoping for the arrival of American troops in Santo Domingo when Wessin's planes were bombing rebel strongholds early in the revolution. But when they did land, the youths said, there was tremendous disillusionment as the result of U. S. iden- tification with the hated Wessin forces and charges that the constitutional movement was Communist-led.

"Suddenly people began to say 'Yankee, go home' and 'Get out of here.' They threw rocks at the house and old friends stopped seeing us," said one Corpsmen in the simply furnished living room of his small, wooden, cabinlike house, which he shared with two other Americans. "Those who have continued to visit us are continually harassed," he said. "Even our maid is insulted. They call her *la gringa* [an unfriendly word for American]."

The youths, who during the first two weeks of the revolution were unable to communicate with the outside world due to a local government cutoff of electricity ("in order to control the people better"), said their best chance for psychological reinstatement in the eyes of the people lay in the fact that they had not evacuated.

"The people are surprised that we are still here despite the danger and the way we are treated," one said. "And I think they respect us for it."

At any rate, a few weeks later, after the United States indicated interest in establishing some form of constitutional government, the youths reported that people had stopped throwing rocks at them, and that some Dominicans had even started visiting them again, though, as one put it, "Anti-Americanism is still strong, just not as violent as before."

A possible upshot of this anti-Americanism is that it may be impossible for any future regime to govern in the Dominican Republic that does not ostentatiously display its independence of American policy. And as a corollary, the Dominican Communists, whatever their number or influence when the crisis started, may very likely gain strength simply by feeding on popular antagonism toward the United States, which previously had been very popular among the Dominicans.

But the repercussions of Washington's action in the Dominican Republic have by no means been limited to that country. They have been felt throughout the world, and particularly in Latin America, where almost all of the democratic countries have indicated strong disapproval of the U. S. intervention. As a result, the Organization of American States, to which all independent Latin-American countries except Cuba belong, has been seriously weakened and the United States highly embarrassed. On the one hand, Washington can find full support for its policy, with few exceptions, only among the Latin-American nations with dictatorial or semidictatorial governments. And on the other hand, by taking action it had deemed necessary to halt Communist subversion in the hemisphere it impaired the hemispheric unity it has always considered a vital factor in the struggle against communism.

And indeed, the OAS had moved a long way toward unity since the First International American Conference was held in Washington in 1890 for the purpose of setting up the Commercial Bureau of the American Republics, which was eventually to develop into the present organization. The OAS had voted unanimously to support U. S. policy during the Cuban missile crisis of 1962, and it had voted to require all members to break off diplomatic and economic relations with Cuba in July 1964, with only Mexico refusing to obey.

The Dominican Republic was another story. First, the United States neglected to consult with OAS members before acting. Second, the United States violated the cherished Article 17 of the OAS Charter, which reads: "The territory of a state is inviolable; it may not be the object, even temporarily, of military occupation or of other measures of force taken by another state, directly or indirectly, on any grounds whatsoever." Third, the United States appeared to take sides with a military dictatorship against a popular revolution that some Latin-American countries are reluctant to believe was seriously threatened by communism. Did such action mean, these countries asked, that the United States would try to crush any popular revolution that might break out against an unconstitutional government on the grounds that it could be infiltrated by Communists? Or worse, did it mean that the United States would not hesitate to send troops to any country where it believed its interests were being threatened—interests that might not always coincide with those of Latin-American countries? Was this the substance of what was rapidly becoming known as the "Johnson Doctrine"?

The concept of nonintervention has deep roots in Latin America. It was born of a fear of U. S. intervention instilled in the Latin mind for more than a hundred years. Latin Americans are suspicious of U. S. private investments, of U. S. government economic aid, of U. S. military missions. Engraved in the Latin memory is President Theodore Roosevelt's "big stick" policy, the U. S. annexation of Mexican territory, the U. S. marine occupations of Haiti in 1915, the Dominican Republic in 1916, and Nicaragua in 1927. Nor is it forgotten that the marines had fostered the rise of dictator Rafael Trujillo in the Dominican Republic and of dictator Anastasio Somoza in Nicaragua.

Anti-American sentiment, therefore, mushroomed in Latin America following the troop landings. Newspapers, political leaders, and labor officials condemned the action in a rising crescendo of criticism. A banner carried by a demonstrator in Buenos Aires read typically: SEND THE ARGENTINE ARMY TO SELMA, ALABAMA, TO PROTECT THE LIVES OF AMERICAN NEGROES. In Venezuela, the Communists, who have been trying to overthrow the democratic government there through terroristic and guerrilla means, are reported to have registered major propaganda gains as the result of growing anti-Americanism. At the same time, Venezuelan militarists and rightists, the government fears, will take heart from American support of anti-Boschist elements in Santo Domingo and try to overthrow the government and set up a junta of their own.

Former Venezuelan President Rómulo Betancourt, a vigorous democrat and anti-Communist, charged in a speech in New York that the U. S. intervention had dealt a "hard blow" to the hemispheric juridical system. "This erroneous step," he said, "could be transformed into a political defeat of unpredictable scope for the United States, and the death certificate for the Organization of American States if the result . . . is the installation . . . of a rightist military dictatorship." He added, obviously apprehensive about possible new U. S. moves elsewhere, that "popular rebellions are being incubated" in all Latin-American countries "where usurping governments exist."

This hemispheric conflict was dramatically reflected in the struggle that has been tearing at the fabric of OAS unity in meetings held in Washington. Well aware of the bitterness engendered among Latins by Washington's unilateral action in the Dominican Republic, President Johnson hoped to remove some of the onus from the United States by obtaining substantial support from the OAS. But U. S.-backed resolutions to increase OAS participation in the peacemaking and occupation machinery in that country were passed after the most intense debate with the barest possible majority—14 of the 20 member votes. And to muster this number, the United States had to push hard for the continued seating in the OAS Council of the Dominican Ambassador, who represented the pre-revolution regime and was kept on by the junta, though the United States said it recognized neither the junta nor the rebel government.

The Administration appeared to have won a victory of sorts when a proposal for the establishment of an Inter-American Peace Force for the Dominican Republic was approved by this minimal majority after President Johnson pleaded that "we need new international machinery geared to meet fast-moving events," particularly Communist subversion. But months after the peace force was set up only four Latin-American countries—Brazil, Nicaragua, Honduras, and Costa Rica—had contributed a total of less than 2,000 troops to it. And of these, the first three are run by authoritarian governments and the fourth, democratic Costa Rica, which dispatched 19 policemen, agreed to participate, not because it supported American policy, but in the hope of diluting this policy.

In other countries that voted for the peace force, criticism from the legislatures, press, and public opinion has delayed or canceled plans for troop contributions. In Argentina the legislature even passed a resolution condemning the U. S. intervention. On the other hand, almost all reformist democratic Latin-American countries—Chile, Uruguay, Peru, and Mexico—voted against the proposal in the first place, and Venezuela abstained.

The United States thus found itself on the side of the dictators and oligarchs in opposition to the kind of government that President Kennedy promoted and President Johnson has said he wishes to promote in Latin America.

Furthermore, if agreement on an inter-American force in the Dominican Republic was achieved only after the most intense diplomatic maneuvering, many Latin-American leaders are reluctant to see a standby force established on a permanent basis, as desired by President Johnson. For even some of those who finally approved the Dominican resolution are wary about how an inter-American force would be used and commanded and under what political circumstances it would be sent into action. And they were not comforted by remarks attributed to Lt. General Bruce Palmer, commander of the U. S. troops in the Dominican Republic, that the United States was keeping tactical control of the Inter-American Peace Force despite the appointment of Brazilian General Hugo Panasco Alvim as commander of this force. Palmer said that he would continue to decide which troops to use, how to use them, and when to use them in carrying out the OAS mission.

"If the OAS and the U. S. government get into a policy conflict," he said, "I would have to follow the guidance of my government."

But if the United States has continued to run things in Santo Domingo under the banner of the OAS, the Administration is not very happy about the sluggishness of Latin cooperation. The failure of the OAS to act decisively in the Dominican crisis, U. S. officials have said, may permanently impair its effectiveness. The OAS, in these dangerous times, cannot afford to be a "do-nothing" group. It can regain its prestige and self-respect only by acting swiftly to establish a full-fledged Inter-American Peace Force or at least to move in that direction, perhaps starting off with a Caribbean Peace Force.

But in the eyes of many Latin Americans, the United States wants an OAS that is not just more responsive to hemispheric crises, but to U. S. policy in the solving of these crises. They view the situation in a reverse light. They feel that the OAS can only enhance its prestige and self-respect if the United States takes into greater consideration the desires of the Latin-American nations and stops trying to mold the OAS into a rubber-stamp organization.

Certainly there is a lot to be said for the establishment of a permanent multilateral force to act swiftly in future emergencies. But the U. S. unilateral action in the Dominican Republic seems, if anything, to have damaged the possibilities of setting up such a force, at least in the true multilateral sense. For such a force to be established and to be meaningful once it is, it would be necessary to convince the Latin-American nations, particularly the democratic ones, that the United States is genuinely prepared to abide by the decision of the majority on whether or how to act; that it won't simply use the force as an instrument to legitimatize action that it intended to take regardless of the majority attitude. Even under such conditions some Latin-American countries would be reluctant to go along with a peace force, fearing that the United States would use the necessary economic pressure to squeeze out the votes it wanted. But if the establishment of such a force is to have any chance at all, the United States, it would appear, must start off by abandoning the unilateral spirit it exhibited in Santo Domingo.

Even less willing than some OAS members to approve U. S. policy has been the United Nations, which sent a special representative to the Dominican Republic shortly after the Americans landed despite U. S. efforts to keep the world organization, which

it cannot control, out of the country. The United States and the
OAS, which resents what it considers an invasion of its prerogatives, have shown considerable irritation with the reports sent
to Secretary-General U Thant by José Antonio Mayobre, the
special representative. These reports have criticized U. S. policy,
including troop activities that Mayobre has considered partisan
and illegal. But many Security Council members have favored
Mayobre's continued presence in Santo Domingo since it has
appeared to moderate the American intervention.

This UN concern with American behavior in the Dominican
Republic reflects the critical attitude of many countries around
the world toward the intervention. In Sweden, the semiofficial
Stockholmstidningen said, "Not in a long time has American
prestige stood so low among the democracies." The British *Man-
chester Guardian* declared in an editorial that the U. S. intervention "invites comparison with the intervention by the Rus-
sians in Budapest in 1956." French Ambassador Roger Seydoux
told the Security Council that the American intervention "seems
to be exercised against those who stand by constitutional
legality," and called for a rapid withdrawal of U. S. troops.
Algeria's government-controlled press service accused the United
States of "gunboat diplomacy," which it said was "not a new
element in American foreign policies if one takes into account
the previous interventions against Panama, Nicaragua, Honduras, Cuba, the Congo, and Viet-Nam." The Syrian Foreign
Ministry said the Damascus government was "deeply concerned
over . . . this aggressive U. S. action, which threatens world peace
as well as the sovereignty and independence of small nations."

And the Communist bloc, of course, has made the most of
the Dominican situation. Russia has used the UN as a sounding
board for charges of American "imperialism," though it has
failed to get the Security Council to formally condemn the U. S.
action. And Cuban Premier Fidel Castro has warned other
Latin-American states that by acquiescing to the intervention

in the Dominican Republic they might invite the risk of seeing marines land in their own territories at some future time. Every people, he said, "may make the revolution it deems most convenient."

To many Latin Americans who long for an end to feudalism and military oppression, such words, in the context of the U. S. effort to contain the Dominican revolution, seem reasonable.

CHAPTER 2

Hell and the Land of God

To UNDERSTAND the revolution that has racked the Dominican Republic it is necessary to understand the historical forces that have made it inevitable. In my travels around the world, which have included visits to almost every underdeveloped country, I have seldom found people who have longed as ardently for democratic political rule as the Dominicans. The reason would appear to be, fundamentally, that few countries have been chained to as ruthless and violent a past as the Dominican Republic, a past that has alternated bitterly between chaos and revolution on the one hand and terroristic dictatorship on the other.

If Juan Bosch had never come to power, it is possible that the Dominicans would be satisfied with somewhat less genuine democracy, not having experienced the real thing. But Bosch did come to power and, whatever shortcomings may be attributed to him, he gave the people complete freedom. For one of the first times in Dominican history, no political prisoners languished in jail; people could say what they wanted; the press could print what it wanted. Bosch spoiled his people. After experiencing such liberty they could never again quietly acquiesce to what had once been the normal expectation of life—oppression, uncertainty, hopelessness.

Bosch's policy offered the appearance of being "soft" on communism, since no one, including Communists, who did not disobey the law or indulge in violence could be jailed or punished under his regime. But in fact, Bosch was building the most powerful kind of barrier to communism—an almost fanatical devotion by the people to democracy and a correspondingly strong resistance to any kind of totalitarianism, whether of the right or the left. It was this popular attitude that accounted for the intense shock felt by most Dominicans when the United States attempted to stop a revolution they had felt was modeled after America's own.

This attempt cruelly recalled their tormented history, which began on January 4, 1493, when Christopher Columbus sighted the part of the Caribbean island of Hispaniola (the other part is Haiti) that the native Indians called Quisqueya, today known as the Dominican Republic.

"There, in that high and mountainous land, is the land of God," Columbus commented on September 12, 1504, when he was about to depart from the island for the fourth and final time. But before he left he was to set in motion a cycle of ungodly brutality that was to plague inhabitants for the next several centuries.

Shortly after his arrival, he wrote in a journal, of the Indians: "They bear no arms, and all are unprotected and so very cowardly that a thousand would not face three; so they are fit to be ordered about and made to work...." In April 1494, the leader of another Spanish expedition, Alonso de Ojeda, accusing the Indians of stealing clothing, reacted in the spirit of that comment. He cut off the ears of one of the local chieftain's men and sent the chieftain with his brother and nephew in chains to Spain. A priest, Barolomé de las Casas, wrote some years later, after the Indians had been enslaved and were growing extinct: "This was the first injustice, with vain and erroneous pretension of doing justice, that was committed in these Indies against the Indians, and the beginning of the shedding of blood, which has since flowed so copiously in this island."

Of an estimated three million indigenous population in 1492, one third had been killed by 1496, and by 1548, according to Fernández de Oviedo, the Spanish colonial historian, probably not more than 500 remained alive. Negro slaves were brought in to replace the Indians.

Hispaniola became Spain's first permanent colony in the New World and its most important harbor. From there, Balboa discovered the Pacific, Cortez invaded Mexico, and other explorers sailed to undiscovered parts of the hemisphere. Spain held on to the island until 1697, when under the Treaty of Ryswick the Haitian portion was ceded to France and the Dominican part remained under Spanish dominion. At the end of the eighteenth century, the French took over the whole island, only to lose it to Negro Haitian armies fashioned from liberated slaves who had been brought into Haiti by the French. The Spanish returned in 1809, but were thrown out again in 1821, when the Dominicans revolted. But independence was short-lived, as Haitian armies invaded the country the following year and imposed an oppressive regime on the Dominicans for 22 years. Finally, in 1844, the Dominican Republic won real independence for the first time under the inspiring leadership of Juan Pablo Duarte. Standing in the hot, dusty square of Santiago, he told a huge, worshiping crowd after he had agreed to run for President in what might have been the country's first free election:

"Be happy . . . and my heart will be fully satisfied even without the office which you desire I may obtain; but first of all, be just, if you desire to be happy, for that is man's first duty; be united, and thus you will put out the flame of discord and conquer your enemies, and the fatherland will be free and safe, and your wishes will be gratified, so shall I obtain my greatest recompense, the only one to which I aspire: that of seeing you peaceful, happy, independent and free."

It took only one day for the Dominican military leader, Pedro Santana, to march on the capital and proclaim himself the first dictator of an independent Dominican Republic. In the next 121 years, the country was to stagger through 23 revolutions interspersed with some of the most vicious dictatorships in Latin-American history, as well as a brief reannexation by Spain, from 1861 to 1865, and two American military occupations.

At one point, in 1866, Dominican President Buenaventura Báez, hoping to save himself from financial ruin, tried to persuade U. S. President Andrew Johnson to annex the country. Anticipating an affirmative reply, Báez hoisted the American flag at Samaná and reassured his people that the United States was "a collection of free and independent republics, united by a common bond, each state possessing its own religion, language, habits, and customs." He even conducted two fixed plebiscites to convince Washington that the people wanted to be annexed.

But the U. S. Senate, under the leadership of abolitionist Charles Sumner, flatly rejected a resolution for annexation favored by President Ulysses Grant, Johnson's successor. "The resolution," Sumner thundered emotionally, "commits Congress to a dance of blood. As senator, as patriot, I cannot see my country suffer in its good name without an earnest effort to save it. Báez . . . is sustained in power by the government of the United States that he may betray his country. . . . The island . . . situated in tropical waters and occupied by another race . . . never can become a permanent possession of the United States. You may seize it by force of arms or by diplomacy, where an able squadron does more than the Minister; the enforced jurisdiction cannot endure. . . . It is theirs by right of possession; by their sweat and blood mingling with the soil; by its burning sun and by unalterable lines of climate. Such is the ordinance of nature which I am not the first to recognize. [The country] is the earliest of that independent group destined to occupy the Caribbean Sea toward which our duty is as plain as the Ten Commandments. Kindness, benevolence, assistance, aid, help, protection, all that

is implied in good neighborhood, this we must give freely; boun-
tifully; but their independence is as precious to them as ours is
to us and it is placed under the safeguard of natural laws which
we cannot violate with impunity."

But in May 1916, President Woodrow Wilson did violate
these "natural laws," dispatching marine units to the country to
bring order after a series of bloody revolts. In familiar terms,
Rear Admiral William Caperton, commander of the force, explained: "It is not the intention of the United States government
to acquire by conquest any territory in the Dominican Republic
nor to attack its sovereignty, but our troops will remain here
until all revolutionary movements have been stamped out and
until such reforms as are deemed necessary to insure the future
welfare of the country have been initiated and are in effective
operation."

The United States demanded that the Dominican government
recognize its authority to collect and disburse all moneys and
that the national army be replaced by a Dominican constabulary
under American tutelage. The government refused, and in November the United States proclaimed the establishment of a
"Military Government of the United States in Santo Domingo,"
which ruled the nation until 1924.

Although the U. S. forces created a civil service, modernized
agriculture to some extent (without breaking up the feudal
estates), improved sanitation, expanded education, and reduced
the national debt, they failed to give the nation what it needed
most—education in democracy. However, as the military government slid into an outright dictatorship American officers were
not lax in providing military training. One of their students was
Rafael Trujillo, who learned from them the efficiency of dictatorship and the means of imposing it.

Having received a commission as lieutenant under the marines, Trujillo rose rapidly in the national police force after
they departed, through stealth, blackmail, and cunning, finally
winning a rigged presidential election in 1930. And thus was

launched one of the most brutal reigns of terror in modern world history.

In a sense, Trujillo, whose firm, thin lips and hard, piercing eyes, magnified behind a pair of thick-lensed spectacles, visually attested to his iron will and quiet toughness, was the "Benefactor of the Fatherland," as he called himself. He built a network of roads, sanitation and water-supply systems, port and docking facilities, an international airport, irrigation systems, luxury hotels, efficient hospitals, sisal, cotton, and cotton-textile plants, a power grid, housing projects, and schools.

But to obtain the revenue for these works, while dragging his country out of the bankruptcy he inherited, he used ruthless means. The funds came from increased prices, high taxes on imported and locally manufactured goods, and "contributions" from the populace—in other words, mainly from the poorer classes. As a result, although a small middle class developed, the living standards of most people remained the same or dropped, despite the country's tremendous economic growth. In 1958, near the end of Trujillo's regime, there were only 7,000 automobiles, 2,000 television sets, and 58,000 radios in the country, reflecting the controlled nature of the economy, which in this respect resembled communism.

Thus, the semifeudal socioeconomic structure characteristic of most Latin-American rural areas was barely touched. Those outside the Trujillo family benefiting materially from the system in varying degree included the armed forces, the new business and industrial elite, the bureaucracy, and the big landowners, particularly the sugar producers.

But even they got only the leftovers. Where did most of the benefits go? To the Trujillos, who obtained control of more than 50 percent of the national wealth and monopolized most major enterprises mainly by forcing or frightening competitors out of business. They ended up owning, among other things, about 65 percent of the country's sugar production, 12 of its 16 sugar mills, and 60 percent of its best land. They had a share of just about every business except, for some reason, drugs. Some 80 percent of the nation's workers worked for them, about half on company payrolls, and the other half on government or military payrolls. Laws were framed requiring the use of alcohol in gasoline, the wearing of shoes by all Dominicans, the sale of meat by approved slaughterhouses. The Trujillos monopolized the production of alcohol and shoes, and ran the only approved slaughterhouse.

Typical of Trujillo's business methods was the encouragement he gave three Poles to construct a chocolate factory at Puerto Plata in 1946. Subsidizing it with the kickback from a 28 percent export tax on beans, Trujillo waited until it was making $1 million a year, then "bought" it at a bargain price, and resold and repurchased it every two or three years for large profits. He added an extra $2 million a year to the family fortune—estimated at more than $800 million—simply by ordering his officials to collect the $2.10 per bag tax charged at the Puerto Plata embarkation point in a cigar box to be delivered to him personally.

His boundless greed and vanity were visibly reflected in the dozens of gaudy palaces he maintained, each serviced by a full staff of servants ready to pamper and feed him at a moment's notice; in his wardrobe of elaborately brocaded and bemedaled uniforms; in his enormous yachts, splendid swimming pools, and countless monuments to himself.

But if Trujillo ran the country like a huge private enterprise to be exploited for the sole purpose of enriching himself and his family, this was the least of his crimes. Thousands of his political enemies, automatically called "Communists," died in secret police dungeons, many of them after suffering hideous tortures perpetrated with electrical devices, nail extractors, decapitation collars, and leather-thonged whips. Young ladies who spurned his advances were found dead in "accidents." Even foes who fled abroad lived in constant dread of kidnapping and death at the hands of Trujillo agents who, after performing their murderous

tasks, were themselves marked for extinction. In 1937, he supervised the massacre of from 15,000 to 35,000 Haitian squatters in
two days.

Yet, despite such horrors, which were largely unpublicized before his death because of the fear of Dominicans, at home and
abroad, to speak ill of him, many American visitors and officials
regarded Trujillo as a "good friend" of the United States who
paid off his country's foreign debts, always voted the "right"
way in the OAS and UN, kept the streets clean, put Communists
in jail, and knew how to keep order in a country that was "not
ready" for democracy.

U. S. congressmen, some of them in his pay, praised him to
the skies. Cordell Hull, Secretary of State under President Roosevelt, described him as "a splendid President, who is outstanding
among all those in the American nations." Cardinal Spellman,
on a visit to the Dominican Republic, embraced Trujillo publicly and called him "Benefactor of the Church."

The beginning of the end for Trujillo probably came on
June 14, 1959, when Dominican exiles, backed by Venezuelan
President Betancourt and Cuban Premier Castro (his Communist inclinations were not yet known), landed in the Dominican
Republic by boat and plane in an effort to overthrow the dictator. Trujillo discovered the plot—some Dominicans say that the
United States threw a naval cordon around the country to prevent reinforcement—and invaders at Constanza were captured
and tortured to death under the supervision of Trujillo's son
and Air Force commander, Ramfis, at San Isidro Air Base.

Trujillo then tried, abortively, to assassinate Betancourt with
a dynamite bomb. As a result, the OAS, which had little inclination to take measures against a hemispheric leader for domestic
crimes, voted unanimously to take action against Trujillo for
trying to export his terrorism. All OAS members were required
to break diplomatic and economic relations with the Dominican
Republic. The United States, though wary of the decision, re-

luctantly joined in it in view of the strong Latin feeling on the issue.

Shortly thereafter, the nation received yet another shock when three young sisters of the prominent Mirabal family were murdered. The girls had been politically active in the student underground against Trujillo together with the husbands of two of them. One of the sisters, Minerva, in fact, was responsible in large degree for the founding of the 14th of June Movement in commemoration of the death of the Constanza invaders, an anti-Trujillo organization that was gradually to be infiltrated by Communists. To Trujillo's fear of the sisters and their husbands was added the humiliation of having been spurned by Minerva when he made advances to her at a social gathering. Seeking revenge, Trujillo imprisoned the girls' father, then the three girls and two husbands. When the girls were released, they drove one day from Santiago, where they lived, to Puerto Plata to see the husbands, who were still in jail there. On the way back to Santiago in a jeep driven by a friend, the vehicle, according to witnesses, was halted by four armed men who dragged the girls into their car. One of the sisters was heard to scream: "Help! Save us! They are *calies* [Trujillo killers] who will kill us. Tell the Mirabal family!" Later that day, the bodies of the girls and the driver were found at the bottom of a cliff. Their jeep, said a government announcement, had failed to make a curve.

A group of twenty Dominicans, including relatives and friends of Trujillo's victims, politicians who coveted his power, and soldiers who had been humiliated by him, began plotting his assassination. About 9:30 P.M., on May 30, 1961, Trujillo and his chauffeur, Captain Socorro de la Cruz, were speeding down the coastal highway from the capital to San Cristobal, where the dictator's mistress awaited him. Unseen in the shadows, a 1958 Chevrolet followed for about two miles. In it were four men, armed with automatics, carbines, and a shotgun. Suddenly, the Chevrolet spurted ahead until it came abreast of the limousine.

A barrage of bullets split the quiet night air, and the limousine came to an abrupt stop. The Chevrolet braked, moved backward and halted about 20 feet from the larger car.

With the three other men in the Chevrolet, Antonio Imbert Barreras, the driver, leaped out. "We four advanced, half crawling, half lying down," Imbert later recalled. "Trujillo by now was standing in front of his car. He screamed something, terror I suppose. He had been wounded in the left shoulder by a shotgun charge. I was lying ten feet from him. I aimed my .45 and shot twice. One bullet hit him in the chin. It knocked him sprawling on his back and he must have died instantly. He never moved again."

But even in death Trujillo had his revenge. Eighteen of the twenty plotters were captured and killed in the next half year, some of them after being horribly tortured. General José René Román Fernández, Secretary of State for the Armed Forces and Trujillo's nephew-in-law, was left for days with his eyelids stitched to his eyebrows. He was drenched with acid, beaten with a baseball bat, castrated, exposed to swarms of ants, and shocked endlessly in the electric chair, until finally a machine gun put him out of his misery.

Also tortured and killed was Dr. Robert Reid Cabral, a physician and brother of Donald, for permitting four of the tyrannicides to hide in his home.

One of the men who escaped, Luis Amiama Tio, hid for more than six months in a narrow closet in the bathroom of an official living in Santo Domingo, emerging only after dark to sleep on a floor mat. He held a pistol to his head at the slightest noise, and he also had hidden on him a capsule of cyanide to be consumed in case he was taken alive.

The second man to escape was Imbert, who lived to play a leading role in the drama that unfolded in the Dominican Republic four years later. In the shooting he had been slightly wounded by a bullet fired by Trujillo's chauffeur.

Trujillo's spirit carried on in the madness of his family, which clung to power. The day after the assassination, Ramfis, who had been in Paris playing polo with Porfirio Rubiroso, his former brother-in-law, flew home on a $27,000 chartered flight to direct the campaign of vengeance and consolidate his family's control of the nation.

Ramfis, though endowed with the same ruthlessness and lust for wealth and women as the elder Trujillo, had little of his father's drive and dedication to work. It hadn't been necessary for him to work, having been coddled and preened all his life. He became a general at nine, being temporarily decommissioned at sixteen so that he would not outrank his teachers at the Dominican Military Academy. After he left school, he was promoted to lieutenant general. When he insisted that he be given a fourth star, for once his father put his foot down and refused. Ramfis embarrassingly flunked out of the U. S. military academy, having spent more time with movie starlets on his yacht than in the classroom. But to prove his toughness as a soldier, he supervised the torturing and liquidation of the 1959 invasion victims.

Now, as Ramfis proved his toughness once more in the new orgy of revenge, an OAS committee arrived and pressured him into reducing his authority and giving more power to the newly named President, Joaquín Balaguer, who, nevertheless, continued to work closely with the ruling family, as he had with the assassinated dictator himself. The Trujillos, hoping for a discontinuation of the diplomatic and economic boycott that the OAS had imposed on the dead dictator's government, agreed to temporize their rule.

Immediately after Trujillo's death, which was not officially announced until two days later, there was little public reaction. The people were still conditioned to fear and silence. Many refused to believe he was really dead, thinking that the announcement might be a trick to draw out his enemies so that they might be tortured and slain. Others, hearing of the terrible retribution taken against the assassins, figured that nothing had really changed, that Ramfis would maintain as strong a hold as his father on the nation. But as Ramfis reduced the pressure on the people they began to stir for the first time, and the United States was now faced with a crucial decision that would have a profound effect on its policy toward Latin America.

Under the Good Neighbor Policy launched in 1932 by President Roosevelt and carried on by Presidents Truman and Eisenhower, the United States had pledged itself not to intervene unilaterally in any Latin-American country for whatever reason. This policy was considered a necessary cornerstone of the evolving United States-Latin American partnership in view of the profound fear of the Latin Americans, spawned in earlier imperialistic days of U. S. domination. In practice, it was used as an excuse for fostering friendship with, and even giving medals to, rightist dictators.

But nonintervention had also permitted Fidel Castro to clamp a Communist hold on Cuba, and now, with the Dominican Republic suddenly released from the grip of a man who had ruled, and in fact owned, the country for 31 years, a new chaos might possibly emerge that Communists could exploit. The United States, President Kennedy decided, could no longer adhere to the principle of nonintervention. But he also decided that future intervention would be of a distinctly different brand than that which had raised the universal hemispheric cry of "Yankee, go home" in past decades. It would be intervention not on the side of the dictators against the people, but on the side of the people against the dictators, whether of the right or the left. This was a kind of intervention, President Kennedy felt, that would be consistent with the interests of both the United States and Latin America. He overruled advisers who held that such a policy could lead to chaos and communism.

Kennedy began to apply American pressure on the new Trujillo regime in July, only a month after the assassination, when university students demonstrated against the government in an unheard-of breach of national discipline. The United States helped to persuade the Trujillos simply to deport one of the arrested leaders, a mild treatment in the Trujilloite context. Other U. S.-fostered measures of moderation followed. Also in July, Conservative anti-Trujillo leaders were allowed to organize a National Civic Union (UCN), and its chief, Dr. Viriato Fiallo, boldly told a crowd of 8,000 people who gathered in Independence Square that the "political power, the economic power, the military power of the Trujillos" must end. On the same day, Manuel Tavares Justo, leader of the underground 14th of June Movement that had been formed to keep alive the spirit of the abortive 1959 rebellion, was released after serving 19 months in prison. He was the husband of the murdered Minerva Mirabal, the main reason why he was selected head of the organization she had helped to found.

On October 17, students again demonstrated, touching off a general strike that closed most shops and businesses in Santo Domingo. Police beat demonstrators mercilessly and demonstrators flung sewer lids and Molotov cocktails at police from rooftops. Finally, riot squads brought the fighting under control, but American pressure again prevented brutal retribution against the rioters. Indeed, under U. S. guidance, Ramfis, in return for a promise from the demonstrators to end the strike, agreed to send abroad his two uncles, Héctor ("Negro") and José Arismendi ("Petán"), who had come to be known as the "wicked uncles" for their efforts to impose a new terroristic regime on the country.

But less than a month later, Ramfis, constantly drunk and fed up with the problems of high office, particularly the American pressures, decided to return to the playgrounds of Europe with a substantial part of the national wealth. After drinking heavily on Saturday night, November 11, he telephoned his uncles, who were in Bermuda, telling them of his plan and advising them to return immediately to take over control of the country. The uncles, in turn, telephoned Dominicans in the army and police

who were loyal to them and told them to prepare for their return. José Angel Savinon, the Minister of Labor in the Balaguer
Cabinet, flew to see them. Balaguer and others have claimed
that he had been the contact man for the uncles, but Savinon
has said that he had tried to persuade them not to come back,
since the United States would not assist a Dominican government in which they participated.

In any event, Héctor and José returned on Wednesday, November 15, and Ramfis departed the following day for Europe
loaded down with booty after vengefully issuing a last-minute
order for the murder of six suspects who had been held in prison
for their involvement in his father's assassination. The uncles,
in league with their followers, immediately set in motion a
plan to depose Balaguer and kill thousands of Dominicans whom
they suspected of opposing the Trujillo family, the massacre to
be carried out probably on Sunday night, November 19.

Meanwhile, Washington found itself caught in the fever of
crisis. Before the return of the brothers, it had apparently decided that the moderation displayed by Ramfis and Balaguer
rendered their government acceptable, at least temporarily.
Thus, on Tuesday, November 14, the day before the return of
the uncles, it had proposed to the OAS that the sanctions against
the Dominican Republic be lifted. But on Thursday, one day
after the return, it withdrew the proposal. It had apparently
heard of the planned massacre and decided to support Balaguer
and those military officers loyal to him, including the Santiago
Air Force commander, General Pedro Rodríguez Echevarría,
whose pilots started bombing the Santo Domingo army barracks.
On Friday, President Kennedy sent a fleet of 14 warships, including two aircraft carriers, bearing marines to Dominican
waters, and three squadrons of fighter jets swooped over the
city to the cheers of the populace. On Saturday, Secretary of
State Dean Rusk announced that the marines would storm
ashore if Balaguer asked for them.

On that fateful weekend, the uncles went to the National Palace to demand, "dead or alive," according to Balaguer, the President's resignation. His office was to be taken over by the dim-witted Héctor, who had already been puppet President from 1952 to 1960, when Balaguer, Vice-President up to then, replaced him to lend "front man" respectability to the Trujillo regime at a time when the tyrant desperately needed a "normalization" of relations with the OAS.

Balaguer, a small, thin, prissy-mannered professor, writer, lawyer, and historian, who had long been a puppet of the Trujillos, now, in this moment of truth, stood up to them. He has said that he told the uncles that if they killed him his forces would never let them leave the palace alive. A U. S. spokesman later explained that "Balaguer could have pushed the button for the landing of the marines. If he had been shot, the marines could have come under the authority Balaguer had given in advance."

Under this intense pressure, the "wicked uncles" threw in the sponge. And on Sunday night, instead of a massacre taking place, Balaguer announced to the nation that Héctor and his brother had agreed, "in a generous, patriotic gesture," to leave for the United States. On the following day, they left, but didn't stay in the United States very long. Héctor was expelled when, in a last desperate move, he telephoned Fidel Castro in Havana to ask for help in returning him to his homeland.

Finally free of the Trujillos, the country went wild. Street signs with the Trujillo name were torn down, and Trujillo statues destroyed. The name of the capital, which had been changed from Santo Domingo to Ciudad Trujillo under the dictator, was given back its original name. Thousands of exiles returned from everywhere. But despite the jubilation, the country had the glazed, shocked air of someone witnessing a miracle. It wept and laughed; it shouted for joy and immersed itself in suppressed hysteria, still conditioned to the silence demanded by Trujillo. Freedom is a complex thing, but to the Dominicans it was simple: an end to Trujilloism.

And the United States, which had long been resented by the Dominicans for its support of Trujillo, was now regarded as their savior. The new Kennedy policy of intervention on the side of the people had appeared to pay off. In his boldness, in his gamble that the Dominicans, if given free reign, would not be stampeded into communism, the President had, in fact, rendered Communist anti-American propaganda virtually valueless, not only in the Dominican Republic but throughout Latin America, despite some rumblings by Latin diehards that non-intervention should be practiced in its absolute form regardless of the consequences.

Nor did Kennedy anticipate withdrawing from the Dominican Republic. Assisted by Puerto Rican Governor Luis Muñoz Marín, who, with U. S. support, had performed a miracle of economic and social development on his own island, he planned to guide the Dominican Republic toward the kind of democratically achieved progress registered there.

Thus, after the last of the Trujillos had departed, American mediators began negotiating with Balaguer and various political groups for the establishment of a caretaker government and the scheduling of free elections. The principal U. S. negotiators were, significantly, two brilliant disciples of Muñoz Marín, who had helped to make the Puerto Rican experiment the success it was—Arturo Morales Carrión, who was later to become Deputy Assistant Secretary of State for Inter-American Affairs under the Kennedy Administration and Special Adviser to the OAS Secretary-General after the President's assassination, and Teodoro Moscoso, who was to be appointed the first U. S. Administrator of the Alliance for Progress.

Spurred by a general strike called by the UCN for the purpose of ousting Balaguer, whose Trujilloite background it deplored, the Dominican leader agreed to set up a UCN-dominated Council of State, which would consist of seven members including himself as President, and, because of their public service, the two surviving tyrannicides, Amiama and Imbert. The Council assumed legislative and executive power on January 1, 1962, to the joy of a nation that now had its first non-Trujillo government in more than three decades.

But the ghost of Trujillo would not disappear. Reports persisted that the "wicked uncles" were about to return. And UCN speakers shouted in Parque Independencia and over the radio that Trujilloism would remain as long as the nation was being led by Balaguer and General Rodríguez Echevarría, whom the President had named Secretary of State for the Armed Forces in gratitude for his role in thwarting the November plot.

Balaguer, in a desperate attempt to win public support, handed out Trujillo properties to workers and peasants; issuing for example, dozens of taxicabs to cabbies after buying them from fleet owners with government funds. As a result of such demagoguery, he became popular indeed, and even today, he possibly could win a free election.

But Rodríguez Echevarría, reared in a military rather than a political tradition, sought to save himself in the only manner he understood. On January 16, hardly more than two weeks after the establishment of the Council of State, the general sent tanks into Santo Domingo and his soldiers opened fire on a crowd outside UCN headquarters, killing six and wounding twenty. He then captured several members of the Council and took them to San Isidro.

Rodríguez Echevarría offered familiar reasons for the coup. The Communists were plotting to take over the government. The bureaucrats were corrupt, and the Council weak and ineffectual. What was needed was a strong military government to prepare the people for eventual elections. But President Kennedy, unlike most of his predecessors, would not buy such arguments. He warned that the United States would not recognize his junta, that promised aid would be canceled, that the Dominican sugar quota would be reallocated, and that the fleet might return. Added to this warning was another, symbolized by a new general strike; the warning of the mob. Rodríguez Echevarría's military colleagues were impressed. Forty-eight hours after his coup, he was arrested and sent to Puerto Rico. And for good measure, as the result of UCN pressure, Balaguer was forced to join him, though it is not clear whether he had been involved in the coup.

The return to democracy touched off the wildest celebrations in the memory of old residents of Santo Domingo. Cheering crowds surged into the streets shouting, "Liberty, Liberty!" The bells of some of the oldest churches in the hemisphere chimed forth the tidings. Women wept, men hugged each other, and policemen and soldiers joined the happy throngs. Music emanated from every house, it seemed, as the city, after decades of silence, let itself go in an uninhibited orgy of joy.

People jammed the National Palace gates to cheer the Council which, to them, now represented the first democratic government they had ever known. With Balaguer gone, it had been immediately reshuffled. Vice-President Rafael F. Bonnelly, a conservative businessman and former diplomat who had joined the anti-Trujillo UCN, became President. Also joining the Council—as Vice-President—was Donald Reid Cabral. They were all heroes in this moment of triumph.

And so was President Kennedy, who had succeeded once more in saving the Dominican people from retrogression into a new nightmare of dictatorship as they slowly, painfully edged their way toward the democracy that most of them had never dreamed they might one day be lucky enough to experience.

CHAPTER 3

Fighting the Ghost

THE Dominican Republic, as it awaited elections the following December, was like a crippled child learning to walk. Slowly, uncertainly, it felt its way in the strange new world opened to it. People began to speak freely for the first time, though sometimes, from habit, they still hesitated before airing political or other controversial opinions, as if the ghost of Trujillo were eavesdropping.

They longed to see what the rest of the world, from which they had been sealed off, was like. The American consulate in Santo Domingo was swamped with a backlog of some 20,000 visa applications, and applicants paid up to $20 just for a good place in the endless queues that perpetually wound around the building. Flights to the United States and other countries were booked solid weeks in advance.

"Since we had never known freedom," a Dominican housewife told me, "we easily accepted the need to keep our mouths shut and never ask questions and never to think about life outside the country. But now we are like children in a candy store. We want to say everything, see everything, taste everything."

Aside from freedom, the future looked bright indeed, with the country showing promise of becoming more economi-

57

cally viable and socially and politically democratic than most
other Latin-American countries. The United States envisioned
it as a showcase of the Alliance for Progress, whose aim was precisely such advance, and put up $25 million in aid to help it
become so. Land was distributed to the peasants. A new tax law
was passed that promised to narrow the gap between rich and
poor. New housing projects were under way. Sugar exports
were booming. Public works gave jobs to 30,000 unemployed.

In registering this impressive record, the government found
itself seriously handicapped by two factors. First, in the last
two years of Trujillo's regime, the dictator and his family sent
an estimated $70 million abroad for their personal use. Second,
the country lacked experienced politicians, diplomats, and administrators. For with the fall of Trujillo, whose personal control reached into the most insignificant bureaucratic niche, the
framework of government all but collapsed.

Yet, the necessity of starting all over again was the mother of
the idealism and the drive that was largely responsible for the
progress of reform. It is also notable that because of Trujillo's
all-pervasive power, his assassination was the equivalent of a full-
scale revolution in most Latin-American countries, where the
forces of progress find it difficult, if not impossible, to overcome
the inert weight of feudal tradition.

In the Dominican Republic, the tyrant's death eliminated
the heart of resistance to reform. It left available for redistribution by the state about $200 million in profits from the Trujillo
properties, representing more than 50 percent of the total value
of the nation's economic production. This meant thousands of
acres of land owned by the Trujillos could be turned over without a struggle to the peasants, and hundreds of industrial and
commercial enterprises could be put to work in the service of
the people.

Martín Díaz, a middle-aged peasant with a rugged, wrinkled,
blatantly honest face, was one of the beneficiaries. When I
called on him in August 1962 at his wooden, thatch-roofed

house several miles from Santo Domingo, he proudly displayed a soiled, much-handled sheet of paper.

"This proves it," he said in rapid Spanish. "This proves that I own this land."

Embarrassed, Martín Díaz, a former tenant farmer, admitted that he couldn't read the deed giving him title to his 10-acre plot of land. But he repeated again and again, "I am a landowner."

Martín's pride was the pride of thousands of peasants who received or had been expected to receive parcels of land under the Dominican Republic's land reform scheme. His former landlord was a relative of Trujillo. Having been confiscated, the farm was given to him, and so he was able to grow corn, beans, peanuts, and tobacco on his own land.

At first he could not believe he had been blessed with such good fortune, or even that El Benefactor had been killed. Trujillo was like an all-pervading spirit. How was it possible to kill him? And when he was finally convinced that the impossible had happened, Martín, like many illiterate peasants, was not sure how to feel. After all, Trujilloism was all that he had ever known. Moreover, he remembered that the Trujillo's relatives had sometimes visited the area and grandly distributed 20-peso notes in the dictator's name.

But once he discovered the exquisiteness of being able to complain openly about his problems and difficulties, he began to understand why his former leader was "bad." He then thoroughly approved the destruction by other local peasants of Trujillo properties in the neighborhood, such as the offices of a banana exporting company and a modern dairy. He even helped to slaughter "Trujilloist" cattle, selling the meat.

Martín, who used to live in a slum at the edge of a nearby town, had built his own house—a cool, floorless, two-room abode with palm-board walls and roof of palm fronds. As a tenant farmer, he had barely subsisted. He would net now, he said, about $300 a year, in addition to his family's food.

And thousands of other Dominicans also saw their living standards rise sharply as salaries of workers in some industries doubled and tripled, as people began eating three meals a day instead of one or two, and as stores did a record business.

But there was another side to the economic and social picture. The skyrocketing salaries, demagogically approved by the Council, which considered such concessions necessary if it was to stay in power for its full term, threatened to put many companies out of business, while tens of thousands of workers had no jobs at all. Moreover, production was slipping and prices were soaring. Sugar mills, which account for about 70 percent of the national economy, were in a particularly precarious state, despite guarantees of large sales in the United States. For aside from the higher wages, no longer could soldiers or prisoners be put to work as they were when Trujillo owned most of the mills. Government corruption was widely reported, and, most important of all, the flight of needed investment capital from the country was tremendous, reflecting the fear of many Dominicans about what the future might hold.

Related problems also plagued the nation. For one thing, Trujillo still haunted the country he had plundered and raped. The Dominicans were a study in psychological distress. Like prisoners suddenly released from a dungeon, they were dazed, uncertain, frightened, suspicious. Most pathetically of all, they were burdened by a gnawing sense of guilt. They spoke of Trujillo's crimes with hatred and bitterness. Yet hardly a Dominican had not at one time or another supported or done business with the tyrant.

"When a man is in power for thirty years, it is impossible not to go along with him and still survive," a Santo Domingo lawyer said in his cramped office as he sat under a landscape on the wall that had recently replaced a photo of El Benefactor. "Yes, I worked for Trujillo. Whether you liked him or not, Trujilloism controlled our life, and the few who uncompromisingly fought it are almost all in their graves today."

Most Dominicans realized this, but they tried to relieve the pain of personal guilt and the fear of being accused themselves by accusing others. Brother turned against brother, son against father. A youth I met tearfully told me that he would never speak to his father again because "he was a dirty Trujilloist."

In this atmosphere of mutual recrimination and distrust, it was surprising that the country was making any economic and social progress at all, or that politicians still thought that peaceful elections could be held.

A new law giving the government the right to confiscate the wealth of all persons who were actively pro-Trujilloist was one reason why the moneyed class kept potential investment funds safely stored away in foreign banks. This law, it was felt, might well be interpreted to engulf almost anyone in the country. But it would have been political suicide for any group to advocate repeal of such legislation at that time.

Political parties—23 had sprung up as the election approached —displayed little subtlety in flinging charges, if only in an effort to extricate themselves from the web of suspicion. The usual reply of the accused was a long report on how party leaders in the past had been imprisoned or tortured. One politician, to cleanse the questioned reputation of his chief, assured me that the latter had been "tortured more" than the leader of another political group, as if the degree of torture proved who was cleaner.

It was particularly ludicrous that almost all of the seven men in the Council of State had collaborated closely with Trujillo. President Bonnelly was once the dictator's administrative secretary, Commerce Minister, and Ambassador to Venezuela and Spain. Monsignor Eliseo Pérez Sánchez had strongly supported Trujillo from his church pulpit. Dr. Nicolás Pichardo had been Trujillo's Minister of Health. Amiama Tio had been Mayor of Santo Domingo. And Imbert had been Governor of Puerto Plata.

The saving grace of these men was that they turned against

Trujillo before his death. But, asked many people, were they any less guilty than thousands of other persons who supported Trujillo, then deserted him in his final years but were now being persecuted?

The question came into bitter focus especially in the cases of Imbert and Amiama, who were actually involved in the assassination plot against Trujillo. They knew they were practically committing suicide by becoming involved. And even when they managed to survive, their ordeal was not over, for Trujillo's relatives had sworn to kill them.

"I know they are planning to kill me," Imbert, a tough, stocky man, told me in August 1962 as he fingered a pistol that perpetually graced his hip. "But they had better shoot straight."

Yet, the very fact that Imbert and Amiama were close collaborators of the dictator for many years helped to explain the determination of the Trujillo family to wreak vengeance on them. The two men who, for whatever reasons, were responsible for bringing to a conclusion an era of terror only to be terrorized themselves, posed the crux of the nation's tragic dilemma. Where should the hatred and the suspicion sown by Trujillo's ghost end?

Nor was Trujilloism the only factor sowing hatred and suspicion. Another one was communism. Three out-and-out Communist parties were outlawed in February 1962, and, in any case, were very weak and enjoyed little support among a people who had suffered too many bitter years to accept any new totalitarian system, right or left.

The Dominican Popular Socialist Party (PSPD) had close relations with the traditional Cuban Communist Party, even sharing the same formal name, and was oriented toward Moscow. It had only 200 or 300 members, many of whom had lived in Cuba for years and were inclined toward intellectual preaching, not action. In August 1965, it changed its name to the Dominican Communist Party, claiming to be the only true Marxist-Leninist group.

The Popular Dominican Movement (MPD), while maintaining links with Moscow and Havana, were more independent of them, tending toward Peking dogma as well as terroristic tactics. It also embraced only several hundred, perhaps 1,000 members. Trujillo had given the party its start shortly before his death when he permitted a Communist leader, Maximo López Molina, to return from exile in Cuba to set it up as a kind of controlled opposition, which he hoped to use as an instrument for pressuring the United States into improved relations.

The Revolutionary Nationalistic Party (PNR) was a minuscule intellectual elite that emphasized indoctrination rather than political action.

But the Communists in all these hard-core parties had infiltrated the legal 14th of June Movement, which was for a while the second largest Dominican party—after the National Civic Union. This party was originally made up mainly of middle-class youths with no particular ideological orientation who had simply been in sympathy with the 1959 martyrs. It was not clear that the masses and some leaders of this party had Communist inclinations. What was clear was that most members were, and still are, young, militantly nationalist, and fervently anti-American with the restlessness and dissatisfaction that characterize youth in most underdeveloped countries scarred by past colonial or totalitarian exploitation. These youths, if scornful of their own families for dealing with Trujillo, regarded the United States with much greater bitterness for having supported and publicly praised him during most of his reign.

In any event, members of these various groups constantly agitated against the Council, which they charged was nothing but a puppet agency of the United States. Hardly had the new American Ambassador, John Bartlow Martin, arrived in Santo Domingo in early 1962 when his official car was burned by rioters. On other occasions, hundreds of youths marched on the American Embassy and had to be disbursed with tear gas and noise bombs. Moreover, demonstrations against the Council and the United States spread to other cities where similar police measures were used. That Cuba was implicated was indicated by Havana Radio programs, supposedly aired by the Dominican "liberation movement in exile," outlining steps to overthrow the government and calling for concerted action by students, peasants, and workers.

But while the Reds and other extremists appeared to be making more noise than they were causing harm, the fear of communism grew among the wealthier classes, which began to suspect politicians who spoke of social reform as being communistically inclined. This suspicion, in turn, fed rumors and counter-rumors that a coup either by leftist or rightist extremists was imminent.

Interestingly enough, in view of recent events, one oft-mentioned danger was the possibility of collaboration between the 14th of June group and some military elements. The central figure in most rumors of this nature was Council member Antonio Imbert. Imbert, the reasoning went, dealt closely with the armed forces and at the same time had good friends in the 14th of June Movement. He could be the catalyst bringing together these two groups. Imbert, it was thought, was particularly hungry for power in order to obtain the protection afforded a president that he would not otherwise have against Trujillo triggermen.

Imbert told me at the time, however, that he saw no chance of a coup taking place. But he defended the 14th of June group as consisting simply of "nationalist youths who will become more moderate when they get jobs." After his ascension to the presidency of the junta formed in May 1965 with U. S. help, he took another view. The 14th of June is a Communist party, he said.

The fear of a Communist takeover led also to talk of a rightist takeover to be achieved by rightist-military collaboration. Many conservative businessmen, if they did not really believe that the Reds could take over, were said to feel that communism, in view of the prominence of its activities, would constitute an excellent excuse for the establishment of a new authoritarian regime favorable to their interests.

Few rightists wanted a return to the brutal, choking totalitarianism of Trujillo. But having learned from the dictator the financial advantages of controlling a nation, they were thought to be pushing for a limited dictatorship only harsh enough to assure that they received a fat slice of the national wealth. After all, some thought, Trujillo had squeezed them out when he was in power. And if leftists of any stripe got into power either through elections or a coup they would be squeezed out again.

The twin issues of Trujilloism and communism, then, gradually developed into the key issues of the electoral campaign that gathered steam as politicians strove to build up voting strength in the event the rumored coup did not materialize. And from the galaxy of parties that had sprung up early in the year, two emerged as the top favorites in the ideological polarization process that took place.

The biggest political organization from the beginning of the campaign was the National Civic Union, which had been created in July 1961 as an apolitical mass anti-Trujillo social movement with the aim of rooting out all vestiges of Trujilloism from the national life, becoming a legitimate political party in February 1962. Still led by its founder, Dr. Viriato Fiallo, it claimed over 500,000 followers, including the leading members of the Council of State. And because the only philosophy it espoused on its creation was anti-Trujilloism, a universally popular one, it did indeed embrace a large segment of the population, from extreme left to extreme right.

The top leadership was in the hands of upper-class professional and businessmen, right-leaning men like Fiallo, a charming, heavyset man with steel-gray hair who looked more like the physician he was than the politician he tried to be. "I can assure you," he said when I visited him at his modestly furnished colonial-style home in Santo Domingo several months before the scheduled election, "that we have the support of at least 70 percent of the population." And he may have been right. The UCN looked like a shoe-in at that time.

Fiallo was a brave man. Although his uncle was General Federico Fiallo, who had been Trujillo's Chief of Staff in the 1940's, Viriato was one of the few Dominicans who had remained in the country yet refused to cooperate with El Benefactor, at one time rejecting an offer to become his Minister of Education. As a result, he was imprisoned for a month in a tiny cell in which he had to crouch on his knees during the whole period, unable to stand up or lie down. Undaunted, he helped to found the UCN as a clandestine anti-Trujillo group while the tyrant was still alive.

But he had no political experience at all, precisely because he had, on the one hand, refused to work under Trujillo, and on the other, stayed in the country rather than fleeing abroad to engage in exile politics. To him, the one answer to good government was the thorough cleansing of Trujilloism from all aspects of public life.

Thus, caught in a web of anti-Trujillo emotionalism, Fiallo, and some of his advisers, failed to see immediately the positive aspects of running a government or the need to give their party a recognizable political philosophy, despite their personal dedication to conservatism and the personal dedication of some business supporters to the proposition that it was time for those who had been squeezed out of Trujillo's monopolistic take to fill the vacuum of wealth.

It followed, paradoxically, that the UCN leaders had little inclination to boot out far-leftist members, who helped to give the party a "grass roots" image and could provide valuable organizational skill. As much as they feared the Reds, they were willing to work with them for "practical" reasons, much as Trujillo had, figuring that they could control them. It was much easier to "use" far leftists who, like themselves, were willing to make deals with their worst enemy for tactical purposes, than

democratic reformers who were less disposed toward such opportunistic associations.

The Communist PSPD, which had allied itself with Trujillo in the mid-1940's until the dictator decided to break up the
alliance in 1947, welcomed this new opportunity to work
through a mass movement. Having already infiltrated the 14th
of June Movement, which had been moderately leftist to start
with, it now bored into the bourgeois ranks of the all-em-
bracing UCN. At the same time, elements of the infiltrated 14th
of June also allied themselves with the UCN.

Under the Balaguer regime, the UCN formed mass organizations with Communist help. It established a trade union confederation—known as FOUPSA, with a Communist, Sanchez
Cordoba, as secretary-general. Fiallo resisted U. S. pressure to
get rid of him until Sanchez Cordoba delivered a Peking-style
speech in May 1962. The UCN also drew up plans for a Peasant
Federation to be led by Carlos Lizardo, another Communist,
though this organization never made headway among the peasants. Still another UCN Communist, Estrella Jacobo, organized
the Public Employees Union, the largest single group of wage
earners in the country.

After Balaguer's ouster, Communists infiltrated the bureaucracy of the UCN-controlled Council of State. An MPD leader,
José Daniel Ariza Cabral, became a subdirector of the Dominican Land Reform Institute. The Minister of Health, Amiro
Perez Mera, was regarded as a fellow traveler. The Economic
Planning Board, Department of Sports, and Dominican Electricity Company were heavily infiltrated.

When UCN leaders decided to convert their organization
into a full-fledged party, they broke its open ties with the 14th of
June, if only in the hope of obtaining American support. But it
was not until October 1962, only two months before elections,
that it forced out Communists and suspected Communists from
leadership in the UCN Executive Committee in Santo Domingo.
Eighteen of its twenty-four members finally resigned, though

some of them, at least, appear to have been non-Communist left-ists. In any event, the UCN chiefs having finally cleaned house, in part, it seems, as the result of U. S. "advice," decided that if they could no longer use the far left as a magnet for mass support, they could at least use it, together with Trujilloism, as an instrument for discrediting the opposition.

The principal opposition was Juan Bosch's Dominican Revolutionary Party, which had replaced the 14th of June Movement as the second most popular political organization after the latter had split into moderate and extremist factions and decided to boycott the elections which it realized it could not win. The PRD had come from nowhere to represent a genuine challenge to the UCN. And the reason lay largely in the magnetic personality of Bosch, who had been virtually unknown in the country when he returned under the Balaguer regime after 26 years of exile.

Bosch, a striking figure with his wavy white hair, searching blue eyes, and craggy Lincolnesque features, was born in 1909 in the interior town of La Vega to poor lower-middle-class parents, a Spanish father who had been a bricklayer and then a merchant, and a Puerto Rican mother whose father had been a small farmer. Profoundly impressed by the poverty around him, he read deeply of his country's social problems and, largely educating himself, prepared for a literary career from which was to flow more than 15 books, many of them on such problems.

In the early years of Trujillo, Bosch spent much of his time writing books: *Camino Real,* a collection of short stories; *Indios,* an anthology of Indian legends; and *La Manosa,* a novel with a revolutionary theme. But he found time to protest the harshness of Trujillo's rule. In 1934, he was jailed with a number of students on the charge that he had been conspiring against the dictator. On emerging from jail, Bosch and his colleagues were given jobs in the government tax office, the kind of magnanimity Trujillo often displayed toward young opponents in the hope of both humiliating them and winning them over.

Bosch played along, and finally asked to be sent abroad so that he could conduct propaganda for the dictator. It is reported that, to convince Trujillo of his sincerity, he even wrote him a letter saying that Santo Domingo was honored to be renamed Ciudad Trujillo. The dictator did send him abroad in 1936, and immediately Bosch began attacking him as a tyrant who had to be deposed. He made his headquarters in Cuba but traveled widely in Latin America denouncing Trujillo and seeking support for a plan of rebellion. In 1939, he helped to found the PRD in exile and modeled its program after that of Latin America's leading democratic social reformers, with whom he associated constantly. They included such men as Puerto Rican Governor Muñoz Marín, Venezuelan President Betancourt, former Costa Rican President José Figueres, and Peruvian reformer Victor Raúl Haya de la Torre. Their program, it seemed to Bosch, offered the best opportunity for democratic social reform. When he wasn't conspiring—in 1947 an exile invasion of his homeland that he had helped to organize failed—he was writing books or teaching at the Institute of Political Science in Costa Rica, a school for democratic reformists sponsored by Figueres.

For a while, he served as political adviser to Cuban President Carlos Prío Socarrás, who was ousted by Fulgencio Batista in 1952. Bosch fled to Venezuela when Batista ordered his arrest for extradition to the Dominican Republic, leaving his family in Cuba. When Castro came to power in January 1959, his family asked him to return, but after observing the new Cuban regime for only three months, he decided instead to bring his family to Venezuela. Even before it was clear that Castro was heading toward communism, Bosch perceived that the Cuban leader was not taking measures he regarded as necessary to make a democratic revolution. Nor is it likely that Castro was sorry about Bosch's decision. The exiled Communist PSPD had for years kept up a steady drumfire of abuse and slander against

Bosch and his party in its propaganda organ that was published for several years in Guatemala.

Bosch returned to the Dominican Republic shortly after Trujillo's assassination and began his uphill struggle to win popular support. At first the UCN, with the help of far-leftist propagandists, concentrated on the theme that while the UCN was genuinely anti-Trujilloist and reformist, the PRD was friendly to Trujilloism and, as Fiallo told me, "to the right of my party." They pointed to Bosch's early association with Trujillo, to the willingness of the Trujillo family to let him and his party return to campaign, and to Bosch's apparent readiness to participate in an election even while the family remained in power.

Bosch replied that his anti-Trujillo activities abroad had reflected his true sentiments toward the Trujillos. He also said that the UCN leadership was naïve and inexperienced and could easily be taken in by the Communists. And when the UCN led a general strike aimed at the ouster of Balaguer, he refused to approve it on the grounds that it would simply give the Communists a chance to come to the fore.

Meanwhile, he took care of Communists who tried to infiltrate his own party. With the PSPD and the 14th of June working inside the UCN, the Peking-oriented Dominican Popular Movement tried to worm its way into Bosch's party. And it had made some headway, having established a foothold in the PRD's youth section before Bosch himself had returned from exile. Bosch, on learning of this, ordered the whole PRD section disbanded, and serious infiltration of the party ended.

But as the electoral campaign matured and the PRD gained strength, the UCN, after finally breaking with the far left, began adding, without easing up on the charge that Bosch was a friend of the Trujilloists, the accusation that he was also a friend of the Communists, if not one himself, though previously he had been regarded as strongly anti-Communist.

The PRD reacted by picturing the UCN as the party of the oligarchs and ultrareactionaries, summed up in the word *tutum-*

potes, an image enhanced by the "bourgeois" look of its leaders, some of whom rode around in sleek cars, crowded the gambling casinos, and frequented fancy restaurants with their stout bejeweled wives. In fact, the PRD charged, the worst Trujilloists, men who had grown rich under the dictator, were actually taking over the UCN. The PRD, on the other hand, Bosch claimed, wanted only to help the poor. He promised jobs and higher wages to the workers, and 16 acres of land to each of 70,000 landless families, to be carved out of Trujillo property at first, and then from the property of the *tutumpotes.*

Behind the demagoguery on both sides, the lines of the political spectrum were, in truth, blurred. Bosch, for example, also promised a 10-year tax exemption to new business firms, while Fiallo, whose party was supposed to represent business interests, told me that no company that showed profits should be exempt from taxation.

Nevertheless, what the campaign did essentially, with the charges and countercharges of "communism" and "reaction" and with Bosch's stress on social reform, was to accentuate class differences. These differences had always been sharp. The top layer of society openly calls itself the "first-class citizens." Landowners and businessmen who are descended from the Spaniards and "hidalgos," Spanish noblemen of secondary rank, of pure blood, this class has traditionally controlled the country, one reason why it despised Trujillo, who was a "second-class" Dominican. "Second-class" citizens are also descended from Spaniards, but not of the pure-blooded hidalgos. They have been gaining strength in business and liberal professions after participation in a century of struggle. And then there are the "third-to tenth-class citizens"—the small shopkeepers, day laborers, white-collar workers, peasants.

As long as each class knew its place, there was a minimum of conflict between them, despite the existence of a latent resentment toward each other. But Bosch was now telling the lower-class citizens that their place was on a higher social ledge, a ledge that the upper class had too long monopolized. The Communists, of course, were saying the same thing, but they had little influence because they spoke in terms of violence, because they rejected God, because they wanted dictatorship when the people wanted freedom. Bosch was offering peaceful transition, God, and freedom, all this and first-class citizenship, too. To the traditional "first-class" strata, there was little distinction between the Communists and the PRD. Both would eliminate its privileges. Somehow the "first-class citizens," most of whom were in the UCN, felt that the other classes would be satisfied with their traditional status, particularly as the UCN was offering crumbs of reform that would to some extent close the social gap. Even Bosch's "educational" program, the UCN thought, could probably not disturb greatly the inertia of centuries.

The UCN made what was perhaps a major tactical blunder when it pledged that once in office it would "clean out" the armed forces, which had been trained and nurtured under Trujillo. In fear of their future, servicemen and their families and friends, ironically enough in the light of later events, threw their support behind Bosch, who remained noncommittal about any military "housecleaning."

But the UCN probably suffered most from the results of a charge by a Jesuit priest, Lautico García, in a local newspaper, shortly before the election, that some of Bosch's writings indicated that he might well be a Marxist-Leninist. This was the signal for a number of priests to tell their congregations that he was a Communist. Bosch charged that some priests even threatened excommunication of persons who voted for his party.

Informally scratching his party from the ballot, he said in a masterful but dangerous political gamble that the PRD would not participate in the election unless the church retracted the accusation. While the country, which had begun to see its first free election in decades go down the drain, sighed in relief,

García agreed to debate the issue with Bosch in a four-hour television drama that ended with Bosch obtaining the retraction. Bosch's grandstand play, it was clear, had cost the UCN many votes.

Several days after the election, *Verde Olivo,* the official organ of the Cuban armed forces, indicated how much of a Marxist Leninist it considered him. "The gesture of Bosch, whose adherence to the policy of the United States, as well as his anti-Communist position, is most notorious," it said, "was interpreted in two ways: either as a last-minute act to enable his chief rival, Viriato Fiallo, whom the U. S. Embassy and the reactionary clergy support, to gain the victory in the electoral farce, or as a reflection of the pressure exerted by the masses of people so that he should not participate in the electoral trickery. A number of democratic organizations, as is known, have denounced the electoral farce and have appealed to the people not to take part in the elections."

From the public's reaction, or lack of it, it was impossible to tell who was likely to win. The calm that prevailed throughout the country would have seemed unusual at election time even in some sophisticated democracies. However, despite the quiet, the streets of Santo Domingo were by no means deserted. Shirtsleeved men and colorfully frocked girls, who are among the most attractive in Latin America, strolled casually in the tropical sun or lounged in the park squares. Some carried beribboned Christmas packages under their arms, though with inflation growing, shopkeepers were not boasting a landslide business.

By standards set during the cruel era of Trujillo, the streets might even have been said to be crowded. Not only did the people have less money to shop with in the dictator's era; they had been afraid of being pulled in by the police at any time for any reason. Habit and residual fear were, in fact, among the most important ingredients of the electoral calm, disguising the true feelings of the people.

"Most Dominicans may seem apathetic about the election,"
one diplomatic observer said as he surveyed from his embassy
window the slow pace of life below, "but in reality they are
quite enthusiastic, and even excited. After living in a national
prison for thirty years, it's understandable that they haven't got
used to expressing their real sentiments yet."

In many cases, people would not say who their favorite candidates were, and in others, they announced themselves for
the candidates they believed the questioner supported. For in
a land where a slip of the tongue once meant jail and torture,
there was still little disposition to trust anyone.

A housewife revealingly told me: "I don't know who I'll vote
for because I don't know who will win."

Political leaders were aware of the reluctance of many people
to identify themselves openly with any political party by appearing at rallies. And they knew that others, once ordered by Trujillo to attend mass meetings in his honor, now had an aversion
to such gatherings. Candidates therefore concentrated on reaching urban voters mainly by radio and newspaper. To harangue
the peasants, they toured the countryside in flag-draped caravans;
no one could accuse anybody of favoring a particular group if
the mountain came to Mohammed.

Nevertheless, it was evident, the average Dominican had a
favorite party and was silently rooting for its candidates. That
was suggested, for one thing, by the extraordinary enthusiasm
exhibited by those who did openly support a party. Among those
Dominicans, the victory of the group they backed was clearly
a matter of life and death for the nation. The favored party
was composed of brilliant anti-Trujilloist social reformers while
the opposition consisted of crooks, Communists, reactionaries,
and pro-Trujilloists.

One notable phenomenon was the tremendous zeal of Dominican women, at least in the cities, for they viewed the election,
perhaps more than many men, as not simply a political contest
but as an idealistic symbol. Milagros Pratt, a beautiful green-

eyed university student and a leader of the women's section of the small Revolutionary Christian Socialist Party, explained: "I—and many other girls—have entered politics because we feel in our hearts that this is the best way we can contribute to the future welfare of our country and our children."

Not the least significant measure of public interest in the elections was the silence of the relatively small far left. In early December, the police discovered a Communist arms cache, but virtually no violence had been instigated as the election neared. The Communists were probably fully aware that to stir up electoral violence would simply intensify popular antagonism toward them.

Furthermore, it was widely felt that the United States would intervene to save the election, if necessary, as it had done to save the nation some months before. Reflecting U. S. involvement, Ambassador John Bartlow Martin was understood to have elicited verbal assurances from Fiallo and Bosch at an Embassy reception that the loser would accept the electoral results. U. S. air-dropped pamphlets taught Dominicans the technique of democratic voting, and U. S. experts trained policemen how to control riots without brutality.

The tacit threat of interference by Washington by no means frightened the Dominicans. After experiencing Trujillo's brutal rule for 30 years, they were determined to prevent the establishment of any new totalitarianism, particularly with elections so near. And they were perfectly willing to let the United States help them do so.

Even on election eve there was talk of a coup, particularly after what looked like a well-organized demonstration by a youthful mob that started throwing rocks and other missiles at some party headquarters. The laxity of the police in preventing the violence gave rise to reports that Imbert was planning to let the riot get out of hand in the hope of forcing a postponement of the election and providing an excuse for a takeover by himself. But Bonnelly apparently ordered the police to take immediate action, and the situation was brought under control. Most Council members, Bonnelly and Reid in particular, were determined that the elections be held—and they expected the UCN to win.

U. S. intentions were thus never put to the test. Despite all the doubts, fears, and rumors, on December 20, 1962, the Dominican people went to the polls to enjoy their first taste of parliamentary democracy. Rain fell most of the day, but this did not discourage a turnout of almost 90 percent of the eligible voters. Nor did the prevailing tranquillity hide their intense feelings in this treasured moment. Most voters, as they waited in endless lines at the polling booths, were still silent, whether Negro peasants in tattered working clothes, housewives with colorful kerchiefs around their heads, or upper-class businessmen in New York-tailored suits. But on every face there was an expression of dignity and exhilaration newly found.

When the votes were counted under OAS supervision, Juan Bosch had, unbelievably, won more than a 60 percent majority, and his party even greater majorities in Parliament. The silent people had spoken at last.

CHAPTER 4

The River Leaves Its Bed

AT HIS inauguration ceremony on February 27, 1963, Juan Bosch was embraced warmly by Vice-President Lyndon B. Johnson, who was representing President Kennedy. About a month later, a photograph of this encounter was published in the Cuban publication *Bohemia*. The caption read: "He is one of us: This is what Yankee Vice-President Lyndon Johnson appears to be saying as he was embraced by the new puppet of Uncle Sam, the slippery Juan Bosch of Santo Domingo."

Though it was highly doubtful that Bosch considered himself an American puppet, or that the United States thought that he would be one, Santo Domingo and Washington were both highly optimistic at the start of Bosch's regime about the future of the Dominican Republic. And the United States was determined to give the new government maximum assistance to make sure that this optimism would prove justified.

Bosch struck the keynote of the program he would follow in his inaugural adress: "Let no one expect the use of hate while we are governing. We are here with the decision to work not to hate, disposed to create not to destroy, to defend and to shelter, not to persecute. Let us join our hearts together in the task of doing away with hate among Dominicans as one does away with weeds in the field to be sown. Let us join our hearts together in the task of building institutions that will give shelter to those who never had it, that will give work to those who seek without having found it, that will give land to those farmers who need it, and security not only to those born here but to all those who wander the earth in search of refuge from misery and persecution. . . . While we govern, liberty will not perish in the Dominican Republic."

Such expansive idealistic promises, capping off a demagogic campaign, put Bosch in difficulty from the start. The masses who had supported him expected overnight miracles of prosperity and social justice. The UCN, already embittered and spiteful in a political defeat they had considered impossible just a few months before, now feared reforms that would destroy their economic and social domination as well. The reactionary clergy feared reforms, too, since they would undoubtedly affect the Church hold on the masses. The armed forces, though having supported Bosch because they feared the UCN more, were wary of a costly reform program that would cut into the military budgets and of a freedom that would permit Communists to return to the country.

To overcome these enormous obstacles, Bosch, it would appear, had to accomplish at least two things. He had to push through immediate reforms in order to keep and consolidate the tremendous popular support he enjoyed when he took power. And he had to reduce the power of the armed forces while his popularity was at its height and before Trujilloite officers had an opportunity to plot against him.

Bosch failed to attain either end, nor did he even try to do so. It is not at all clear that even if he had tried he could have hung on to power. He might, in fact, have accelerated his downfall. But if the political wisdom of his tactics are arguable, what those tactics showed about the man are not. They showed that Bosch's acute sense of social justice was strongly flavored with economic conservatism. And they showed, more importantly, that he was virtually incapable of resorting to expediency at the expense of principle. His cautionary and moralistic approach may well have been a questionable instrument of policy in a situation calling for drastic action, but it also accentuated the tragedy of his fall. Rare indeed is the Latin-American leader who in his actions is neither demagogic nor opportunistic.

The United States, which was determined to keep Bosch in power and make its democratic experiment work as an answer to communism, realized the need to maintain strong popular support as a counterweight to the powerful forces ranged against him. Ambassador Martin and his staff urged him to start instituting reforms immediately. The United States, they assured him, would back him to the hilt. It had already poured in funds amounting, in 1962, to over $22 for each Dominican, more than triple the average per capita contribution to the rest of Latin America as a whole. Now it was ready to accelerate its assistance to programs that called for land reform, food distribution, agricultural credit, extension services, rural roads, a vocational agricultural school, farm cooperatives, low-cost housing, school expansion, and a corporation to run the Trujillo commercial properties.

Martin, and also Newell F. Williams, who was director of the U. S. Agency for International Development in the Dominican Republic, got along quite well with Bosch. A distinguished magazine writer and author, Martin, after writing speeches for President Kennedy during the 1960 campaign, had been selected Ambassador on the basis of an illuminating report he had prepared on the Dominican Republic following a visit there. His literary background, political liberalism, and straightforwardness soon earned him Bosch's friendship and trust. In a recent book, Bosch wrote: "In truth, Martin and Williams did not appear to be agents of the U. S. government but rather two Dominicans as anxious as the best of Dominicans to accomplish the impossible for us."

But Martin and Williams found Bosch a stubborn customer.

Oddly enough, unlike most other recipients of U. S. aid who can never get enough, Bosch said, "Wait!" American assistance, he maintained, would do the most good when the programs he had in mind were sufficiently developed to be able to absorb large-scale funds efficiently. Without proper planning, he said, the programs would be wasteful and amount to demagoguery. To the exasperation of U. S. officials, Bosch, who had been demagogic in his campaign speeches, promising immediate and drastic reforms, was proving to be not enough of a demagogue in action. In fact, he displayed in some ways the mentality of a conservative American businessman.

Bosch's central economic aim was to create new sources of production in order to keep pace with consumption, and create capital for further development. He regarded the oligarchs as having more the mentality of "colonial traders" than of "industrial entrepreneurs," and felt that such thinking had been reflected in the policies of the Council of State. Figures appeared to bear out this appraisal. In 1962, the Council had vast financial resources at its disposal as the result of the lifting of U. S. economic sanctions, new U. S. sugar legislation favoring the country, the doubling of world market prices for sugar, the confiscation of Trujillo's wealth, and the granting of large-scale U. S. economic aid.

Yet, government development investment formed less than three percent of the gross national product that year as compared to 10 percent in the period from 1956 to 1958. It dropped to $14.4 million from $30.5 million in 1961. On the other hand, Council funds were squandered as the result of corruption and ineptitude. The Council, for example, sold about 60 percent of the 1963 sugar production in advance at an average price of 3.5 cents per pound, though the price was almost four times higher at the time of delivery. Income and net profit taxes, meanwhile, amounted to only $1.7 million between January and May 1962, as against $14.1 million during the same period of 1963 mainly under Bosch.

On taking office, Bosch immediately abolished more than 150 bureaucratic and diplomatic positions, including 15 in the Dominican Embassy in Washington. He then reduced the salaries of all government officials earning over $500 monthly. His own plunged from $5,000 to $1,500 a month, and those of his cabinet ministers from $2,000 to $1,000.

In his savings campaign, which reduced government expenditures by almost $200,000 a month, Bosch even appealed to government employees to preserve paper cups and used carbon paper. He also revoked the right of Dominicans traveling abroad to draw $250 from local banks, as a means of cutting off illegal imports that had fetched highly profitable prices at home. The result of this policy was a balanced budget, and within a few months a near elimination of the national deficit.

A large balance-of-payments surplus also seemed in view. Gross foreign exchange reserves were in May 1963, two months after he took office, double the figure recorded in January, reaching $43 million. And that was after payment of more than $20 million of commercial arrears owed American and other foreign suppliers. The nation's improved foreign reserve position permitted it, moreover, to reduce import restrictions, and to repay a $9 million debt to the International Monetary Fund in advance of the repayment schedule.

Nor did Bosch ignore the future. With world sugar prices high and sugar accounting for about 70 percent of the Dominican economy—large sugar sales helped to explain the nation's relative prosperity—he imposed a new tax on sugar producers to reduce inflationary pressures during periods of price fluctuation and provide additional revenue for development purposes. Thus, all earnings above a ceiling of 5.8 cents a pound had to be deposited in a special government fund.

At the same time, he fitfully reorganized all ministries and agencies that were to participate in reform projects, giving special attention to the Agrarian Institute which was responsible for land reform. He believed that the Institute as organized under the Council threatened to become an overburdened organization on the style of Cuba's, a kind of state within a state, with the job of building roads, schools, and almost everything else connected with land and living improvement. He laid plans to streamline the Institute and decentralize the various aspects of agrarian reform. He was ready to start distributing former Trujillo-owned land to the peasants on a large scale in September, when he was ousted. Only 1,300 families had been settled on land in the seven months he was in office, but by the end of September the number was to have increased to 4,000, accelerating to 20,000 by the termination of Bosch's term in 1966.

With the American aid that he did accept, he established vocational schools for agricultural education, savings and loan associations, a poultry industry. Private builders constructed new housing.

Though unemployment was critical, Bosch, after a few months in office, had put 11,000 persons to work on public works, including schools, with the help of a $200,000 fund granted under the Alliance for Progress. He used some U. S. aid to encourage the growth of small business. For example, he sold American road-building equipment on easy terms to young engineers willing to form small companies and sign maintenance contracts with the government. Previously, such machinery had been administered by the Ministry of Public Works, leading to inefficiency and corruption.

Bosch went on the radio time and again to report to the people on the progress the country was making and the plans he was developing. But if his approach was probably justified from an economic point of view, the U. S. Embassy was probably right in a political sense. The people expected, however unreasonably, quick results, and to keep them on his side while he played for time, he might well have thought less in orthodox economic terms. For even a political genius would almost certainly have had a hard time satisfying the demands of the long-underprivileged Dominican people, and Bosch, inexperienced as were all Dominican politicians, was no such genius.

The facts of life were that unemployment remained high, disgruntled job seekers waited in long lines outside the presidential palace, per capita income declined as the population growth outstripped the gross national product, businessmen, with little trust in Bosch or their own country, were investing abroad, and the peasant population, representing over 70 percent of the total, was clamoring for land.

Moreover, Bosch could find few good administrators, and the fact that more than half of the population was illiterate slowed down efforts to introduce new techniques in industry and agriculture. Even plans to use soldiers on civic-action projects had to be curtailed because there weren't enough literate officers to run the program. Needless to say, there was also a severe shortage of trained professional and technical personnel to perform the tasks of development. Nor would there have been enough capital available for substantial development even if U. S. aid had poured in, with Dominican industries suffering from underinvestment in capital equipment and the land reform program slowed by the high cost of resettlement.

In any event, Bosch made it clear that he had no intention of depending strictly on American funds for long-range development, often criticizing the Alliance for its red tape and conditional nature. If he could make more advantageous arrangements with financing organs in Europe, he planned to do so. And in fact, after his election and before his inauguration, he visited not only Washington but the capitals of Europe investigating loan possibilities.

One of his most controversial actions, which some people point to as evidence of his administrative incapacity, was an arrangement he made with a group of European businessmen who had formed a company called Overseas Construction, Ltd. In a deal calling for the expenditure of $150 million for a series of hydroelectric projects, the company was commissioned to

parcel out contracts to various firms. It obtained the services of
General Electric Company of England, then dissolved itself.

Bosch's opposition questioned the need of Overseas Construction's services and of the advance payments that were made to
General Electric, and accused him of agreeing to overcostly conditions. Bosch replied that the arrangement was a perfectly honest one, and that in the end the country would gain since it
wouldn't have to wait for the sluggish Alliance machinery to
start grinding. A saving in time, he said, was sometimes more
important than a saving in immediate expenditures. Whatever
the merit of his plan, which never got off the ground, no dishonesty was ever established. And, according to *Listin Diario,*
the Reid Cabral government was trying in early 1965 to renew
at least some parts of the General Electric contract.

Thus, for a while after Bosch took office, one saw fewer and
fewer tractors, trucks, and half-tracks marked with the hand-
clasp emblem of the Alliance for Progress lumbering along
Dominican roads. His unusual attitude toward U. S. assistance
appeared to be rooted partly in his strongly nationalistic sen-
sitivities, which instinctively led him to seek a reduction of
America's powerful influence in his country, however appreciative he was of the U. S. effort to protect democracy and promote
reform. And this aim was fed by what he considered the need
to win over the ultranationalistic, anti-American youth, particularly those in the 14th of June Movement, by following as
independent a line as possible. He wanted to develop a Mexican-
type relationship with the United States, warm but unbinding.
He didn't want to be anyone's "protégé."

Bosch's reluctance to push through reforms before plans had
been perfected and his reservations about unrestrained cooperation with the United States, whether justified or not, played
into the hands of his enemies. For with the people starting to
grow impatient and the United States expressing some irritation
with Bosch, his foes felt less pressure on them to accept him with
all his faults.

The armed forces held the key to Bosch's future. They, after all, had the guns, the same guns that had kept the Trujillos at the helm for over 30 years. And they, as well as Bosch, had the support of the Kennedy Administration. One reason why that Administration had felt it could afford to gamble that the country would not go the way of Cuba lay in their continued existence as the real source of power in the country. Thus, Washington had provided the democratic revolution with both a shield against communism and a sword over its head.

Nor was Bosch himself prepared to cleanse from leadership the undemocratic, Trujilloite elements, as the UCN had promised to do in the electoral campaign. He rejected the advice of some advisers that he balance the power of the armed forces, or replace them, with a militia loyal to him and his principles, though his enemies accused him of trying to set up a militia. He was convinced that any effort to take on the armed forces would spark a coup and possibly civil war before democracy was even born. He preferred to take his chances with the armed forces' sword over his head, figuring that even if it eventually dropped, democracy could at least get started. And maybe, with luck, young officers, trained in constitutionalism, particularly in U. S. schools, might come to the fore before the Trujilloites struck. At any rate, he was certain that the people, once they tasted democracy, would in the end never settle for less.

But the military sword was a menacing one, indeed, for Trujillo had conditioned his officers well, keeping them under his thumb with an effective mixture of terror and patronage. One such officer was Miguel Atila Luna, who became Air Force chief after the dictator died. Atila Luna, a tall, slim man in his mid-thirties, served Trujillo faithfully for 14 years. He admitted to me as he ground a cigarette stub into an ashtray in his office at San Isidro Air Base that, having been fed almost from birth on the myth of the dictator's greatness, he only realized his boss was bad after his assassination.

Atila Luna and his fellow officers learned to respect the use of brute power to achieve desired ends. They learned conversely not to think for themselves. For Trujillo, fearful that he might train a Frankenstein monster that would someday destroy him, demanded absolute obedience from his soldiers, and was careful not to allocate many responsibilities. His secret police made sure they kept in line. Any sign of disloyalty automatically meant torture and death.

But at the same time, Trujillo showered favors on his officers, particularly those most willing to bow and scrape before him and dedicate themselves unreservedly to a single aim—the satisfaction of his every tyrannical whim. They lived in expensive homes and drove duty-free automobiles, and sometimes, if the dictator learned one was in debt, he would send him a check for the total amount. His officers could be proud, too, for they led the most powerful war machine in the Caribbean, including 17,000 troops, 12,000 national policemen, light, medium, and heavy tank battalions, and squadrons of fighters, bombers, destroyers, and frigates—all occupying their own tiny country of 3.5 million people at a cost representing about 40 percent of the national budget.

The Trujillo officer could be particularly proud if, like Atila Luna, and also Wessin, he was in the Air Force. For the dictator, to make doubly sure against an army uprising, built up an elite Air Force at San Isidro, under his son Ramfis, that included not only planes but the best tanks, artillery, and infantry units and an Armed Forces Training Center.

Under the Bosch government, officers and enlisted men continued to be paid the salaries they received under Trujillo— $70 a month for a private, $600 for a general—but officer privileges and opportunities for smuggling and corruption, which had produced not a few millionaires, were drastically cut down. And with the expensive reforms envisaged by Bosch bound to cut deeply into the national budget, the armed forces would inevitably have been reduced in size and power. Atila Luna was particularly incensed when Bosch rejected his request for a $6 million aircraft order from Great Britain. Not only was this a sign of the coming cut-down, but he was deprived, according to Bosch, of $1 million in commission.

But if officers like Atila Luna were concerned primarily with the monetary profits of military leadership, some were mainly alarmed by the threat being posed to the military's traditional role in society as the "guardian of the nation" in partnership with the Church. The job of the armed forces, as they saw it, was to maintain to the degree possible the social status quo, with each class in its natural place. The only alternative was communism. And this kind of thinking was intensively fostered by some Jesuit priests, who viewed the Church's role in society in the same light.

Such priests found Wessin, who was a colonel at the time, in command of the Air Force tank units and training center, particularly amenable to such logic. A paunchy, swarthy, beetle-browed man with an immobile expression and retiring manner, Wessin is a man of simple taste. He modestly refuses to wear the many decorations conferred on him by Trujillo, and he lives with his wife and two sons in a $12,000 concrete house that some of his fellow high-living officers might use as a shed. Wessin, whose father was a Lebanese shopkeeper who had emigrated to the Dominican Republic in 1920, joined the Air Force as a private in 1944 at the age of twenty and rose quickly in the ranks.

He was the ideal Trujillo military officer, obedient, unimaginative, tough and, if need be, cruel. As a guardian of Trujillo, he was a guardian of the nation, for Trujillo was the nation. When Trujillo was gone, it was a simple matter substituting for the dictator as an object of devotion other forces representing the status quo that the tyrant had, during more than 30 years of uninterrupted rule, come to personify. And one of the most powerful of these forces was the reactionary element in the Church, which is still largely unresponsive to the new liberal tenets of the Vatican. Except in Trujillo's last years, when he stepped on its toes, it supported the dictator in return for his agreement to abide by a Concordat he had signed with Pope Pius XII.

Wessin was one of the officers who helped to overthrow General Rodríguez Echevarría 48 hours after the latter had ousted the first Council of State in January 1962. His respect for power, at that time the overwhelming power of the United States, which was then ranged on the side of the people, was reflected in that episode, as were his views on loyalty to anyone he considered vulnerable to the exercise of such power. Wessin, as an Air Force transportation officer, had been accused by Ramfis Trujillo of stealing large quantities of gasoline, and jailed shortly after the elder Trujillo's assassination. But Rodríguez Echevarría, as Air Force chief in Santiago, had him released and assigned as his assistant, the two men having trained together in cadet days.

Wessin went along with his chief when the latter was made Secretary of the Armed Forces. But when Rodríguez Echevarría tried to take over the government, American officials apparently convinced the general's protégé that he should turn against his benefactor.

"Wessin was so scared when he, together with several other officers, came to arrest me," Rodríguez Echevarría told me, later, "that I was sure he would shoot me. Finally, a major persuaded him to leave the room before he pulled the trigger. I was very sad that Wessin betrayed me." (The major was Rafael Fernández Domínguez, who was to become a rebel leader in the 1965 revolution.)

Once Bosch came to office, the dilemma in which the armed forces had found themselves gradually dissolved in a natural realignment of forces. The UCN's hatred of the armed forces had been a unique and unnatural situation. In almost all other Latin-American countries, the status quo civilian forces and the armed forces were traditional partners, since it was in the interest of each to support the other against the encroachment of social change that would reduce or destroy the power of both. But in the Dominican Republic, the situation had been distorted by the extraordinary advent of Trujillo.

The dictator, far from being an ally of the traditional oligarchal families, despised them for their socially exclusive attitude that, in fact, excluded him from their circle as a rather lowbrow man of mixed blood, his mother having been, though he tried to cover up the fact, a Haitian mulatto. One of his most satisfying actions while in office was his takeover of the exclusive Club Unión that had once blackballed him and his order that its name be changed to "Club Presidente Trujillo." But far more meaningful for the traditional rulers was his monopolization of the Dominican economy from which they could eke out only limited leftover benefits. The armed forces they could once depend on were ranged on Trujillo's side against them. Thus, after the dictator's demise, the UCN, which largely represented upper-class interests, wanted revenge.

But when Bosch came to power, the UCN awakened to the realities of the situation. It was time to forget old hatreds and jealousies. The simple fact was that the oligarchs and the armed forces were in the same boat. The power of both was being threatened by Bosch's reform schemes. And so the vested interests pursued an entente with officers like Wessin, using primarily "religion" as a common platform for attacks on Bosch.

The civilian rightists started laying the groundwork for an anti-Bosch entente with the military almost as soon as Bosch was elected, possibly before he assumed office. Boschist leaders say they are responsible for the death of General Miguel Rodríguez Reyes, a strong supporter of constitutional government who might have become Bosch's armed forces chief had he lived. They maintain that Council of State members had asked Rodríguez Reyes to participate in a coup against Bosch, and that he had refused, and had, in fact, tried to dissuade other military plotters from doing so.

It was then, claim the Boschists, that Bonnelly ordered the

general to go with an Army unit to wipe out the influence of
a group of fanatical Dominicans who were fostering voodoo
practices of Haitian origin in the village of Palma Sola near the
Haitian border. Members of the Trujillo family, Bonnelly is
understood to have argued, were using the sect as a center of
conspiracy aimed at their return. A more subtle reason for sending troops appears to have been rooted in the fear of Dominican
coffee plantation owners that the cult's influence might seriously
disrupt production, since its day of rest was Monday, a working
day. Many workers simply didn't show up on that day.

General Rodríguez Reyes was surprised that he, a top general,
was to be used for an action that might have required the leadership of a lower-ranking officer, particularly since cult members
were unarmed. And he told his family that he was puzzled by
the assignment. But he went, and reportedly tried to use peaceful means in dealing with the group, which was called the Cult
of Liborio after its leader who first formed it to resist the American Occupation that started in 1916. The general was mysteriously killed, apparently with stones and clubs. Some Boschists
claim, however, that he was murdered, and that he had been
sent on the mission to provide an excuse for his death. Others
say that at the least the Council was hoping to discredit him,
since it was known that the cult would violently resist the troops,
provoking them to shoot the unarmed villagers. At any rate,
the Army did indeed shoot, killing scores of people. It was supported by police units under the command of Colonel Francisco
Caamaño, who himself was almost killed in the fight. It is not
clear whether he was responsible in any degree for the massacre.

Former Council members have vigorously denied that they
had engaged in a pre-inaugural plot against Bosch or that they
had any ulterior motives in sending Rodríguez Reyes on his
fatal mission. Wherever the truth lies, immediately after Bosch's
inauguration, Horacio Julio Ornes, president of the Revolutionary Vanguardia Party, a small conservative group, accused Bosch
of planning a program of "Communist indoctrination" of the

armed forces. With blatant opportunism joined to a genuine fear of social reform—which amounted to communism in many rightist minds—the electoral campaign slanders were thus carried over into Bosch's regime, and hardly a day passed when he wasn't called a Communist, charged with giving Communists jobs, or in other ways promoting communism. Fiallo finally came out with an accusation that Communists were filling "key posts" in the government, though he refused to say who they were, perhaps because the naming of names might have brought out the fact that infiltration had really begun under the Council of State.

Bosch's enemies also charged that he was allowing a Communist, Dato Pagán, to conduct Marxist classes in a public school building. Yet, Pagán had been granted a license to use the building by the UCN-dominated Council of State. Bosch was planning to evict Pagán at the end of the school term, but because he would not take action before then he was accused by those who had agreed to the classes in the first place of promoting communism.

Bosch may have erred in not closing the classes immediately, but in his view that would have looked like suppression when the same result could be achieved by letting the license run out. Why, he felt, should he be unnecessarily provocative, particularly when pressure was being exerted on him strictly for political purposes? Why should he make a martyr of Pagán?

Bosch was also severely criticized for permitting Dominicans to travel to Cuba. Actually, after the first group went, he put a restriction in all new passports forbidding such travel, but, as in the United States, there was no law he could use to enforce this restriction. He was, in fact, drafting a constitutional amendment permitting enforcement at the time of his ouster. (Most of those who visited Cuba, incidentally, were former members of the UCN.)

Nor were the rightists interested in explanations. Behind their charges was not necessarily logic but fear. And this fear was fed by some of the laws that Bosch tried to push through, particularly those embodied in the new liberal Constitution, which, written with the assistance of U. S. Supreme Court Justice William O. Douglas, was considered basically excellent by American experts but contained several loosely framed articles spawned by overzealous reformers. A U. S. Embassy official told me while Bosch was in office: "Bosch admits there are defects in the Constitution, but they can be corrected, for the Constitution itself provides ways to do this. But it is necessary to have enough time to know what changes would be wise."

Capitalists were aghast at Article 19, which said that the workers have the right to share in the profits of industry and agriculture without specifying what percentage should go to them. Property owners were shocked by several articles. Article 23 prohibited very large private landholdings, or *latifundios*, without indicating how many acres constituted a *latifundio*. Article 28 required landholders to sell that portion of their land exceeding maximum levels to be set by law. If no private purchasers were available, the landholder had to sell the excess land to the government, which would resell to peasants when they chose to buy. And Article 32 said that if the value of land and building increased as a result of state-instituted improvements in the area, the owner had to pay a share of the increase in value to the government. No maximum proportional share was specified.

Such provisions, cried some people, could be used to deprive capitalists, if expediency so required, of all their holdings. In other words, they left the door open to communism. And their fears grew when Bosch later backed a law, if unsuccessfully, whereby the Minister of Public Properties could seize any land or property that had been acquired by a public official illicitly, that is, through the use of his public position. The law would also apply to land or property acquired by a third person profiting from his relationship with a public official. Since almost everyone with money had made it at least with the passive cooperation of Trujillo, the law, it was feared, would permit, even more dangerously than the Constitution itself, the confiscation of almost any property the government wanted.

At the same time, some Dominicans complained, Article 25, which said that "only Dominican citizens have a right to acquire land," except under special circumstances, would discourage foreign investment.

There were other controversial articles as well. Some men balked at Article 47, which stated that a husband had to obtain the approval of his wife in order to dispose of jointly owned properties. Some women, and the Catholic Church, opposed Article 49, which, designed to protect children born out of wedlock, prohibited public officials from inscribing the "character of the affiliation" of a child's parents on a birth certificate. The Church also was dissatisfied with Article 37, which gave the state control over education while ignoring the Concordat that had given the Church the prime role. Nor was the Church pleased with the failure of the Constitution to characterize the state as a Catholic nation, or with proposals for legal divorce and civil marriage.

Furthermore, rightists protested Article 66, which provided that no Dominican citizen could be deported without due process of law—a provision that Bosch defended with special vigor in view of Trujillo's policy of deporting anyone on the slightest whim.

The nerve center of the civilian campaign to paint Bosch as a Communist was Rafael Bonilla Aybar, a radio-television commentator and tabloid publisher. His compelling voice boomed throughout the nation that Bosch and his associates were Communists. His handsome Caesar Romero face, aflame with indignation, appeared on almost every TV screen.

Businessmen basked in what they considered confirmation of their own fears. Some women saw him as a hero on a white horse having come to save them from a fate worse than death. Workers and housemaids devoured his gossipy revelations of corruption in the upper class, which he cleverly interspersed with his anti-Bosch charges.

To get his message across even more dramatically, Bonilla began holding meetings of Christian Reaffirmation, one in a different city each week. Although these meetings were ostensibly intended to rekindle religious faith among the people, they were actually gatherings to further discredit Bosch as a Communist. As soon as Bosch came to power, Bonilla had begun putting out a daily tabloid, called *Prensa Libre,* devoted to the same end. Not surprisingly, he used the presses of the UCN, which is believed to have financed his activities.

Ironically, Bosch's fanatical opposition to all forms of suppression furthered Bonilla's aim. Even some of Bosch's enemies were at a loss to understand how he could stand by and permit Bonilla to proclaim to the people day in and day out that he was a Communist. On one occasion, Bosch did crack down, to Bonilla's benefit. Charging that the commentator had misused funds of *La Nación,* which Bonilla had once edited, the President dispatched the chief of police to arrest him in the middle of a telecast. The spectacle of Bonilla being dragged off to jail while thousands watched sent his TV rating skyrocketing.

Bonilla concentrated mainly on trying to turn the armed forces against Bosch. He started with a big strike against him. As a supporter of the UCN, he had, in the electoral race, strongly backed the party's attacks on these forces as "Trujilloist." When Bosch won the election, Bonilla saw the need for flexibility. He embraced the officers he had been calling "criminals." He enlisted the help of ultra-rightist priests and businessmen who gave the military "friendly advice."

Through his radio, TV, newspaper, and Christian Affirmation propaganda, he helped to create a climate of anti-Communist panic—fed further by scare telephone calls supposedly from Communists—that gave the impression to the unsophisticated military leaders that the nation, and even the United States, was clamoring for a coup. And so Bonilla—and other rightists—

joined in common cause with the military to set the stage for the tragedy to come.

The reactionary priests were glad to foster this reconciliation. On the one hand, they presided at Bonilla's Christian Affirmation meetings. And on the other, they conducted "religious" classes for the armed forces, which Wessin made mandatory for his troops. Wessin himself, whose modest office at San Isidro is adorned with a small bust of Jesus wearing a crown of thorns, on his cluttered desk, and a painting of Christ on the wall, attended three-day religious seminars and was an excellent pupil. With the information he absorbed, he personally began lecturing officers and writing in the Air Force news sheet on Communist theory and methods of detecting subversion. Even Atila Luna, who has never been known for his spiritual interests, recognized the value of the religious classes.

"The Air Force is far more religious than the Army and Navy," he told me. "We have better priests."

Aside from the fears aroused by Bosch among military leaders as to reforms that would cut into their privileges and lead toward communism, these leaders were infuriated by his efforts to seek a military showdown with the dictatorial Haitian government of President François Duvalier. Although Bosch claimed that Duvalier was persecuting and threatening Dominicans in Haiti, the militarists believed that Bosch was only stirring up a nationalist crisis artificially, using them in the process, to maintain his waning popularity at home.

Bosch's determination to be the very antithesis of Trujillo and to keep his country completely free from persecution of any kind unless sanctioned by law helped to speed his downfall. For as much as he despised communism, he refused to deprive the Communists, or for that matter, the Trujilloists, of their constitutional rights, taking the same stand that the U. S. government has always taken toward its own Communists, who cannot be punished or deported without due process of law any more than common criminals can. Nor would he forcefully break up far-leftist demonstrations, fearing that once the police were unleashed the old Trujillo brutality would return with "communism" becoming once more an excuse to arrest anyone for any reason.

Moreover, he felt that Communists out in the open were no more dangerous than Communists underground but, in fact, were easier to handle, since, on the one hand, they could be watched and, on the other, they would be less likely to resort to guerrilla warfare, as in Venezuela. In the latter respect, he assumed the same attitude toward the Communists as toward the armed forces, which he also refrained from attacking head-on in order to avoid violence and bloodshed.

He felt, furthermore, that suppression of the Communists would help to unite them at a time when the different Red groups were excoriating each other with almost as much gusto as they were denouncing the other parties.

But most important of all, Bosch wanted to show the restless, cynical youths of leftist bent whom he hoped to convert to moderation and democracy that moderation and democracy could lead to the desperately needed social reform and economic development for which they longed.

"The youth of the country are the future of the country," Bosch told me in his hotel room in San Juan after he had been overthrown. "They are not Communists. They come from conservative middle-class families. They are suspicious of democracy because the United States, with its imperialistic past in Latin America, is a democracy. They are suspicious of it also because they think it works too slowly. I wanted to show them that you can have democracy and still be independent and make extraordinary progress. If they can't be convinced of that, then our future is bleak indeed."

In discoursing on democracy, Bosch spoke to his people simply, in the way a teacher might speak to his children. He was starting from scratch, he knew, and if democracy was to succeed in a country that had known only dictators, he believed, the people had to understand the responsibilities as well as the benefits of such freedom. In a radio speech delivered in April 1963, he said:

"The President is humble, democracy must be humble. In a democracy, all must comply with the law.... There is no room for privilege among those who must comply with the law. All Dominicans must respect the law. In the social and economic fields, management must respect the law and fulfill it, and the workers must respect and comply with the law....

"It is not easy to be always calm. The Lord, who was always calm, once lost His temper and drove the traders from the temple with a whip. We will never use the whip because we know that Jesus used it once but imposed His authority with sweetness over millions of men. It is not easy to maintain serenity, but I will do so no matter what. This is because it is our duty to maintain this democracy until the last day of our mandate. The law is not a whip. The law is the bed over which the river runs. As long as the river flows over its bed, the river does good. But when the river leaves its bed, the river sweeps away crops, houses, and isolates people. No one here should leave the river bed. To do so would be to harm the country. We will maintain the law, no matter what."

But if Bosch refused to suppress Communists unless they were caught disobeying the law, he made it clear what he thought of communism when he said at an Army ceremony in March 1963: "There is no longer room for personal dictatorship from which we have been suffering. There is only one clear dilemma: communism or democracy. And communism means death, war, destruction, and the loss of all our blessings."

This was one of the few times that Bosch came out with an open denunciation of the Communists, and his refusal to do so more often gave the accusations of "pro-Communist" hurled by his enemies a certain credibility among Dominicans who didn't like him anyway. When I asked him why he was so reluctant to state flatly that he was anti-Communist, if for no other reason than to counter the charges, he indicated again that he didn't want to look as if he were simply rubber-stamping American propaganda tactics, as valid as those tactics might be for the United States, since that would reduce his chances of wooing to democracy the misguided youths who tended toward the far left not because they favored communism, but because they had one strong sentiment in common with the Reds—anti-Americanism.

Since anti-Communist statements, he said, are associated with U. S. thinking, for him to make them constantly would stiffen their resistance to his efforts to reach them. They had to be led toward democracy, he maintained, through the positive tactic of showing them what democracy has to offer, not through the negative one of telling them how bad communism is.

At the same time, it was evident that Bosch, perhaps an unreasonably proud man, felt it was beneath him to have to deny constantly that he was pro-Communist and to have to prove to anyone that he wasn't. His record, rooted in democracy and blasted by the very Communists he was supposed to favor, spoke for itself, he believed.

In terms of action, he was less timid. Despite charges that he collaborated with the Reds or let them infiltrate his government, he tried, in reality, to rid the government of the far leftists who had been permitted to infiltrate by the Council of State. When he found the Economic Planning Board riddled with suspected Reds, he rendered it largely ineffectual by transferring most planning authority to a semipublic organization, the Inter-American Center of Economic and Social Studies (CIDES), which, supported by American foundations, developed an agrarian reform program, compiled the government's budget, and prepared population and manpower studies. Ironically, the organizer of this center, Sacha Volman, a staunchly anti-Communist Rumanian-born U. S. citizen, was one of the main targets of the slander campaign, though he was successfuly stealing the Communists' thunder.

To end Communist influence in the Land Reform Institute, Bosch divided its functions among various ministries. The Department of Sports was eliminated through drastic reduction of its budget. Many Communists were ousted individually from other ministries.

Bosch also tried to counteract the activities of a Communist-controlled trade union movement that had taken root in 1961, when the UCN saw nothing wrong in dealing with Communists, by setting up a free trade union center affiliated with the Inter-American Regional Organization of Workers, which embraces the AFL-CIO. He squelched Communist-led strikes of government employees and teachers on the grounds that these walkouts violated laws regulating strikes, purging Red leaders. He ended Communist control of the electrical workers, too.

Bosch prohibited Dominicans from accepting scholarships to study in Communist countries. He ordered his embassies to reject all visa applications submitted by foreign Communists. He kept Dominican Communists under close police surveillance. And he selected a reputed pro-American, Pedro Alvaro Bobadilla, as director of the government newspaper, *La Nación,* to keep out far-leftist influences.

Bosch's enemies conveniently ignored such accomplishments. His moral stubbornness and imaginative approach were made to order for them. But, it must be added, so were his personality and temperament. Bosch, for all his dedication to democratic principles, is, oddly enough, not a man of tolerant disposition. He often cannot accept a dissenting opinion. In one case, for example, just before he took office he asked an American official and longtime friend for his frank opinion on how the United States would feel about the appointment of a particular individual as Ambassador to Washington. When the official diplomatically indicated that such an appointment would probably not be regarded with delight, Bosch walked off in a huff and actually went to the trouble of withdrawing an invitation to his inaugural ceremony that he had sent him. Indeed, Bosch, after a disagreement with his friend, Puerto Rican Governor Muñoz Marín, only agreed to invite him after Venezuelan President Betancourt, another friend, indicated he would not come unless Muñoz were there.

If Bosch exhibited such sensitivity in his relations with his most ardent supporters, he was, of course, far less tolerant toward his political foes. He viewed them as his mortal enemies rather than as political opponents to be tactfully dealt with, though his foes regarded him with no less intolerance. He was, for example, furious at Betancourt for receiving some UCN visitors, and he even refused to let Bonnelly, the Council of State chief, officially turn over the government to him at his inauguration because he suspected him, as a member of the UCN, of having tried to keep him out of office. When, as President-Elect, he visited Washington, he failed to show up at an OAS luncheon that had been arranged for him, pleading illness at the last moment, though associates made it clear that he was "angry" at the OAS for having given strong support to the UCN-dominated Council of State he had so despised. He did try to get some oppositionists, including Reid Cabral, to enter his government, it is true, and they refused. They might well have refused in any event, but he did nothing to ease their feeling that he wasn't a man who would compromise, even on the smallest issues.

Moreover, though his enemies resorted to Dominican McCarthyism to discredit him, his own constant attacks on them as *tutumpotes* lent a strong and unnecessary class flavor to his attacks. The upper class viewed such attacks as an attempt to instigate mass uprisings against them, to stir new class hatreds and also racial resentments, since most upper-class people were white, and most lower-class members Negro or mulatto.

"He spread hate, hate, hate," one prominent physician told me in describing why he himself "hated" Bosch.

Certainly some political opponents who might have been willing to suffer through Bosch's term for the sake of preserv-

ing democracy decided otherwise when he seemed to go out of
his way to antagonize them.

Nor did even his best friends derive comfort from his tendency to react emotionally, and sometimes irrationally, to situations requiring coolness and a tough skin. For example, his
threat to resign from the presidential candidacy because someone called him a Communist was not regarded as the ultimate
in emotional maturity. He was even thinking of resigning just
before the election until his aides persuaded him to change his
mind, arguing that he would probably win the election. Was
it possible, some observers asked, that one day he would pull
a Jânio Quadros, that is, suddenly resign his office in a fit of
pique as President Quadros did in Brazil in 1961, leaving chaos
in his wake?

But if Bosch lacked a tolerant spirit, he did not vent his intolerance in violence, force, or dictatorship. He refused to let
his bitterness and prejudice dilute his moral convictions, to
sway him from the path of democracy. Paradoxically enough,
the uncompromising attitude that might be considered anath-
ema to democracy was most prominently applied in his support of democracy itself.

But whatever the shortcomings or accomplishments of the
Bosch regime, such factors were really irrelevant insofar as they
were related to its survival. Those who were determined to oust
him were not interested in waiting to see what Bosch would do
or not do. According to Bosch, he learned about and thwarted
a plot that had been planned for March 9, only ten days after
he took office. He claims to have broken up another plot in
April. Then, in mid-July, at a meeting at San Isidro with Wessin, Atila Luna, and other high officers, Bosch was told that the
group was "very worried about the activities of certain political
segments. We also wish to tell you that you can count on us
in any step undertaken against them." This was an obvious reference to the Communists.

Bosch flatly refused to cooperate, explaining angrily that to take action against any one political faction would open the door to action against other groups in the future.

"We have not returned to this country to persecute," he replied. "We are affirmative, not negative. If the armed forces persist, they must look for someone else to rule because I am not willing to lead a dictatorship—total or partial—in the Dominican Republic."

But his ouster, he added prophetically, would result in civil war. He castigated the officers present for involving themselves in political affairs, and ordered two officers, including a chaplain, discharged from the Air Force for allegedly instigating the confrontation. Then, in a radio speech, he alluded to the danger that he might soon be overthrown.

It is possible that this prospect could have been avoided, or at least delayed, if he had agreed to the officers' "advice," or even had he been more diplomatic in rejecting it. But, right or wrong, that would not have been Bosch. He was prepared neither to compromise what he considered a matter of principle, nor to give the armed forces the impression that he might. And as a matter of fact, in his view, two principles had been involved. One was that no group could be punished unless found to disobey the law; and the other that political policy was not the business of the armed forces, but only of the civilian leaders. Unless these two principles were honored, he believed, democracy could not be a reality.

Ambassador Martin, seeing that a coup was in the making, tried to dissuade the rightists and militarists from taking such action, warning that the United States would cut off diplomatic ties with, and economic aid to, the succeeding government. But he could not back up this warning with a threat that the United States might resort to armed force if necessary, as in the case of the Trujillo family plot, to preserve democracy. Washington was reluctant to make such a commitment again despite its tremendous investment in the Dominican experiment. For one thing, while it backed Bosch, it was not overly happy about his disturbingly independent attitude. For another, the more "pragmatic" advisers around President Kennedy, who felt that the United States had gone too far in defense of Latin democracy while ignoring "traditional friends," were increasingly making their influence felt, particularly after the failure of the United States to force the ouster of the Haitian tyrant, François Duvalier. Nor did the independent-minded Bosch himself want to depend on U. S. marines to keep him in power.

But Martin's efforts appear to have been undercut most seriously of all by some U. S. military attachés who, in their constant consultations with the Dominican military leaders, seem to have been influenced by them rather than vice versa. Bosch has written:

> I never had proof that the U. S. military in Santo Domingo conspired to overthrow my democratic government, although I frequently heard rumors to this effect; but I am sure that if a captain in the mission would have said that the government should be overthrown, it would have been done in an hour because such a captain has more authority over the Dominican military high command than the people, the Constitution, and the President.

But if the U. S. military role was not clear, it was clear that some of the attachés greeted Bosch's fall with a delight that contrasted most markedly with the deep dejection of top Embassy civilian officials. Bosch, one of them told me after his overthrow, was leading the country to communism. On the other hand, the armed forces were a moderate institution, actually "left-of-center" politically. They were primarily concerned with economic and social problems. "Can you blame Wessin for being upset?" the attaché asked.

Atila Luna told me shortly after the coup that the armed forces had decided on Bosch's overthrow "two months ago," that is in July, at about the time of the San Isidro confrontation. Apparently to strengthen the case for a coup, security chief

Antonio Imbert, who favored a coup, gave Bosch on September 19 a three-page document that purported to show—though no evidence has ever been made available—that the Communists planned to set up a Red government the following January; in other words, contradictorily, the Communists planned to overthrow a man whom his enemies, including Imbert, accused of being a Communist or Communist sympathizer himself. This information, said Imbert, was obtained from an informer who had been present at a secret meeting of Communists and left the President with little choice. He had to "crack [Communist] heads." Imbert knew what Bosch would say—that he didn't intend to usher in a period of terrorism.

The following day, the rightist civilians played their role in instigating the armed forces to act. Businessmen in Santo Domingo, spurred by an extremist group called the Dominican Independent Action Committee, which has been compared to the John Birch Society by the moderate newspaper *Listin Diario,* went on strike against Bosch's policies, closing down stores everywhere except in the working-class districts. With radio stations inciting businessmen to join in the strike, Bosch finally clamped down, temporarily closing three stations.

He meanwhile heard that Wessin was about to move against him. On September 24, according to Atila Luna, he came to him and asked for his support in dismissing Wessin and seven other officers. "I refused," Atila Luna said. At 12:40 the next morning, the Air Force leader went on, an associate called him and said that Bosch was meeting in the National Palace with Defense Minister Victor Elby Viñas Román and the chiefs of the Army and Navy. "Bosch was evidently trying to turn the other services against the Air Force," he said.

Atila Luna had hit upon a key point. He and Wessin knew that the Army and Navy leaders, as well as Viñas, an Army man, harbored little affection for the Air Force, whose elite, tank-backed status gave it by far the dominant voice in intra-service affairs. Not surprisingly, Atila Luna immediately telephoned

Viñas at the palace and, according to the Air Force chief, said
that he would send two colonels to the meeting. Other reports
suggested that up to that moment, Viñas and the two service
chiefs with him had been seriously thinking of acceding to
Bosch's demand that Wessin and several other officers be transferred to lesser posts. But Luna's telephone call, in the form of
a warning, apparently sealed Bosch's fate.

When Luna's colonels arrived, Bosch would not receive them,
but the three military leaders present spoke with them anyway
in another room. According to Luna, all five men then decided
to carry out a coup immediately.

Bosch and his wife, who was in Puerto Rico, meanwhile made
telephone calls to the Presidents of Mexico, Costa Rica, and
Venezuela, and the Governor of Puerto Rico, in a desperate
appeal for support to discourage the military leaders. Bosch
also spoke with Ambassador Martin, who apparently felt out
the Dominican leader about whether the dispatch of U. S. warships might be helpful. Bosch reportedly replied in the negative, maintaining as he always had that he didn't want to rely
on U. S. marines to stay in power. Apparently as a result of a
signal from Martin, Washington planned regardless to dispatch
at least one warship, probably the aircraft carrier *Okinawa,* to
Dominican waters, but had abandoned the idea because of hurricane conditions in the area. U. S. officials said, however, that
this plan had been motivated only by the need to assure the
protection of American citizens in case of violence.

Martin tried but failed to contact the military leaders in a
last-ditch effort to talk them out of their plan. It was too late,
anyway. At 3 A.M., Viñas placed Bosch under arrest in the palace.
Atila Luna then arrived and the military leaders called the
chiefs of the opposition political parties to ask them to form a
new government. Bosch later told me that some junior officers
had contacted him while he was under arrest and offered to
launch an immediate counter-coup, but that he had vetoed the
idea in order to avoid bloodshed, particularly when the chances

of upsetting the military traditionalists at that time were slim. Several weeks before, he had rejected a proposal by the same young officers to strike first and eliminate the traditionalist threat. At that time, too, he sought to prevent bloodshed. And so he paid the wages of timidity.

The American-supported experiment in democracy was over.

CHAPTER 5

Chewing at the Grapes

THE COUP hit the White House like a thunderbolt, even though such an event had long been considered possible, if not likely. The very foundations of its new pro-democratic policy in Latin America seemed to have crumbled. U. S. Alliance for Progress leaders were equally shocked and privately indicated that drastic policies should be instituted to prevent similar setbacks in the future. Such policies would apparently involve an indefinite suspension of aid to regimes coming to power by force. Only the more traditionalist State Department viewed the coup with relative dispassion.

The military had set up a rightist civilian junta composed of three businessmen in the hope that the United States would find such a "front" government acceptable. But Washington, as Martin had warned, immediately cut diplomatic relations and economic assistance, and even pulled out its large aid mission to emphasize it meant business. The U. S. Embassy bluntly told the junta that only agreement to return to constitutionalism would bring American recognition. It supported a solution, favored by the Boschists, whereby Juan Casasnovas Garrido, Senate leader under the deposed regime, would be named as President. This could be done constitutionally, since Bosch himself had been exiled to Puerto Rico. Casasnovas, who had already declared himself the legal President, was being hunted by the police.

Democratic opponents of the junta exulted, predicting that the tough U. S. attitude would encourage an early counter-coup by dissident members of the armed forces who favored constitutional government. The Communists and fellow travelers, who had charged that the United States had fomented the coup, found themselves, on the other hand, in an embarrassing position.

The military leaders seemed undismayed. "The United States can do whatever it wants. Somehow we will keep going," Atila Luna told me. To prove it, he pointed to the last year and a half of Trujillo's rule during which the OAS nations had no relations with his regime. "We somehow got along," he said with a sense of pride, ignoring the fact that the international boycott encouraged Dominicans to defy and eventually destroy Trujillo.

But Manuel Tavares Espaillat, a member of the three-man junta, was less optimistic when he received me in the National Palace. "Without U. S. assistance," he said, "within two years either the Communists will take over or we'll subsist in isolation like Spain."

The fact that there were few pro-Bosch street demonstrations offered the impression that most people didn't care about Bosch's ouster. But this lack of demonstrative reaction appeared to be due not to apathy, but to decades of conditioning under Trujillo. There had also been little immediate reaction when news came of the dictator's death and following the coup of General Rodríguez Echevarría that lasted two days. Now few Dominicans were prepared to risk the wrath of the Trujilloist army that was again running the country.

But an undercurrent of tension nevertheless swept the nation, and the masses were ridden with fear as the nation reverted to virtual police rule, complete with beatings of demonstrators, mass arrests, and hunts for elected political opponents in hiding. Even some members of the business class, which supported the coup, began to wonder whether they had judged the situation correctly. For what started as a bloodless coup could, it appeared, end in a river of blood that might well engulf their class. "Perhaps," one businessman said, "we were a bit panicked."

Rumors of potential violence abounded. The largest labor federation, the 50,000-member autonomous Confederation of Christian Syndicates, threatened a general strike—which, however, never came off. Two of the four other labor federations announced their opposition to the new regime. The National Federation of Peasant Brotherhods, to which the great majority of peasants belonged, also turned its back on the junta, as did the Federation of Agrarian Peasant Leagues. Professional groups similarly demanding an immediate return to constitutional government included the Dominican Medical Association, the Dominican Dentists Society, and the Dominican College of Engineers and Architects.

A survey I made of some 500 people from all classes suggested massive disapproval of the coup. The usually unemployed and raggedly dressed members of the poorer classes voiced their views in many cases only after initially hedging their answers for fear that frankness might land them in jail. Considerable persuasion was necessary to convince them that I was not a police agent. But once trust was established, they poured out their feelings to me, competing with each other to talk when crowds gathered around me in the street, and virtually refusing to let me go when I visited them in their remarkably clean board shanties.

They told me, almost to a man, that the coup represented a return to the dreaded police rule of Trujillo days. On the waterfront and in factories, workers echoed this same sentiment. Among middle-class people, there appeared to be some division, but even the majority of them denounced the new regime.

Significantly, among the poorer groups, which had voted overwhelmingly for Bosch in the election, there was considerable disillusionment over his inability to make good on his promises, particularly regarding the creation of jobs for everybody. Some blamed him personally, but most blamed the rightist opposition, and said they would vote for Bosch again. But their enthusiasm for him was obviously far less than that which they expressed for constitutional government.

Armando Gómez was typical. The oligarchal and military leaders said Armando and poor people like him were not ready for democracy. That they couldn't think for themselves. Therefore, it was perfectly all right to overthrow Bosch, who came to power only because of their support.

Armando, a forty-five-year-old tailor with a gaunt black face creased with wrinkles, did not dispute his ignorance, for school was an impossible luxury in a world where people scrounged for every hour of work and every morsel of food. After inviting me into his home, a blue-painted two-room structure of splintered boards in which he lived with his wife and five children, he reacted even before I could ask my first question:

"I don't care who is in power. I like all governments."

Dressed in a tattered white shirt and brown patched trousers, Armando spoke with a suspicious air, conditioned to fear by Trujillo police rule. But after our second cup of coffee, served by his stout, motherly wife who kept the sparsely furnished house as clean and neat as would her middle-class counterpart, Armando began speaking with finer distinctions.

During Trujillo's regime, he said, he was never interested in politics. What was the good? Trujillo made all the decisions and the people had to obey or face the wrath of the police. And this had seemed the normal way of life.

But after the dictator was killed, his world suddenly changed. The police no longer were brutal and employers began paying higher wages to avoid strikes. As a part-time worker in a clothing factory, Armando said, his salary—when he was working—rose from about $1 to $2 a day.

If this was "democracy," he was all for it.

But since the coup, Armando lamented, he had been confused. Maybe he had misunderstood what "democracy" meant. His boss had told him, he explained, that under Bosch there had been no real democracy. Only by overthrowing Bosch was it possible to have real democracy, his boss had said.

This was a puzzling argument. Before the election, he had been told that democracy meant the freedom of the people to choose their own leaders. He, like most people of humble birth, voted for Bosch because he believed he would give them a better life. Armando was deeply disappointed because Bosch had not kept all his promises in the seven months he had been in power. But he couldn't understand why he was thrown out of power before his four-year term was up.

"Now the police is strong again. But is that democracy?" he asked. "I had thought that democracy was like a contract, or like marriage. If a strange man tried to take my wife from me, I wouldn't let him. Because she is my wife and I have the papers to prove it. It's like a contract between me and my wife. Well, if the people voted for Bosch and he is supposed to be President for four years, isn't that like a contract?"

Armando paused for a moment, sipped his coffee, and said sadly, "I wish I was smart like my boss. Then maybe I could understand democracy."

The support I found for constitutional government among lower-class people like Armando appeared to be a fairly strong insulation against extreme leftism, though some said they would vote for the 14th of June Movement before they would support a rightist party—an indication that if the democratic left, as represented by Bosch, continued to be suppressed for long, the movement toward Castro communism would be likely to grow.

Without the democratic safety valve, support for the group already appeared to be considerable among younger members of the middle class, who thought less in terms of employment and freedom than in terms of immediate social reform. The coup seemed to many of them a measure of the vast difficulties standing in the way of reform through democratic means. Significantly, a left-wing faction of the student federation (FED) won majority control in January 1965 for the first time.

This attitude seemed to dovetail with the more positive, but similarly reasoned, statements of the Castro government. Two days after the coup, an editorial in the Cuban organ *Hoy* said "it simply revealed the degree of decomposition and the crisis through which so-called 'representative democracy' is passing." Bosch's "overthrow was inevitable," the editorial said, because he did not understand "that the middle way does not exist."

In overthrowing Bosch, ostensibly to reduce Communist influence in the country, the rightist-military forces had, in fact, helped Castro to "prove" to some people who had been willing to give democracy a chance that perhaps communism was the only answer after all.

But while popular fear and bitterness coursed silently through the veins of the nation, indications that such sentiments might eventually find an outlet for expression in revolution grew. One such indication lay in the increasing disunity of the armed forces. For weeks after the coup, rumors of an impending counter-coup that could lead to civil war were almost as thick as the rumors of military intentions that preceded Bosch's ouster.

On October 24, one month after the coup, I cabled a story to *The Washington Post* from Santo Domingo that "a new armed strike might not come for weeks, or possibly months, if at all, but the reports that one is being planned reflect the uneasiness characterizing intra-service relations. These reports have been fed by the discharge of dozens of officers from the armed forces since the coup. It appears that most of these officers were opposed to Bosch's overthrow and strongly favor an immediate return to constitutional government."

Although most of the officers discharged were of junior rank, including a few majors, some colonels still in the forces, I had learned, supported their cause. This cause, moreover, was feeding on the growing intra-service rivalry for power. If Army and Navy leaders and Viñas had gone along with the coup only with reservations, such reservations could possibly grow into outright defiance of the Air Force that might find expression in a counter-coup.

During the period immediately after the coup, I received a number of hints about pro-Bosch activities within the armed forces from a young man I met one evening in the casino of Hotel Embajador. While we both followed the fortunes of people seated around the roulette wheel, we started talking. On learning I was an American reporter, he took me into the adjoining lobby and over a drink assured me that it was just a matter of time until a counter-coup restored constitutional government. I asked him how he knew, and he smiled with the puckish expression of a child trying to keep a secret from his parents.

"I can't tell you anything now," he replied. "I'll have to speak with some people first. But meet me here tomorrow at about the same time. My name is Héctor Aristy."

I wasn't very impressed at that first meeting by Aristy or his assurances of a counter-coup. For one thing, he wasn't very impressive-looking—at least from a political point of view. Short and immaculately dressed, he had the tough, sinister good looks and cocky air of a youth gang leader, with long wavy black hair, a bronze complexion, and slightly Oriental eyes. Furthermore, it was hard to tell whether he spoke seriously or had some ulterior motive in mind. He had all the earmarks of an actor, looking fiercely grim when he discussed the new junta, profoundly reverential when he talked about Bosch, balefully conspiratorial when he predicted future trouble, and humorously lustful when he made remarks about pretty girls who happened to pass by.

The next evening he took me by car, via a circuitous route, to a house in the country where several pro-Bosch politicians were waiting for us.

"We're all against the junta," Aristy explained, as we sat in straw chairs on the front porch of the house. "And we're doing something about it. We're organizing a constitutional network within the armed forces that will soon strike. A couple of colonels who are working with us are supposed to show up here tonight—if they feel they can come without being followed. That's why I've brought you here tonight, so you can see for yourself. We want the American people to know that the Dominican people are not going to accept a new dictatorship. We trust that you won't use any names."

We talked over beer for about two hours, but the colonels didn't arrive.

"I guess they decided it was too dangerous," Aristy said. "But you can be sure we're serious."

I later learned that they were serious indeed. Aristy had initiated his plot by contacting a Boschist politician, Dr. Hernández Almanzar, who had a stock of guns and knew some Army officers ready to participate in a counter-coup. When an article I wrote concerning the possibility of a counter-coup appeared in *The Washington Post*, Aristy, who was suspected of leaking the information, was warned by the military to leave the country immediately. At great personal risk, he stayed anyway. Soon afterward, according to him, one of the officers involved in his plot got "cold feet and talked," and the government broke it up. But the military made a fundamental error. They left Aristy alone to keep on plotting.

If the government thus frustrated initial plans for a counter-coup, it was deeply concerned about the continuing refusal of the Kennedy Administration to recognize it or to resume economic aid. Businessmen in particular were feeling the pinch sharply, unable in many cases even to get credit from other countries, which were reluctant to take chances in a nation abandoned by the United States and disintegrating economically.

Persistent reports have suggested that some supporters of
the junta formulated a plan to create an artificial "Communist
crisis," in lieu of the real one that never materialized, and
thereby frighten Washington into renewing relations and aid.
These reports revolve around the launching of a "war of liberation" against the government by Tavarez Justo, the leader
of the 14th of June Movement, a group of his followers, and
also members of the leftist but anti-Communist Revolutionary
Social Christian Party in the northern mountains.

According to these reports, Maximo Bernard, a 14th of June
member, persuaded Tavarez Justo to begin the guerrilla struggle after convincing him that Imbert, who had had dealings with
the 14th of June Movement in the past, would support the operation, if only for his own conspiratorial purposes. But Imbert
and other junta backers, the reports say, saw to it, with the help
of Camilo Todeman, a German-born technician at the San
Cristóbal arms factory, that the guerrillas would receive defective weapons. In late November, the small band, whatever the
basis of its decision, took to the hills.

At about that time, President Kennedy was assassinated. On
succeeding him, President Johnson was immediately faced with
the apparent problem of communism in the Dominican Republic. His reaction was not long in coming. Recognition was
granted in late December. Two days later, the Army and police
killed almost a score of guerrilla fighters, including Tavarez
Justo—when it was no longer necessary to keep Washington in
a state of fright.

Immediately afterward, junta president Emilio de los Santos,
a respected businessman, resigned, giving no reason. But the
reason was understood to be that he had opposed the killing of
youths he had considered merely misguided—some of them, at
least, not even being Communists but simply nationalists. Was
Taverez Justo himself a Communist? According to a U. S. labor
official who had spoken to him often, he probably was a Castroite, but not a convinced one. "With responsibility," said the

official, "he might well have become a moderate." Other Americans who knew him thought he was more anti-American than Communist.

De los Santos was succeeded by Donald Reid Cabral. A youthful-looking man with blue eyes and blond hair that betray his Scottish heritage on his father's side, Reid was a wealthy automobile dealer before he started dabbling in politics after Trujillo's assassination. The torture and death of his physician brother for his involvement in the Trujillo death plot served to intensify his desire for public service, and he eagerly accepted an offer to become Vice-President in the Council of State that paved the way for the 1962 election that Bosch won. But as a member of the oligarchy, distant from the problems of the masses, he had never enjoyed great popularity. And, despite his affability, his lack of a strong personality and his limited speech-making talent did not produce an image capable of overcoming the social disadvantage.

But if Reid suffered from these handicaps before he joined the junta, his shortcomings were magnified in the popular view by the very fact that he was the leader of a government installed and supported by the armed forces that had overthrown the constitutional regime. Few people believed him when he said that he regretted Bosch's ouster. If this were true, they argued, why had he agreed to work for and with the perpetrators of the coup?

But U. S. officials were delighted that "Donny" Reid had gravitated to the top, since they knew from Council of State days that he was pro-American, honest, and courageous. If he did a good job, they felt, the people would gradually accept him as their leader. He wasn't a constitutional leader, but he did permit some freedoms—though the danger of a police crackdown on oppositionists was always implicit in the lack of guarantees, and, indeed, sometimes materialized in the form of killing and brutality. In some cases, corpses were left in public places as a warning to others. Also, a number of pro-Constitution trade union officials were jailed on unproved charges of "subversion."

Particularly optimistic was Ambassador William Tapley Bennett, Jr., who replaced Martin after the resumption of diplomatic relations. Reid and Bennett became close friends, seeing eye to eye on most measures and policies considered necessary to build from the debris of the September coup. In fact, when the ruling "triumvirate" headed by Reid was reduced to two men in June 1964—Reid and Dr. Ramón Cáceres Troncoso, who dealt mainly with economic matters—many Dominicans began referring to Bennett as the unannounced third member.

Bennett, a tall, redheaded, bespectacled man of serious demeanor, has displayed aggressive leadership qualities that his retiring manner does not suggest. As a student at the University of Georgia, Bennett, who was born in 1917 in Griffin, Georgia, was president of his fraternity and of the intrafraternity council, a cadet colonel in the Reserve Officers Training Corps, and a member of the debating team. He also won top scholastic honors, being voted to membership in Phi Beta Kappa and the Sphinx Society, the university's highest undergraduate academic honor.

His youthful successes spilled over into his diplomatic career, which started in 1941 when he was sent to the Dominican Republic for nearly three years as a political officer and economic analyst, never dreaming that he would one day be a key figure in Dominican history. When he was reassigned to Washington, Latin diplomats remember him as a man who listened to them and cared about their problems. In 1948, when democratic elements in Costa Rica revolted against the Army, Bennett, according to Costa Rican diplomats, displayed considerable sympathy for their cause, though in that case the Communists were supporting the armed forces for their own purposes. He was described by Dr. Milton Eisenhower, with whom he worked on hemispheric problems for a while, as "an engaging, sensitive, tireless worker."

After serving as the deputy director of the State Department's Office of South American Affairs from 1951 to 1954, Bennett filled posts in Vienna, Rome, and Greece before being sent back to the Dominican Republic in 1964.

Although associates know him as a warm and charming person, he projected an image of aloofness to the Dominicans that hurt him, particularly since he succeeded Martin, whose unprofessional informality and earthiness had deeply impressed the people, even those at the village level. Bennett seemed to them like the traditional U. S. diplomat they had previously known, a man who dealt mainly with the upper classes and didn't understand the lower.

And Bennett and most of his political aides—none except CIA officials had held positions in the Embassy before the resumption of diplomatic relations—were in fact not given to folksiness. In their eyes, there simply wasn't time for that. They felt they could contribute most to the people's welfare by encouraging the government to develop the national economy and get rid of corrupt elements. And this concentration of effort seemed to be paying off. Reid was doing a fine job. He had no popular mandate, but the people would one day appreciate what he was doing for them. And though constitutionalism was important, in the Dominican context it was more a word than a vehicle for promoting progress. Certainly, in the Embassy's view, the unconstitutional Reid was doing more for his people than did the constitutional Bosch.

This thinking led Bennett and his aides to give scant attention to Bosch's Dominican Revolutionary Party, even though this party, whatever its merits or shortcomings, polled about two-thirds of the vote in the 1962 election.

"We had almost no contact with Bennett," PRD Secretary-General Antonio Martínez Francisco told me shortly after U. S. troops landed. "He wasn't interested in us or in what we were thinking. Although I'm Secretary-General of the PRD, I was invited to only one Embassy party after he arrived. And when we did see other American officials once in a while, they did not regard us with much sympathy. Even though we had won the election by an overwhelming margin, the Americans regarded us as not worthy of having any say in the running of our own country."

Bennett, it seems, made an important miscalculation. In earlier days it may have been possible to pursue policies without reference to the people. But not after Bosch had given the long-exploited peasants and workers a stake in the government for the first time. The Dominicans were no longer people who would accept the political fate meted out to them, good or bad. They had never really felt cheated before Bosch because they had never had anything that they could be cheated out of. But Bosch had given them something—a sense of power and importance. And now they did feel cheated. And Bosch's failure to give them immediate material benefits gradually faded from memory as the realization of what they had lost when he fell simmered gradually to a boil.

The frustration of the lower classes was fed in the months after the coup by the violation of human rights, the abandonment of most reform plans, by nepotism, and by vast corruption. Guarantees of habeas corpus and judicial process before deportation were suspended. Scores of political opponents were jailed. The tax on sugar producers intended to control inflation in periods of price fluctuation and provide more money for development was abolished.

Friends of the UCN and the military swallowed up the key political and diplomatic jobs at salaries phenomenally higher than Bosch had paid. Eleven relatives of Rafael Bonilla Aybar, the anti-Bosch commentator and publisher, were awarded some of the best positions. His uncle became Ambassador to the United States and to the OAS; his father, consul in Puerto Rico; a cousin, Ambassador to the United Nations; another cousin, Secretary of Industry; and still another, Director of Tourism.

Government corruption got so out of hand that Finance Min-

ister Pedro Manuel Casals resigned in protest in December
1963. He cited, for example, payment of $125,000 to the former
Council of State leader, Rafael Bonnelly, for a trip to Europe.
He also denounced the "intention" of the government to sell
the former Trujillo industries to "their own vested interests"—
at low prices—on the grounds that they were unproductive. He
said that these state-owned industries were making money, particularly under the Bosch regime.

But the bitterest pill of all was the massive corruption in
which military leaders, in a burst of nostalgia for the privileged
days under Trujillo, indulged greedily and openly. One officer
sent two Dominican Air Force planes to Puerto Rico that returned loaded with contraband furniture. About 3,500 cases of
contraband whisky were discovered in a warehouse outside
Santo Domingo. They were removed to police headquarters, and
that was the last to be heard about them. When a Dominican
merchant ship carrying American cigarettes ran aground near
Puerto Plata, it was unloaded by soldiers who disappeared with
the contents in military vehicles.

Customs agents received high fees to let such goods, as well
as television sets, stoves, foodstuffs and other items, into the
country without inspection. These articles were then sold to
the public through a black market operated by duty-free military canteens. It was considered the privilege of a canteen officer
to steal—provided his superiors shared in the 10 to 30 percent
kickback.

The fruit of such corruption was painfully visible in the
luxurious homes that many top officers built for themselves—
using enlisted men for the construction work—while the living
standards of the poor plummeted still further. Even Trujillo
had never been as good to them. Nor did they have to be loyal
now to anybody but themselves. Yes, the overthrow of Bosch
had been a profitable act indeed for the military. But not for
the country, which, within a few months after the coup, ran
up a $45 million balance-of-payments deficit, partly because of

the illegal importations, while payments on the astronomical commercial foreign debt halted completely.

Such conditions produced major violence in the hungry slums of Santo Domingo when in May 1964, 5,000 taxi drivers and dock workers went on strike, throwing garbage and soft-drink bottles at 4,000 troops and policemen who patrolled among their ramshackle dwellings, and symbolically burning tires taken off automobiles of the wealthy they hated. Over 1,000 people were arrested, two were killed, and scores were injured. The strike was specifically in protest against new import levies on luxury items, including automobiles and spare parts, an austerity measure proposed by the International Monetary Fund to stabilize the Dominican peso. But that was simply the occasion for an explosion that would probably have come anyway.

Finally, with the United States threatening to continue withholding economic aid—it had resumed such assistance after the granting of diplomatic recognition in only token amounts—Reid, an honest, well-meaning man himself, took the bull by the horns. He abolished the canteens which had been used for black market purposes and ordered that all overseas flights by the Air Force be cleared with him. Then he started to transfer and fire top officers who were involved in corruption or suspected plots against him. In this effort, he obtained the support of Wessin, who was only too glad to see officers who threatened his own power removed from their positions.

Reid first dismissed Atila Luna, one of the most insatiable of the contrabandists, and several other Air Force officers. He then removed General Belisario Peguero Guerrero as chief of the national police force. A protégé of Imbert, Peguero was both corrupt and a major threat to Wessin, who demanded his removal. When Reid and Wessin learned of plans for a military coup involving Peguero and the Army's quartermaster general, Colonel Neit Nivár Seijas, the latter was dismissed and retired. There was also teamwork when General Viñas, who had become Secretary of the Armed Forces, ordered three of Wessin's close aides transferred. Reid canceled the order, dispatched Viñas to Washington as a delegate to the Inter-American Defense Board, and took over Viñas' portfolio for himself. Reid then replaced General Salvador Augusto Montas Guerrero, the Army chief. He was the first cousin of Peguero.

As the corruption eased off, in the government ministries as well as in the armed forces, the United States started injecting shots into the Dominican arm to stem the trend toward chaos. The United States loaned more than $10 million to the country to finance economic stabilization and stimulate development. The International Monetary Fund and private U. S. and Canadian financial institutions lent $50 million to pay off the balance-of-payments deficit. But the Fund—and the U. S. Embassy —exacted from Reid, in return for such bounties, a severe austerity program, including cuts in the national budget and curbs on the import of luxuries that pleased neither the poor nor the rich.

By early 1965, the economy had shown some signs of revival. Industries had started to expand, and new ones were springing up. Controls over public revenues and expenditures had been incorporated into the national budget. Reform of the customs service had begun. Some 3,000 land titles had been distributed to landless farmers. Funds had been appropriated for rural roads, irrigation, electrification, and farm credit systems. The white fences of experimental farms were becoming a common sight in the countryside.

But the Reid government was far from out of the rough, and it wasn't being helped by climatic and international economic conditions beyond its control. A drought hit the country in January which yielded only half an inch of rainfall during the first four months of the year. The water shortage in Santo Domingo was the worst in 14 years, and water was sometimes available for only two hours in the morning—unless one purchased some from "water peddlers" who suddenly appeared on the streets.

World sugar prices had nosedived so low that the country, it appeared, would lose $30 million in 1965 selling sugar below the cost of production. Coffee and banana prices were also low. The drop in total exports resulted in the unemployment or underemployment of almost 70,000 people in Santo Domingo alone. Many government workers were being paid in chits, which few merchants would accept. Tourism plummeted, with Hotel Embajador reporting almost a one-fourth drop in reservations over the previous year. The newspaper *El Caribe* reported that the internal debt in October 1964 was $223 million and the external debt $194 million.

At the same time, the lower classes were infuriated by a Reid decision to put off promised elections to September 1965, with campaigning prohibited before June 1. The military officers who had lost their lucrative jobs plotted to get them back. And all classes grew increasingly dissatisfied with the austerity program.

Reid and the United States thus had considerable reason for worry. On the one hand, the corrupt militarists might attempt a coup at any time that could produce a strictly military government dedicated to the vandalization of the country. And on the other, even worse, the Communists were in an excellent position to profit from the deep discontent among the lower classes. In fact, the United States sent Reid intelligence information that many Communist leaders who had been deported after Bosch's overthrow were slipping back into the country. Some critics of the Reid regime, though offering no proof, have said that Reid didn't need such information, that Antonio Imbert, his security chief, ironically enough, had let them in as a means of building up a new "Communist threat" that could prove useful in exacting from the U. S. further financial and political support—as Trujillo had done.

"They entered the country with regular visas granted by the Reid government even though in many cases they were arriving directly from Moscow or Havana," according to Antonio

Rosario, who was the Caamaño representative in Washington.

Ambassador Bennett, sensing that an explosion was building up, sent several warning messages to Thomas C. Mann in early spring. In one, he wrote: "We are almost on the ropes in the Dominican Republic." In another, telegraphed in early April, he said with a curious obtuseness in view of the availability of ciphering devices: "Little foxes some of them red are chewing at the grapes. It is impossible to guarantee a good harvest in view of many unfavorable aspects of local scene. It is however fair to say that a diminution of our effort or failure to act will result in bitter wine."

Significantly, Bennett sent the latter message about the same time that reports circulated that Reid had decided to run for President in the September election and to bar as opponents the two exiled former Presidents, Bosch and Balaguer, who were regarded as the nation's most popular politicians. (Despite such reports, Reid denied after his ouster that he had intended to run.)

Until then, the leaders of Bosch's party had tried to keep the lid on the growing desperation of the poorer classes in the hope that the September election would result in a new PRD victory. Secretary-General Martínez Francisco told me during the subsequent revolution that he had warned U. S. officials that if Reid ran for President, particularly to the exclusion of Bosch, "there would be trouble. But they didn't seem to care what we said."

U. S. officials say they were "surprised" by the reports of Reid's decision to run in the election and to exclude Bosch and Balaguer from it, and maintain that they told him that they would not work with him if he became an outright dictator. However that may be, few Dominicans believed that Reid, who listened so closely to Bennett, would have reached the reported decision without the Ambassador's nod. By the same token, Bennett, who listened closely to Reid, is believed to have felt that the PRD was a rabble-rousing, Communist-infiltrated party that, however it had fared in the 1962 election, had a nerve withholding its cooperation from Reid. And the subsequent disclosure that U. S. officials were cool or opposed to the return of Bosch when it appeared that he would be coming back after Reid fell did nothing to dispel the feeling that the United States would not necessarily have supported an election in which the unpopular Reid would have been pitted against the very popular Bosch.

An interesting question to ponder is how and why the Communist danger was growing—both Reid and Bennett claimed that it was—when the armed forces were supposed to have deposed Bosch mainly to end this danger. A corollary question is, how was it possible for Communist leaders to filter back into the country so easily? Did not the new Communist threat indicate at the least that Bosch's policies were no more likely to lead toward communism than Reid's? It could, in fact, be argued that communism, however weak it still remained, had gained strength under Reid since the overthrow of representative democracy had persuaded many fence straddlers that only extremism could do away with military and police oppression and lead to the reforms they demanded.

In any event, Reid's reported decision to run for President convinced the PRD leaders that the time was about ripe to act. The people who had voted for Bosch in 1962 were now militantly supporting him again, having forgotten their disappointment over his slowness in improving their living standards. And, over the preceding several months, the Boschists had built up the means to strike effectively at the appropriate moment— thanks in considerable degree to one man.

He was a young Army officer, Colonel Rafael Fernández Domínguez, a short, stocky man. Fernández came from a well-known military family, his father, General Ludovino Fernández, having been one of Trujillo's top, and most brutal, commanders, who was particularly renowned for his handling of thieves. Any man caught stealing a second time was automatically hanged.

In 1958, after 13 men had been convicted of robbing the Bank of Canada of about $200,000, he had them shot with explosive bullets. Their grotesquely maimed bodies were then displayed in Santiago's baseball stadium as a lesson to other would-be criminals.

His son Rafael, determined to clear the family name, became an ardent constitutionalist. But though a devoted follower of Bosch, he had been smart enough to evade the dragnet of the traditional militarists after Bosch's overthrow that resulted in the discharge and imprisonment of dozens of young constitutionalist officers. Nevertheless, suspected as a possible troublemaker, he had been "exiled" to military posts in Dominican embassies abroad. While in Madrid, Fernández, several months after the coup, at the suggestion of a PRD leader, Ramón Vila Piola, flew to Puerto Rico to see Bosch. He returned to Madrid and began planning a counter-coup. He continued his plotting when he was transferred to Santiago, Chile. Then, whenever he was able to find an excuse to return home for a few days, he would go over his plans with Bosch during stopovers in San Juan, and try to implement them in Santo Domingo.

Late at night, he would steal out of his brother's house, where he stayed, and meet secretly at the homes of co-conspirators— leaders of the PRD and of the allied Revolutionary Social Christian Party and a group of young officers in their thirties and forties, including Colonel Miguel Angel Hernando Ramirez, commander of the 16th of August military camp, who was to lead the revolt if and when it took place.

According to Caamaño, in late 1964 "we made an agreement of honor that if by June 1 presidential elections had not definitely been fixed, we would rise in arms." Other rebel leaders said that Caamaño himself joined the plot about a week before the revolution broke out.

By April, elections appeared to be fixed, but not the kind that the conspirators would accept. Was there any reason to wait until June, some of the plotters began to ask, especially since Reid had, ironically, played into their hands by purging many senior officers—some of the same ones who had thrown Bosch out—who would now probably go along with a revolt, however it started?

Other plotters, however, favored waiting until the purged officers, who became known as the San Cristobal group as distinguished from Wessin's San Isidro group, struck first, whereupon the PRD-led rebels would try to take over the revolt. But even these plotters had begun to fear that Reid had managed to pacify the San Cristobal officers by buying them off.

To make as certain as possible of Reid's intentions, Caamaño, almost as soon as he joined the plot, went to see him. According to rebel officials, Caamaño said that many young officers wanted him to take a stronger stand against corruption, which, he said, riddled the Armed Forces. And they wanted him to deliver a statement assuring completely free elections. Reid, the rebel officials said, replied that he saw no reason why he should take orders from "a bunch of kids."

"I happen to be one of those kids," Caamaño responded.

In any case, Caamaño departed convinced that Reid had little intention of heeding his demands. The plotters decided to strike on Monday, April 26. The plan was to send forth three truck-loads of soldiers from the 27th of February military camp. Two would wait at Parque Colón, and the third, with Caamaño and two other rebel leaders—one a military officer and the other a PRD official—would go directly to Ozama Fortress, arriving there at about midnight. Caamaño would tell the commanding officer that the men had come to reinforce the guard because of rumors of an impending coup attempt.

As soon as the conspirators entered the fortress, they would take over the guardhouse where the officers were located, and Caamaño would solicit the support of the Cascos Blancos, the police troops that he himself had trained when he had been in the national police. If his entreaties failed, the other two truck-loads of troops, at a signal, were to come and fight the defenders.

Troops from all other military installations, including San Isidro, were then to be asked to join the revolt.

But as details of the plan were being worked out, Reid, apparently getting wind of the plot, dismissed, on Thursday, April 22, seven suspected Air Force officers. Then one of the plotters found at staff headquarters a list of other officers to be arrested. Also, the civilian pilot who had been assigned to bring Bosch home as soon as the revolt broke out—the brother of exiled General Rodríguez Echevarría—had been mysteriously fired from Quisqueya Airlines.

There was no time to wait.

CHAPTER 6

Rebirth of a Cadaver

SATURDAY was always a quiet day at the American Embassy in Santo Domingo. It was closed to the public, and only a small number of persons came to work. But Saturday, April 24, was even quieter than most. Fewer officials than usual were in town that weekend. Ambassador Bennett had left the evening before for the United States, first to see his mother in Georgia, then to consult with policy makers in Washington about the rumblings in Santo Domingo, feeling that this might be his last opportunity to do so. In a routine report to the State Department filed on Thursday he had mentioned talk of a possible coup attempt that weekend, but he dismissed it as one of the "usual Santo Domingo rumors," apparently seeing little significance in the arrest of the seven officers.

Also out of town were 11 of the 13 officers in the United States Military Advisory and Assistance Mission, who were attending a conference in Panama. And the U. S. naval attaché was off on a weekend dove-shooting trip with Imbert.

Nevertheless, Deputy Chief of Mission William Brewer Connett, Jr., a slim, dedicated man who was left in charge of the Embassy, did not feel apprehensive about the burden of responsibility that would be his for the next few days. One of about 30

foreign service officers in the Embassy, he saw no reason why
the rumor of a weekend coup was any more valid than one that
had indicated the possibility of a coup taking place several days
previously. That "D-Day" had passed without incident, as had
all others. Certainly there was a danger, both from the military
right and the Boschist left, possibly even in conjunction with
each other, and that's why the Ambassador had gone to discuss
the situation in Washington—while he could still get away. But
who knew when and if Reid's opponents would finally act?

Certainly not Chief of Staff Marcos Rivera Cuesta, who had
been promoted by Reid from Army chief shortly after he had
replaced General Montás Guerrero, the cousin of Police Chief
Peguero, in that position in February. He had heard that more
officers were plotting against Reid, but he would soon take care
of that. Late in the morning, he telephoned from his office at
the 27th of February military camp to the 16th of August camp
several miles away and ordered four suspected officers based
there to come to see him immediately. When they arrived,
Cuesta accused them of plotting against the government and
ordered an aide, Captain Mario Peña Taberas, to arrest them.

But instead, with the support of about 25 soldiers present,
Taberas, who turned out to be another of the plotters, pulled
his pistol and arrested Cuesta as well as four other high officers.
It was now about 1 P.M. Captain Taberas then telephoned a
local radio station, said to be owned by a former PRD official,
and reported the revolt. The station flashed the news. Immediately people started swarming into the streets, honking automobile horns, and shouting, "Bosch! Bosch!" But their glee was
short-lived.

Within minutes, Radio Santo Domingo, the main government station, with its powerful multiple transmitting facilities,
was denying the report. Meanwhile, Taberas telephoned José
Francisco Peña Gómez, a slim Negro PRD leader and well-
known radio commentator, and told him in detail what had
happened. Peña Gómez, who described to me several days later,

as he sat on his bed in a dumpy bedroom at rebel headquarters, how the revolt got under way, said that at about 2:30 P.M. he, accompanied by three sergeants and some 15 civilian PRD followers, "but not Communists," rushed into a studio at Radio Santo Domingo. They cut off the announcer who was denying reports of a revolt, and Peña Gómez began shouting into the microphone: "The government of Reid Cabral has fallen! Go into the streets and celebrate! Viva Bosch!"

While Peña Gómez spoke, his supporters barricaded the door so that government officials trying to enter to cut him off could not get in. Finally, at about 4:30 P.M., police broke in, arrested Peña Gómez and his associates, and took them to police headquarters where the commentator was placed in solitary confinement.

But it was too late. Though Reid was still in office, the people thought he had been ousted and had poured into the streets once again, dancing, singing, and renewing their cries of "Viva Bosch!" They paraded with huge banners reading CONSTITUCIÓN CON BOSCH, and turned Parque Independencia into a seething, merrymaking mass of humanity.

Washington at this point was concerned though not yet alarmed by developments. "It looks like Reid will be able to handle the situation," a U. S. official said. But "as a routine precautionary measure . . . if evacuation of Americans should become necessary . . ." President Johnson sent the aircraft carrier *Boxer,* with 1,500 marines aboard, and other naval craft to Dominican waters.

Reid, meanwhile, ordered a curfew and, after the police had cleared the streets, went on radio and television from the National Palace to announce that most military units remained loyal to him, that the country was calm, and that he had given the rebels until 5 A.M. to surrender or be crushed. With the lie about Reid's fall exposed and the crowds off the streets, both Reid and his American supporters sighed with relief as the coup appeared doomed.

In the next several hours, Reid had a rude awakening. He found that he could rally only about 500 troops in Santo Domingo to his side; about 1,200 were in rebellion. He called Wessin, who had helped to get him into this predicament by supporting his military cleanup. Certainly he would help him. But Wessin, for all his tanks, offered his regrets. To attack the rebel-held camps he would need more infantry than he controlled, Wessin said. Tanks could too easily be destroyed with Molotov cocktails. He had to join the rebellion or endanger his own position. He suggested that a three-man junta be set up.

When the 5 A.M. deadline passed without incident, Reid, and the public, knew he was through. He had lost the support of the armed forces, with many younger officers favoring Bosch and most senior ones opposed to him because of his crackdown on them for corruption and suspected plotting.

In desperation, Reid called the U. S. Embassy's Connett to the Palace, told him about Wessin's proposal, and felt him out about the possibility of American armed help. Connett obliquely said "No," pointing out that such a move would be politically impossible, particularly in view of the U. S. failure to take such action when Bosch, a constitutional leader, fell, and also physically impossible, since warships couldn't arrive in time to save him.

Rebel troops had started moving from Hernando's 16th of August camp toward town at about 1 A.M., before Reid's deadline was up. He telephoned the commander of the 27th of February camp, and asked him to order his men to join the march. When the commander hesitated, Hernando asked gruffly: "Are you with us or against us?" His threatening tone belied his true strength at that time—only 250 men as compared to 2,000 in the 27th of February. But the commander of the latter did not know the comparative figures and, fearing an attack, nervously replied: "We are with you." And his troops joined the march on Santo Domingo.

As soldiers from the two camps started out for the city, other units already in town, under the command of a Lieutenant Núñez, established themselves on the Palace grounds. According to Héctor Aristy, who was now one of the civilian leaders of the rebellion, Aristy paved the way through a daring ruse. Dressed in an army officer's uniform, he entered the palace grounds and demanded: "Who's commanding here?" A captain appeared, and Aristy shouted: "Come to attention. Don't you know how to behave before a superior? How many armored vehicles have you got?"

"Eleven," answered the captain, as he stiffly drew to attention.

Aristy then ordered the officer to move his men outside the palace grounds. When they had gone, Aristy called for the waiting rebel force nearby which took over the grounds, complete with armored vehicles.

At about the same time, rebel forces, arriving from their camps, took over Radio Santo Domingo, and others remaining at the 27th of February camp broke into the arsenal and loaded several army trucks with rifles, machine guns, grenades and pistols for distribution to anybody who wanted them. The radio immediately blared forth the news that the arms would be available at Parque Independencia and other points. Before the day was out, from 3,000 to 5,000 civilians had these weapons, and hundreds of others had Molotov cocktails made with gasoline siphoned without cost from station pumps and tank trucks.

With the revolt blossoming into a full-blown revolution, Reid and his junior partner Ramón Cáceres resigned and turned over their government to General Montás Guerrero, whom Reid had replaced as Army Chief only two months before. They were allowed to go into hiding.

Santo Domingo went wild. But while members of the lower classes were out celebrating on the streets, those of the urban elite sat at home and watched television in horror. Across their screens they saw parading a constant stream of shouting, weeping, laughing men, women, and children, most of them raggedly

dressed or wearing parts of uniforms, all of them pathetically
seeking an outlet for their suddenly unleashed emotions, emotions which, except during their brief experiment with democracy, had been suppressed for decades under the Trujillo heel.
In this orgy of release, people simply said what they wanted
to say at the moment. A minister screamed, "Christ, Christ."
A little girl yelled, "Mommy, I'm going to die for my country."
And there were also cries of "American imperialism" and men
who wore beards and Castro-style caps amid the incredible as-
sortment of workers, secretaries, waitresses, and students who
offered the face of the revolution to stunned watchers in a two-
day marathon performance. It was hardly likely that Communists, whatever their power or numbers, would have missed an
opportunity like that to contribute to the chaos, though their
contribution is hard to measure.

The question now arose: Who would control the chaos? The
younger officers and their seniors had joined in an unholy alliance to get rid of the Reid government, but each group for
their own reasons. It was still unclear on early Sunday which
group would come out on top. Some officers offered their support to the highest bidder. Caamaño told me that Imbert, Atila
Luna, and General Reid Santa María, three generals who always
wanted to be on the right side, presented themselves at the Juan
Pablo Duarte camp and solicited support for a military junta
composed of themselves.

"Aristy wanted me to arrest them," Caamaño who was at the
camp, said, "but foolishly I let them go. I wasn't yet looking
at the situation from a revolutionary viewpoint."

Caamaño at that time was under the command of Colonel
Hernando Ramirez. Both Colonels were determined to bring
Bosch back and, at a meeting of the original plotters and representatives of Wessin at the National Palace, demanded that the
1963 Constitution be reactivated and PRD leader Rafael Molina Ureña be installed as Provisional President until Bosch
returned. As president of the Lower House of Congress, he was

constitutionally next in line, since both Bosch and the Senate president were out of the country.

Some of the young officers protested. They wanted not Bosch, but new free elections. And not unexpectedly, the demand infuriated the supporters of Wessin, who had been responsible for Bosch's overthrow in the first place. They insisted instead on a military junta. The key figure in the situation appeared to be Air Force Chief General Juan de los Santos Céspedes, who hadn't made up his mind which side he would support. Later, he telephoned his answer to Molina Ureña and Hernando from San Isidro. Unless they agreed to abandon their plans, his planes would bomb the palace within five minutes. They refused.

Some of the young plotters, however, disagreed with this decision. Aside from those who did not particularly wish the return of Bosch in any event, even some Boschists began asking how they could defy the power of San Isidro. Then Captain Peña Taberas, a quiet-spoken but ardent constitutionalist, said with devastating effect: "As a patriotic Dominican citizen, I, for one, prefer to fight for the Constitution than give in for the sake of peace. We are at a crossroads, and must choose between right and wrong. There can be no compromise."

That convinced most of those present—even as four of the Air Force's five P-51's dived on the palace in rocket and machine-gun passes. Molina Ureña was sworn in at about 5 P.M. while bullets peppered the palace. The revolution was now a shooting war.

Infuriated rebel mobs which earlier in the day had consisted of singing, shouting, banner-waving demonstrators were now converted into civilian armies determined to destroy and kill despite the radio pleas of rebel leaders that they "must not loot, must not destroy the patrimony of the Dominican Republic." The mobs attacked the homes of Trujilloist and Reid supporters, set fire to the headquarters of three anti-Bosch political parties, and machine-gunned several Latin-American embassies. The Guatemalan Ambassador barely escaped violence when at about 7 P.M. a mob of some 200 poured into the Embassy grounds and demanded the right to search for Bonilla Aybar, the anti-Bosch commentator, who they believed might be in asylum there. When the Ambassador refused, only the timely appearance of a police detachment seems to have saved him from attack.

But the bitterness of the mob was perhaps reflected most dramatically of all in the scores of dead bodies that lay on the moonlit streets and in the garbage-glutted gutters of Ciudad Nueva, the downtown Boschist stronghold, that night—most of them policemen. They were the symbols of Dominican oppression, the symbols of death, torture, and corruption. Any policeman, armed or not—some changed into civilian clothing but were still shot when recognized—was fair game to people unleashed with guns in their hands after a lifetime of submission to guns.

Elsewhere in the country, the people didn't have guns, but, when rebel-controlled Radio Santo Domingo announced that Bosch was coming back, they streamed into the streets, dancing, shouting, demonstrating, and in most cases were not hindered in their merrymaking by the police or military. For it looked on Sunday as if the Boschists would win, and the local police and military leaders wanted to be on the winning side.

In Puerto Plata, the local army commander went on the air and encouraged the people to rejoice, though he asked them not to drink too much. "The Army is with the people," he proclaimed. Only when it appeared later that Wessin's forces were winning did he order the people off the streets and start arresting hundreds of them. In San Francisco de Macarís, the police did nothing to stop dozens of youths from dashing off on commandeered trucks to Santo Domingo to obtain arms and fight the Wessin forces—until, again, it looked as if these forces were winning.

The situation in Santiago was critical for the rebels. At about 1 A.M., Sunday, a rebel official, Papi Ginebra, telephoned from the 27th of September camp to an influential rebel supporter in that city. He asked Pedro Casals Victoria, the young, good-looking Finance Minister in the post-Bosch regime who resigned, charging vast government corruption, to take over several radio stations in the city and announce the revolt. Casals telephoned local supporters, including Antonio Guzmán, who had been Bosch's Minister of Agriculture and was to play a leading role in U. S. peacemaking efforts later in the revolution.

At about 3 A.M., Casals received another telephone call from Santo Domingo informing him that troops had marched into the city proper. From 9 to 10 A.M., rebel supporters took over three local Santiago radio stations that were owned by constitutionalists and announced this news, calling on people from the whole area to gather in Santiago to show their support for the revolution. The police, which at first opposed the revolt, began closing the stations, but then seemed to have a change of heart when it became clear that the Army, and also the Air Force, was backing Reid's ouster.

At an 11 A.M. meeting in Guzmán's comfortable middle-class home, rebel representatives met with Colonel Domingo de la Mota, commander of the Santiago Army garrison. Rebel officials who were present say that the colonel agreed to back the revolt against Reid but said that the people must be told not to damage any property. Nothing was said about Bosch being asked to return after the revolt succeeded.

While a crowd of people gathered in the streets in an exultant mood similar to that which had captured Santo Domingo, the question of military loyalties became more fluid following the split between San Isidro and the Boschist leaders in the capital. Casals suggested that the rebels in Santiago hold off announcing that Bosch must come back until a later time in order to keep the Santo Domingo split from spreading immediately to Santiago. But Guzmán and others vetoed the idea, arguing that Bosch represented the spirit of the revolution. They joined in demanding the return of Bosch.

When the Wessin forces started bombing the National Palace in the capital, Molina Ureña telephoned Casals and urgently requested that he get Air Force units in Santiago to send planes to bomb San Isidro. Casals and other rebel leaders tried to persuade local Air Force chiefs to dispatch the planes, but they wouldn't commit themselves. It was evident that they had decided to back Wessin. Rebel leaders then went to see Major Méndez Lara, second in command of the Army fortress, and asked him to attack the Air Force base and capture it. Méndez Lara said that Air Force tanks were going to attack the Army fortress and that the Army would have its hands full just defending itself.

Meanwhile, Molina telephoned Casals again and said almost desperately: "Where are the planes? We're being bombed incessantly. Send the planes immediately."

Casals replied: "It's impossible. The Air Force is going to attack us."

While waiting for the anticipated Air Force attack, Méndez set up 50-caliber machine gun and bazooka emplacements, and rebel officials distributed about 300 Molotov cocktails to civilians. Méndez said he would give arms to civilians but only to ones who were known to be responsible. However, the arms were never distributed. Nor did the expected tank attack materialize.

But while the Army units waited, the U. S. consul in Santiago, Francis M. Withey, according to rebel sources, came to the fortress and told Army leaders that the United States supported Wessin, and that he appeared to be winning the struggle in Santo Domingo. It would be unfortunate, the consul reportedly stressed, if the Santiago garrison found itself fighting brothers in arms.

At about 3 A.M. on Monday, Méndez told Casals that two rebel tanks would soon be arriving from Santo Domingo and that the people should be informed so that they would not attack them by mistake. The tanks were being sent for an assault on the Air Force base. Five pilots accompanying the tanks were to fly the bombing raids on San Isidro as soon as the base was secured.

General de la Mota, after meeting the tanks, led them to the Army fortress, and dispatched the pilots to the air base, the reverse of what had been planned. The tanks were then locked up in the fortress, and the pilots fell into the hands of the Air Force. De la Mota had apparently betrayed the rebels.

Casals called Molina and advised him to dismiss de la Mota immediately and make Méndez, who appeared to be loyal to the rebels, the Army commander, pointing out that Méndez had indicated he would take command only if he were legally promoted to the position. For some reason, however, Molina did not act. Then a rebel commander in Santo Domingo exhorted Casals to lead "an attack by the people" on the fortress in order to get the tanks needed to capture the Air Force base.

"But the people have no arms," Casals argued.

"Never mind, attack anyway," the commander replied.

Local rebel officials immediately contacted the commander of the La Vega army garrison about 40 miles away, and he apparently offered to provide 44 machine guns. But at about 4 A.M., a rebel truck that had been sent to La Vega returned empty. The commander had changed his mind. At the same time, the police, which now also supported Wessin, destroyed the three rebel-controlled radio stations.

Meanwhile, the crowds that had gathered on Calle El Sol, armed with only a few hundred Molotov cocktails, iron pipes, stones, knives, and clubs, were beginning to get out of hand. They wanted to attack the fortress regardless. Finally, the police started rounding up small groups of demonstrators, and as the day wore on, it became clear even to the fanatics that the pro-Wessin forces had full control of the situation. The crowds gradually and reluctantly dispersed, angry but helpless.

As the revolution gained momentum on Sunday night, I flew from Washington to Puerto Rico to see Bosch and to try to get into Santo Domingo from there, though Wessin's troops had closed all Dominican airports to traffic. The next morning, it was not hard finding the apartment building in which Bosch and his family lived, once I had gotten near. Scores of Dominican exiles, supporters of Bosch, stood in front of it in noisy groups, excitedly discussing the latest news from Santo Domingo and predicting when Bosch would return there. Upstairs on the second floor, where more Dominicans stood around in a patio listening to news broadcasts, a Bosch aide led me into the exiled President's small, modestly furnished apartment.

I found Bosch in his bedroom where he had been trying to take a brief nap. He sat on the edge of his unmade bed looking like a cadaver fighting for a spark of life. His blue eyes were bleary and bloodshot from 48 hours of sleeplessness, but they still reflected the familiar cold fire. And though the frozen lines in his thin, brooding face were deeper than ever, they yielded quiveringly as he smiled in greeting.

"Well, didn't I tell you?" he said. "It was inevitable. After tasting democracy, my people could not accept its loss."

Bosch was now in fact a political cadaver sparked to life. At least, this was his interpretation of what the events unfolding in his homeland meant. As I spoke with him, seated in a chair beside his bed, he expressed confidence that "within a few hours" he would be asked by the rebel government to return from exile to take over power once more. And he invited me to fly back in the same plane with him. He appeared certain the pro-Bosch forces would win the civil war.

The arrival in Puerto Rico that afternoon of a Dominican fighter plane carrying an officer who had defected from the anti-Bosch Air Force appeared to bolster this confidence, as did an abortive attempt by some 50 flag-waving pro-Bosch Dominicans to take over the Dominican consulate in San Juan.

Bosch had not changed since the last time I had seen him, shortly after his ouster from the presidency. His every remark, facial expression, and shrug revealed a complex mixture of intellect, arrogance, stubbornness, idealism, and, most important of all, faith. Faith in himself and in the people he had led.

"Some observers say that the Dominican people are not ready for democracy because they have had so little experience with it," he said between nervous puff on a cigarette. "But I say they are ready for democracy precisely because they have suffered so much without it."

He then picked up a copy of *The New York Times* and pointed with mixed anger and disappointment to an editorial in it that reflected regret over the ouster of Reid.

"Under that government, generals became millionaires overnight," he said. "It is strange that its fall should be regretted by some Americans."

With a child's hurt look, he told me that he could not understand why the U. S. government had not tried to contact him, particularly in view of its stated support of constitutional government. Even if it didn't like him, he said, it was strange that it had made no effort to at least find out what he was thinking, since he was, after all, a rather key figure in the revolution. He nevertheless predicted that the United States would strongly support him when "I return to power. For your country has the very democratic tradition I have tried to develop in the Dominican Republic."

Bosch, dressed in unbelted trousers and open white shirt put on hastily, said, as he ran his fingers through his wavy white hair, that he had not known about the planned rebellion by his followers.

"I knew that the people would rebel sometime, but I did not know when. One big mistake many people made was that the armed forces were against me. As this rebellion shows, only about a score of top commanders opposed me because I would not let them become millionaires. They represent the last remnants of Trujilloism."

Why did he not return to Santo Domingo immediately to rally his people behind him? He replied that there was no plane available, and that all the airports in the Dominican Republic were closed anyway. But after my talk with him I met outside an exiled Dominican congressman who had somehow obtained a small plane and hoped to fly to his country that night and land secretly in an interior area apparently controlled by rebels. He had asked Bosch to go with him, he said, but the Dominican leader had put him off. Days later in Santo Domingo, PRD leaders told me that they had asked Bosch to return on Saturday, immediately after Molina Ureña was sworn in, but that he insisted a plane be sent for him complete with an official escort composed of representatives of the three armed services.

"He wanted to return not as a man sneaking into the country, but as the President, with all the symbolic trappings," one PRD leader said.

Another Bosch associate told me that the ex-President was frightened most of all by the possibility that U. S. officials would prevent his departure and thereby make him look foolish. Several of his followers tried to leave San Juan in a boat three times to test this possibility, the associate said, and each time they were prevented from leaving.

But aside from such factors, Bosch—whose failure to return has been attributed by some observers to physical cowardice or lack of true leadership qualities—appears, in fact, to have simply miscalculated the course of the revolution. It was obvious in his talk with me that he expected a quick and overwhelming rebel victory. Therefore, he apparently felt, it was better to wait until calm was restored so that he could make a truly triumphant return as befitted a man who, as President, saw himself as the Rousseauistic incarnation of the national soul. But victory proved elusive, and by the time this became clear, Santo Domingo was in utter chaos and the U. S. marines were landing, leaving it to historians to speculate on the effect Bosch's return in the first days of the revolt might have had on ensuing events.

Stranded in San Juan because of the closure of the Dominican airports, I visited Bosch again the following day, on Tuesday,

and he no longer seemed as optimistic about a quick rebel victory as he had been the day before. And with good reason. On
Monday morning, the Air Force had made rocket runs against
the 27th of February barracks and had resumed strafing attacks
on the National Palace. The Wessin forces had also set up radio
facilities at San Isidro Air Base and by early afternoon were
warning that "the plan to clean up the city is going into effect
now!" This appeared to indicate that Wessin's tanks were about
to cross Duarte Bridge, which separated the road to San Isidro,
ten miles away, from the downtown part of Santo Domingo
where the rebels were entrenched.

The rebels fought back mainly with their own television and
radio stations. They paraded the families of Air Force officers
before television cameras and warned the Air Force that they
would be taken to Duarte Bridge to be the first casualties if the
tanks actually moved across the bridge. Both TV and radio
announcements volunteered the names and addresses of other
Air Force families who, it was advised, should be herded to the
bridge. A frantic radio announcement screamed: "To the
bridge! Don't let the tanks pass! Use your Molotov cocktails!"

Bosch, who had been in frequent telephone contact with his
forces in Santo Domingo, was now clearly worried. And he appeared completely disillusioned by the failure of the United
States which had backed him so strongly when he had been in
power, to come to his support now. No American official had
yet bothered to contact him. In the pathetic hope of winning
American support before it was too late, Bosch, in this second
interview with me, dramatically appealed to President Johnson
to back the constitutionalist cause.

"I hope President Johnson will support my government since
it is the only constitutional one," he said. "I'm sure that his
heart and feelings are with the Dominican people." He then
added after a pause: "And the Dominican people are backing
the constitutional government."

Unable even to imagine that the United States would back

the militarists, he complained, ironically, that his "people are disappointed by the neutrality of the U. S. government, especially since the only opposition to the constitutional government is a military group which has proclaimed it wants a military junta." He maintained that the democratic principles espoused in the Punta del Este Charter, which gave birth to the Alliance for Progress, were at stake in the war. And he stressed that the United States was a leading promoter of that declaration.

"We need now more than ever the comprehensive backing of the U. S. government and people," Bosch said contemplatively, "because this is the first time in history that the Dominican people are fighting for a constitutional regime. They are fighting, in fact, for something they learned from American history. They are fighting the same fight Washington and Jefferson fought."

He added that he was sorry to see evidences of "disenchantment in U. S. government circles" about the ability of democracy to survive in his country. He emphasized that young officers who had learned democracy in U. S. training institutions were leading the struggle for his return.

Bosch didn't realize it at the time, but nothing he might have said, it appears, would have influenced Washington to support him. The American Embassy's Connett, in the early stages of the revolution, advised Washington to contact Bosch for a discussion about his return. But shortly afterward, he counseled against his return apparently because of the Communist support he was receiving. The Embassy advised that the United States should not commit itself to either side, recommending that the best solution lay in the establishment of a military junta which would rule until elections could be held. This was also the solution that Wessin proposed.

Washington, except for a few subordinate officials who favored Bosch's return, thought these recommendations made sense. Constitutional government in Latin America was no longer the vital concern that it had been under the Kennedy Administration. And so Johnson Administration leaders decided that since, in their view, Bosch had not been a good President when he had been in power, and since he didn't know how to deal with Communists, particularly armed ones, the United States should make no effort to get him to Santo Domingo, or even to contact him. Under President Kennedy, some U. S. officials had even advocated sending marines if necessary to keep Bosch in power before he was ousted. Now the United States would do what it could to keep Bosch out of power—a decision apparently made even before concern had arisen over the Communist role in the revolution.

This and other major decisions were reached by President Johnson with the advice mainly of Mann, White House Adviser McGeorge Bundy, and Defense Secretary Robert S. McNamara, but also of Secretary of State Dean Rusk, Undersecretary of State George W. Ball, CIA Director Admiral William F. Raborn, Jr., Undersecretary of Defense Cyrus K. Vance, Assistant Secretary of State Jack Hood Vaughn, and State Department officer Kennedy M. Crockett.

Washington's attitude toward the Boschists appears to have hardened on Monday, April 27, after the U. S. Embassy sent a message saying that the Communists were seriously threatening to take over the revolution. The Embassy may have based this report on information it received from the loyalist leaders, who had an obvious interest in calling the revolution "Red," since it also reported the same day that Wessin and De los Santos had requested U. S. military intervention, apparently on the basis of the Communist threat, and were told not to expect such help.

The loyalists' request for aid on Monday, when they appeared to be winning, would indicate that Wessin and his colleagues were far from sure that their soldiers in the end would attack the rebel masses gathered at one side of Duarte Bridge. In any event, the Embassy for the second time recommended to Washington on that day that it support a plan for a military junta and

later elections as approved, or suggested—it is not clear which—
by Wessin. It also advised that a U. S. show of force in the area
might be useful at a later time.

Before making such recommendations, Embassy officials had
talked with representatives of both sides. On Sunday, Monday,
and Tuesday they conversed with the leaders of small anti-Bosch
political parties, and, according to one Embassy official, all
proposed creation of a military junta to be followed by elections.

U. S. officials said they also spoke with PRD leaders daily.
At about 6 P. M., Sunday, three such leaders, including Secretary-General Martínez Francisco and Antonio Guzmán called
at the Embassy and asked Arthur E. Breisky, the second secretary, to appeal to the Wessin forces to halt their bombings,
which had just started. Martínez and Breisky offered me conflicting versions of how the conversation went.

According to Martínez, "Breisky yelled that the revolution
was controlled by the Communists, and we denied this. He
said, 'Now you're looking for help. Why don't you tell your
people to surrender?' He picked up the telephone and slammed
it down on the desk in front of us, and said: 'Here, call your
military leaders and tell them to surrender.' We refused, of
course."

Breisky said that he had told the three men that he agreed the
Air Force should stop bombing, but that it was time that Dominicans of goodwill on both sides acted responsibly. He said
he pointed out politely but firmly that they had a lot of nerve
asking the Embassy to get the other side to give in, and that the
situation was now favorable to the Communists. He told them
that the Embassy couldn't intervene on their behalf. They replied, said Breisky, that, as good Dominicans, they understood.

Whatever words Breisky used, the rebels regarded his remarks
as calling for surrender to Wessin, a suggestion that would have
been consistent with the Embassy's recommendation to Washington that an effort be made to set up a military junta as favored by Wessin.

At any rate, the Embassy did manage to get the Air Force to
stop its bombing raids on four different occasions, though only
for a short time in each case. Embassy officials tended to blame
the Wessin forces less for resuming their air attacks than the
rebel forces for refusing to halt their mob actions.

To the rebels, this was incomprehensible. In their view there
was no comparison between the two forms of violence. The mobs
killed individuals whom they regarded as enemies, mainly the
armed policemen who had for so long suppressed the people.
But the planes were shooting into crowds, killing anyone in
the way, men, women, or children, by the dozen or even the
score. It was almost impossible for them to believe that this was
happening, this mass, indiscriminate murder. On the other
hand, U. S. officials saw killing as killing. If there were no mobs,
there would be no strafing or bombing. It was a question of
cause and effect, and the rebels were the cause.

With the situation rapidly deteriorating into chaos, American
and other foreign civilians who wished to leave were advised on
Monday to gather the next morning at Hotel Embajador, from
where they would be taken to the port of Haina, about seven
miles away, for evacuation to San Juan in U. S. naval vessels.
At about 7 A.M. the following day, Tuesday, April 27, some
1,000 people, mostly Americans but also other foreign nationals,
were gathered at the hotel. Babies were crying, older children
were playing hide-and-seek, husbands were embracing their de-
parting wives. Suddenly about 25 young civilian rebels brandishing rifles and automatic weapons came rushing up and encircled a large group of evacuees standing in front of the hotel.
"Get down on the ground!" the rebels yelled, and then started
firing at the hotel façade, breaking a few windows. When the
firing stopped, the terrified evacuees got up and ran into the
hotel lobby for protection. But the rebels followed and threatened them for four hours.

"They knew we were Americans and they were absolutel

delighted that we were so terrified," David Sofaer, a New York
businessman, said later.

At one point, the evacuees were told to lie down on the lobby
floor and rebels fired in terrifying bursts over their heads. Rebels
even refused to let mothers obtain milk for their babies. Tension
was relieved somewhat only when a group of young Americans
started singing. Meanwhile, the rebels conducted a futile room-
by-room search for Bonilla Aybar, whom they had been unable
to find at the Guatemalan Embassy. They thought that he might
be at the hotel trying to evacuate. As Dominican policemen arrived to take the Americans to Haina, they finally departed.
Miraculously, nobody had been killed or hurt. But that incident
was to contribute materially to an atmosphere that later in the
day proved conducive to a momentous decision on the part of
the United States.

The evacuation was under way when, later on Tuesday, Ambassador Bennett returned to Santo Domingo. He had rushed
from Georgia to Washington during the weekend and had participated in high-level discussions there on Monday before leaving for his post. A presidential jet flew him to San Isidro Air
Base, but, unable to cross besieged Duarte Bridge, he went by
helicopter to the *Boxer,* which now lay offshore, and from there
to the Embassy. He found the Embassy a scene of confusion
and anxiety. Some employees were leaving for Haina by automobile to evacuate their families. Others were on their way by
helicopter to the *Boxer.* Shots had rung out in the vicinity during the day, and there was fear of a full-fledged attack on the
Embassy.

But the Ambassador received instructions from Washington
that undoubtedly pleased him. He was to press for the establishment of a military junta, as his subordinates had advised during his absence. Such a junta, the Administration felt, could
best bring about law and order, protect American lives, and prevent a Communist takeover of the country.

Bennett's instructions sharply contradicted American assertions made after the troop landings that U. S. policy was to remain neutral in the conflict. Indeed, they show that even before the decision was made to send troops, the United States had flatly decided to take sides with the Wessin forces and to help stop the revolution. And they show that no thought was given to the possibility of dealing with Bosch and other rebel leaders with a view toward cleansing the revolution of important Communist influence without destroying the revolution itself—which President Johnson himself was later to characterize as basically democratic.

Meanwhile, the civil war seemed to be going the way the Administration was hoping it would. Wessin's tanks had started to edge over Duarte Bridge, bombing of the National Palace continued, and the Navy, which had previously remained aloof —like the Army, it had never been happy about the Air Force's elite status—threw its support to Wessin on Tuesday and had started firing rounds into the city, apparently in coordination with the Air Force. Moreover, overnight, it seems, Boschist army supporters in Santo Domingo had dwindled from about 8,000 to some 1,000, while a regiment of troops from San Cristóbal was en route to help Wessin. The military defections were due not only to the calculation that Wessin was now likely to win, but to a growing fear that they would be dominated by the armed civilians, perhaps the Communists among them. They had been willing to participate in a military revolt involving only professional soldiers, but not in a popular revolution whose ramifications they could not foresee.

So defeatist had the rebel side become that about fifteen of their military leaders, led by Hernando Ramirez, hearing that the Ambassador had returned, voluntarily came to the Embassy on Tuesday morning to ask him to help "end the bloodshed." Benjamin J. Ruyle, the chief political officer, suggested to the group that to discuss a settlement it would be best to have Provisional President Molina Ureña present. At first the officers, apparently ashamed of their efforts to forsake the PRD and

Bosch, were reluctant to agree, arguing that Molina was in the
National Palace, which was being bombed almost constantly.
Ruyle said, however, that despite the risks he himself would go
to the palace if they would accompany him.

Several of the officers agreed, and they drove with Ruyle to
the palace. The great beige building looked like a relic in the
wilderness. Shattered windows and bullet holes and crevices in
its battered hulk attested to the severity of the air attacks. Mahogany trees that had stood like rigid sentinels on the sidewalks
surrounding the palace now resembled petrified corpses as they
lay in the deserted streets.

The group of men entered and found Molina sitting in a
room off the main corridor with several advisers. His eyes were
sunken and he looked like a broken man. His starched collar
and pressed suit seemed strikingly incongruous amid the shattered glass littering the floor and the overturned furniture in
this desolate tomblike setting. The newcomers came to the point.
They said that enough people had been killed and that fighting
should stop. Ruyle suggested that Molina return with them to
the Embassy to discuss ways of ending the war. But Molina, his
pale face suddenly flushed with anger, replied that he would
never betray the revolution. He flatly refused to go. Finally, one
of his advisers, Luis Homéro Lajaré Burgos, a naval officer who
was Molina's Director of National Security, persuaded him that
under the circumstances there was little choice. With tears in
his eyes, Molina gave in.

Molina, with the others, then drove to the Embassy, where
they arrived shortly before 4 P.M. As he was about to enter, the
Provisional President drew himself stiffly to attention, removed
a pistol from his belt, and dramatically handed it to a marine
sentry. All arms had to be left at the door anyway before one
could enter, but Molina's manner reminded Embassy officials
of a proud general surrendering to the enemy.

The group, together with the officers who had been waiting
for their colleagues' return, then entered the Ambassador's

office. The tone of that meeting has since been bitterly disputed. The rebels have said that the Ambassador mocked and humiliated them in refusing to mediate the dispute and virtually asking them to surrender to Wessin. The Ambassador, while declining to be quoted, is known to feel that he was simply firm with them, politely refusing to mediate only because he didn't have the authority to do so. Thus, there is no disagreement on the Ambassador's reply to the request for mediation, but only on its motivation and the manner of delivery.

No information on the meeting had been published up to May 3, several days after American troops had started landing, and my curiosity was naturally aroused when an Embassy official remarked to me on that day, rather offhandedly, that perhaps the Ambassador had been a little too abrupt when the rebel leaders had come to see him. When I pursued the subject, he said only that one of the leaders had angrily said as he was leaving the Embassy that the talk with the Ambassador had convinced them that they must go on fighting "to the bitter end."

I immediately went to Caamaño's headquarters in the heart of Ciudad Nueva and saw Aristy, who was now Caamaño's chief political adviser. When I brought up the subject of the Embassy meeting, his lively face twisted in a scowl.

"You want to know what happened?" he said. "Well, Caamaño will tell you. Bennett is responsible for everything that's happened. Wait until you hear the story."

He took me into Caamaño's office, which was seething with rifle-carrying aides, most of them dressed in varying mixtures of civilian and military clothing, and introduced me to the colonel, who was wearing a rumpled suntan uniform open at the throat.

"Let's tell him what happened at that meeting with Bennett," Aristy said. He looked toward me and added: "You'll be the first reporter to have this story."

Caamaño, a barrel-chested man with a round face embroidered with a thin moustache, sat down at his small, scratched-up

desk, ordered his aides to leave the room—all except Aristy—
and, pointing to his thick forearm, said to me in a voice scald-
ing with bitterness: "I get goose pimples just thinking of it.
I'll never forget that moment of shame. It was the decisive moment of this war."

After a pause, he added, his hand wiping his sweaty brow:
"I'll never forget how your Ambassador laughed at us when we
asked him to help us end the bloodshed. Imagine, we were
ready to agree to peace on any terms just to stop the killing.
And the Ambassador laughed at us. It is because of that we decided, in our shame, to fight to the death. This is what happened.

"On the day that the Air Force started to bomb the city and
National Palace, we saw people being killed by the bombing and
we were desolate. It was horrible seeing Dominican blood being
shed like that. The officers in our high command then decided
to go to the American Embassy to make an agreement with the
San Isidro people through U. S. mediation.

"To stop the bloodshed we decided to accept more or less any
kind of agreement at that moment. Unfortunately, in the belief
that Bennett would help us solve the terrible problem, we told
him of our wish.

" 'Mr. Ambassador,' one of us said, 'we have come here to ask
you to mediate between Wessin's troops and ourselves. We
would agree to the formation of a military junta, though we
think elections should be held soon.'

"But Bennett replied: 'You should have realized before you
started the trouble that you couldn't hold out. Now it's too late.
You started this, you are responsible for all that has happened.
You hold the solution in your hands. Go and see Wessin your-
selves. You are finished.'

"Our eyes filled with tears of shame for having gone to see
him. I told him, 'Mr. Ambassador, it's a pity that you do not
appreciate men's humanitarian feelings and sense of honor and

responsibility. But I can assure you that you will see that there
are men of honor in our country.' "

Toward the end of the conversation, Caamaño said, a telephone call came through from La Romana, an American-owned
sugar company in the town of La Romana. The voice on the
other end said that the rebels in the area were arming civilians
and there was fear of attack on the American property. One of
his group, Caamaño said, tried for 30 minutes to call the rebel
commander in the area to order him not to arm civilians.

"After we got through," Caamaño said, "Bennett dismissed
us, saying that there was nothing more to talk about. One of
the officers present, Lieutenant Héctor Conde, took off his military cap and ripped off his insignia, saying, 'I can't endure this
shame.'

"As we were about to leave, I said, 'Mr. Ambassador, before
twenty-four hours are out, you will be interceding to stop Wessin's forces from being wiped out.' "

Caamaño paused, then said in a low, suppressed voice: "That
was the decisive moment. We went back to our headquarters
and decided to rally our troops at the bridge. Out of pure shame,
we went to the bridge to fight to the death. Finally, we pushed
Wessin's forces back. And I was right, Bennett did have to inter-
cede to help him within twenty-four hours."

Ambassador Bennett offers a different version of what happened, which is known to go like this: He politely told the rebel
leaders that he could not help to mediate the war because he had
no authority to do so. But he suggested that they deal directly
with the Wessin forces in ending the bloodshed, having received indications that the latter would be prepared to negotiate
peace. He said that he thought it was time for them to face up
to their responsibility, since it was their action that initiated the
fighting.

The United States, he said, had loyally backed Bosch when
he had been in power. The effort to bring him back had failed,
so it was necessary to start again. He said he looked forward to

early elections, supervised by the OAS if the Dominican people so desired. He said he spoke with equal firmness to the Wessin forces in asking them to stop their bombing attacks. His staff, he said, had succeeded four times the day before in getting them to halt the attacks, but each time, the rebels had tried to turn the lull to their military advantage.

The Ambassador emphasized that the Communists had unquestionably taken advantage of the situation and that the PRD had tolerated and encouraged them. He said that people who talked, acted, and dressed like Castroites could be seen on rebel television. And when the telephone call from La Romana came through he pointed to that as an example of Communist activity. (The feared rebel attacks there never materialized.)

The rebels, the Ambassador is known to have reported, would not admit to any of his charges of dealing with the Communists, calling them "details." Bennett said they were important details which were not compatible with their talk of democratic methods. (Caamaño told me that the rebel leaders denied having given arms to known Communists or tolerating the Communists in any way.) The Ambassador also said the incident at the Embajador Hotel that morning had been disgraceful and said the rebel leaders were responsible for it. The latter replied the band of attackers had not been under their control.

U. S. officials argue that the Wessin forces probably would not have agreed to negotiations through mediation in any case. But since the rebels were prepared to accept Wessin's terms it would seem that they might have agreed. In any event, Bennett, who perhaps could have obtained authority to mediate within minutes, did not bother to find out whether they would agree or not. Unforgivingly bitter toward the Boschists, in their eyes, for having sparked the overthrow of Reid Cabral, he was seen as not wanting to give them the face-saving satisfaction of a negotiated settlement even if such a settlement might have been consistent with American aims. He wanted them, they were convinced, to suffer the humiliation of abject surrender. And

as a result, he forced them to keep fighting until the marines had
to be called in to keep them from winning.

According to PRD leaders, this was not the only case of what
they regarded as Embassy arrogance and hostility toward the
rebel cause on that fateful Tuesday afternoon. There was another, they say, involving the second secretary, Breisky. Again I
received two versions of the story. PRD Secretary-General Martínez Francisco told me that Breisky had come to see him at
about 4 P.M. and said, apparently because of the rebel military
mission to the Embassy, "It's all over. You might as well quit."
Then, on his way out, Martínez said, Breisky approached two
rebel tanks that were standing on the street and, repeating the
tidings to the operators, advised them to leave.

"The drivers got out of the tanks, spit at Breisky, and left,"
Martínez said.

A neighbor who had seen what had happened then yelled
out, the PRD leader went on, "History will condemn you."

"Breisky walked over to him," said Martínez, "and asked for
his name. Then he said, 'You're lucky you're still alive.' "

According to Breisky, he noted that the tank guns were
pointed at houses along the street, and "people asked me to do
something about that, and I agreed. I went over to the operators
and said, 'Do you mind if I suggest something? Would you
please move your tanks.' They said that their side had lost and
that they were afraid. So I suggested that they just leave the
tanks and go away. And they did."

But once more, whichever story is more accurate, the rebels
were left with the impression that the United States regarded
them not simply as representing one side in somebody else's
civil war, but as an enemy to be destroyed.

Not all the rebel leaders, as a result, discovered a second battle
wind. Molina Ureña, whose nerves gave out under the constant
pounding of bombs, found himself unable to continue the fight
after conditioning himself to defeat, and fled to asylum in the
Colombian Embassy within an hour after the meeting with Ben-

nett. Five other PRD leaders also took asylum in various embassies, as did the rebel military leader, Hernando Ramirez, who
had a recurrence of a severe liver ailment. This left Caamaño
as the top military-political leader.

It was about this time, the Administration has said, that the
Communists took control of the revolution, filling the leadership vacuum left by the flight into asylum by PRD and rebel
military leaders. The rebel argument is that there was in fact
no leadership vacuum, for Caamaño and most of the rebel command not only continued to lead the fight but did so in a far
more vigorous manner than previously, thanks to the American
Ambassador. The rebels further claim that the abandonment of
the struggle by a few PRD leaders was not a decisive factor. For
one thing, in an armed battle it is the military and not the political leaders who direct the course of the fighting, they say, and
that is what Caamaño and his fellow non-Communist officers
were doing. As for their political inspiration, the people still
looked to Bosch, even though he was not in the country, and
not to Molina or other PRD leaders.

Furthermore, it is argued, only six of the PRD's nineteen
executive committee members went into asylum, while the
others remained at their political posts. And except for Molina
and one other, the asylees emerged after two or three days to
resume their jobs. The rebels maintain that a PRD liaison official had uninterruptedly been present at their headquarters
since the revolution started. Although I couldn't verify this, I
myself saw some on my first visit to the headquarters on Sunday,
May 2, only four days after U. S. troops started landing.

PRD officials, moreover, have scoffed at a statement released
by the U. S. Embassy—and repeated in so many words in a presidential speech—that said: "There is little room for doubt that
the PRD civilian leaders of the revolt, with the exception of
Bosch . . . have all at least privately recognized the capture of
their revolt by the extreme left." PRD leaders told me that all
members of their party who took asylum did so temporarily

because they thought at the time that the Wessin forces were about to win and they were on his death list.

"None of us took asylum because we thought the Communists were winning control of the movement," said Peña Gómez, who was in asylum for two days. "The Communists never had control of our movement."

PRD Secretary-General Martínez Francisco added: "It is possible that some Communists have tried to attach themselves to our movement, but it is ridiculous to say that they have ever had any control."

These statements flatly contradicted, without necessarily disproving, of course, U. S. Embassy statements specifically declaring that both Peña Gómez and Martínez had said privately to American officials before going into asylum (Martínez took refuge at the Mexican Embassy for only a few hours) that they feared the Communists were taking over the revolution.

Molina himself tried to leave the Colombian Embassy after two days to return to his post. As he was about to depart hidden in a Red Cross ambulance, however, an American officer and the papal nuncio, Monsignor Emanuele Clarizio, arrived and persuaded him to stay in asylum for safety's sake.

No one denied to me that Communists were participating in the revolution. Indeed, Communists wouldn't be Communists unless they played a role in every revolution in the hope of turning chaos to their advantage. There is no way to keep them out. But at the same time, they are wary of joining revolutions they feel haven't much chance. Peña Gómez, in fact, claimed that the Reds, far from pushing for the revolt, had refused to join it at first, and had even tried to obstruct it. Unable to differentiate between revolutionary and nonrevolutionary elements in the armed forces, he said, they had doubted the popular nature of the revolt.

The U. S. government, after the landing of American troops, issued list after controversial list of Communists who were supposed to be involved in the fighting, each hopefully more accurate than the preceding one. It issued an uncheckable document purporting to show how and where the Communists operated in the revolution. But it couldn't offer any evidence that could stand up showing that the Reds had done anything more than participate in the rebellion, that they had controlled anyone other than themselves.

Whether the United States was justified in sending troops to the Dominican Republic can be argued either way. What is far more difficult to justify was the effort to smear a democratic revolution as Communist-controlled in the Trujillo manner, particularly without any evidence to support this contention. For although this smear may have been motivated by tactical rather than by pro-rightist ideological considerations, the propaganda effect was the same. The United States emerged in the world's eyes as the partner of the old order in trying to prevent social progress.

Thomas C. Mann himself, in an interview with Max Frankel of *The New York Times* shortly after U. S. troops landed, said: "I think it is standard Communist doctrine, as well as proven tactics, for Communist groups to form popular fronts and to try to take over from within all kinds of movements. But there really is no problem, as far as our policy is concerned, unless and until the Communists succeed in actually capturing and controlling a movement.

"It is a matter, essentially, of control and, fortunately, most people in Latin America understand the difference between a liberal and non-Communist left, if one can call it that, and the Communist left. And as long as this distinction is kept in mind there really isn't any political problem."

Yet, despite this very reasonable statement, the United States did see a problem even at the beginning of the revolution before the Communist issue clearly emerged. It wanted to keep Bosch from reclaiming his constitutional leadership and was prepared to deal with the military to do it. Nor, indeed, has Mann himself ever said in public that the Communists at any point *controlled* the revolution. The most he has said is that the Communists "succeeded in organizing, arming and moving into the streets very sizable paramilitary forces."

Even if there had been substantial evidence of Communist control it would still have been a mistake to attempt to discredit and fight a revolution rooted in democracy, whatever measures would have been required to purge the Communist leadership. But on the contrary, little evidence has been offered that the Communists were in control, and it is not certain that they could have gained control, lacking a power base. It wasn't simply that the Dominican Communists are very few in number. As I pointed out in my book *Subversion of the Innocents*, a study of Communist infiltration in the underdeveloped world, it is possible for a handful of Communists to take over a country under certain circumstances. Certainly if the revolutionary leader is a great popular hero who happens to be a Communist, as in the case of Fidel Castro, that leader, once in power, can impose a Communist government.

But no U. S. official has even suggested the possibility to me that the popular leader of the Dominican revolution, Bosch, or the military leader, Caamaño, might be Communists. Nor has such a possibility been held out by any diplomats or other responsible observers.

At the same time, the Communists enjoy negligible sympathy among the masses who recall their "deals" with Trujillo, and they can find little political apathy to exploit, as in many underdeveloped countries. Indeed, the Dominican masses fear and despise the Reds more than do their counterparts in most other nations, since, having experienced harsher dictatorship than most, they are more sensitive to any kind of suppression and, conversely, more appreciative of democracy. If sympathy for communism is to grow, or resistance to it is to lessen, opening the door for eventual Communist control, the reason is likely to lie in the failure of democracy, particularly if the

United States, the symbol of democracy, tarnishes the credibility of that system by frustrating it in the Dominican Republic.

It is highly doubtful, moreover, that the Communists could have mustered the armed strength to assert control over a hostile people. The armed forces, even if they had collapsed in the face of the revolution, might have fallen in with the "people," but not with the Communists. Certainly units based in the interior, which had been sitting on the fence waiting to see who was winning before committing themselves to the support of either side, would not have thrown in their lot with the Communists, who have failed to infiltrate the armed forces to any significant degree. As a rebel officer told me, the worst that might have happened is that there would have been a civil war within a civil war.

"Do you think that after all we've sacrificed we would let the Communists steal our revolution?" this officer asked. "If they even came close to doing so, the great mass of our fighters would fight them no less tenaciously than we're fighting the military traditionalists, and we would, of course, have more support from elements of the armed forces than we have today."

Thus, without the numbers, the popular leader, the public sympathy, or the armed might, and divided into four bitterly competing groups, the Communists would have had a hard time indeed gaining control of a revolution embracing most of the population, and would have had even greater difficulty maintaining their control. Nor would the United States, if it had to intervene as a last resort, be likely to have much trouble sweeping out the Reds once it was established that they really were in control.

This is not to say that the United States necessarily made a mistake by going in under the circumstances that existed at the time of intervention. Perhaps the Administration did have intelligence it could not make public which left it with no choice. Perhaps its action did save many lives. But it should be noted that there is another side to the argument also, an argument that many Latin-American democrats are using.

At any rate, the Communist issue had become almost academic in the minds of U. S. officials when the rebel leaders left the Embassy. For it looked as if Wessin had just about won, fulfilling U. S. aims, at least its temporary ones. In telephone conversations with U. S. reporters stranded in San Juan on Tuesday night, Embassy officials assured them that all was over but the mopping up. The rebels, they said, had come to the Embassy and indicated they were through. Headlines in Wednesday morning newspapers read that the civil war was over and the Boschists defeated. My office even suggested by telephone that morning that perhaps I should come home, rather than continue my efforts to go on to Santo Domingo.

But the Embassy had completely misjudged the situation. In the first place, Caamaño and his invigorated command leaped into the battle with a fighting spirit they had not displayed before. They pushed, cajoled and ordered their followers to batter back Wessin's tanks regardless of the cost. On Tuesday night, several tanks had already crossed the Ozama River and established a bridgehead on the rebel side. It looked as if they could not be stopped. And Caamaño and his fellow revolutionaries were among those who were not sure they could be. But no longer was it a question with them whether they would win or lose. It was a question of honor. It was a question of fighting until all of them were dead.

Caamaño's "moment of decision" was a vital moment not only for the revolution, but for himself. It was a moment of personal rejuvenation for a man who had never understood nor had much faith in himself. Like many young Dominicans born in the Trujillo era—he was born in 1933, three years after El Benefactor came to power—he grew up with the dictator's curse over his head. His father, Lt. General Fausto Caamaño, was known as Trujillo's "butcher" for having supervised or permitted the mass murder of 15,000 to 35,000 Haitian residents—

no one is certain of the figure—during one 48-hour period in 1937.

Francisco was only four years old at the time. But as he grew older, he heard many stories about what happened. He could almost hear Trujillo's dry, ominously quiet voice as he told a crowd of Dominicans at a church dance in Dajabón, near the Haitian border, on the evening of October 2, 1937:

"I came to the border country to see what I could do for Dominicans living here. I found that Haitians had been stealing food and cattle from our farmers here. I found that our people would be happier if we got rid of the Haitians."

Francisco could picture him as he paused, stamped his foot, pointed his finger at the audience, and added coldly: "I will fix that. Yesterday 300 Haitians were killed at Bánica. This must continue."

And so it did, under the supervision of the Army, which was under the control of his father. It was all very systematic and efficient, though lacking the scientific refinements of Hitler's methods of genocide. Soldiers rounded up Haitians in all the border towns, most of whom were part-time sugarcane cutters, and, in general, followed a simple procedure. They divided the prisoners into couples, tied the right arm of one to the left arm of the other, and, while villagers watched, led each couple about 20 feet from the crowd and told them to squat down on their heels. Then a soldier with a machete brought it down on each victim in turn amidst the cheers of the crowd and the horrified shrieks of those waiting their turn to die. Only the Haitian children seemed disinterested. They didn't know what death was or that they were to die.

There were, of course, variations in the system. In one case, for example, a soldier asked a young Haitian woman to raise her left arm. When she did, he plunged a dagger into her breast. By some miracle she lived to tell her story to doctors at a hospital. Sometimes, if a child was very young, a soldier would simply take it by the feet and swing it against a tree.

Francisco, as he heard the stories, could almost see the wounds as they were inflicted, particularly the machete wounds, which were not clean like those from the dagger, which left only a purple mark. Because of the heaviness of the machete and the dullness of its blade, it tore the skin crudely, leaving a wide, red gash bubbly with blood, a grisly symbol of what a man had to do to survive in a vile world.

The youth both accepted the reality and rebelled against it, torn between a son's longing to believe in his father and his hatred for everything his father stood for. Caamaño's elder brother, Emerson, found a way out of the agonizing dilemma. In 1958, a close friend of his who was apparently involved in a plot against Trujillo came to Emerson and, indicating that the police suspected him, asked him for help. Emerson then seems to have told his father in confidence about the situation, asking him to use his influence on behalf of his friend. Instead, General Caamaño reportedly informed Trujillo that the young man was plotting against him. A short time later, the body of Emerson's friend was found floating in the sea. Emerson himself was then found dead. He had been playing Russian roulette, according to the official word. But few Dominicans doubted that he had committed suicide.

Francisco, on the other hand, continued to live with his frustration, bitterness, and sense of guilt, all of which are reflected in his unstable, rebellious military career. At fifteen, he was sent by his father to Riverside Military Academy, a preparatory school in Gainesville, Georgia. But before he finished his first year, he was suspended for three months after getting into a fistfight with another cadet. He went home and didn't return, enrolling in the Dominican Navy's midshipman's school instead. He became a naval officer, but after tangling with superiors, shifted to the tiny Dominican Marine Corps.

In 1954, he went to Coronado, California, for Marine Corps amphibious training, and a year later took an officers' course at the Marine base at Quantico, Virginia. He returned home

bubbling over with ideas for the reorganization of the Dominican marine infantry. After working out a plan, he submitted
it to the Navy chief, and it was rejected within five minutes.
"We can't change things in this country," the naval leader
reportedly told him. Caamaño was infuriated. "Well, why did
you bother to send me for training in the United States?" he
remarked. In his new frustration, he learned to despise the
traditional militarists not only for their cruelty and corruption,
but for their arrogance and unimaginativeness, qualities which
he saw in sharp contrast to what he says he regarded as the
understanding, open-minded attitudes of the military leaders
he had met in the United States.

He finally moved to the Army, and from there to the Air
Force infantry, winning promotions as he shifted, some people
say because of his father's influence. In 1962, when the Council
of State replaced the assassinated Trujillo, he was switched to
the national police and put in charge of the Cascos Blancos.

Caamaño's force, together with the Army forces, were sent in
December 1962 to eliminate the voodoo "threat" in Palma Sola.
In the struggle that ensued, he was assaulted with clubs and
struck with his own machine gun, and was hospitalized for several weeks. But the Army, as already indicated, killed scores of
people. (Communists and other extreme leftists charged that
hundreds had been massacred.)

Caamaño's role in the killings is ambiguous. He claims that
he was knocked out of the fight and therefore couldn't have directed the slaughter, which Juan Bosch characterized in a recent
book as the "bloody episode of Palma Sola." But his association
with an event that brought back searing memories of his father's
great crimes intensified his feelings of guilt and his efforts to
overcome them with toughness, bluster, and, sometimes, drink.

In November 1964, he accused his police chief, General
Belisario Peguero Guerrero, of corruption and plotted against
him. Reid then transferred him back to the Air Force. Bitter
toward Reid, he not unnaturally joined the Boschists who

were plotting against his new boss, Wessin, Reid's protector. But if Caamaño's motives for joining in the plot might have reflected in the beginning more the rebel than the constitutionalist—he had done nothing to help Bosch when he had been overthrown, though he explains that he had had little choice at that time but to obey orders—he had obviously discovered in his support of a popular and meaningful cause an instrument for fighting his past and coming to terms with himself. He had found a rebellion that eased rather than aggravated his torment, one conceived in hope rather than hate. And ironically, it was the American Ambassador who put into true focus for him the distinction between the disorder in which he had been reared and the revolution he hadn't understood, though only the future can tell how long this distinction will remain in focus.

But as Caamaño and his rebels plunged ahead with what looked like a losing cause, they had a better chance of pulling a military "miracle" than they—or the American Embassy—suspected. For Wessin, though he had 26 tanks and elite Air Force infantry units comprising some 5,000 men, controlled no unified command, nor did any other general. He had little influence over Air Force General de los Santos, who owed his job to Reid and had only decided to join Wessin at the last minute. And he had little reason to trust General Montás Guerrero, commander of about 1,000 troops who were moving into Santo Domingo from San Cristóbal on Tuesday night to support him. Wessin had backed Reid when he had ousted Montás Guerrero from the job of Army chief shortly before the revolution.

Moreover, from the start of the constitutionalist revolt, many Air Force pilots proved reluctant to bomb the people and were made prisoners. Nor could Wessin be certain of the loyalty of his common soldiers. It was one thing to depend on them to carry out a coup directed against an opposing group of officers. It was another to depend on them to fire into crowds of civilians,

simple people like themselves. And certainly they would be
affected by the knowledge that some of their own families had
been herded to the firing line. Adding to Wessin's troubles was
the growing problem of keeping the air base in operation. It
was short of food, gasoline, communications equipment. Electric power had been shut off.

Wessin's fears, which apparently accounted for his request
for U. S. military aid on Tuesday, proved not without foundation. Several tanks had, after eleven tries, managed to cross
Duarte Bridge and were followed by a stream of junta troops.
The rebel forces backed away, and it looked as if they were
indeed through.

Then, a remarkable thing happened. Near the entrance to
the bridge, about a dozen 75-mm. guns stood abandoned. Suddenly an unidentified man dashed from a nearby house to one
of the guns and pointed it at the lead tank as it advanced into
rebel territory. He fired it and there was an explosion. The shell
had miraculously hit the tank and knocked it out. For some
seconds there was an incredible silence. Then people materialized from everywhere, it seemed, and began attacking the remaining tanks, their guns ablaze. Wessin's infantry soldiers
started retreating, and so did the besieged tanks. The great
military might ranged against the motley mixture of some 3,000
(Caamaño put the figure at 10,000) professional and amateur
soldiers with their outdated rifles and homemade explosives had
begun to disintegrate.

At the moment when the tanks started to recede, history
reached a turning point for the Dominican people. In a sense,
it was the climax for them of more than 450 years of suppression, subjugation, and hopelessness. They had experienced brief
stretches of freedom, such as under the Bosch regime. But the
military sword had always been poised, ready to fall at the least
provocation. Always had they been at the mercy of men with
guns. Now, for the first time in history, the people had guns,

and they had forced the tanks to retreat. They were beating the armed forces that symbolized their centuries of misery. They were lifting the sword from above their heads. They realized for the first time that they possessed a strength they had never before imagined could be theirs. And Caamaño shared in this realization as he stood on the edge of a personal as well as a military victory—a victory over his father's ghost, a victory in partnership with the people his father had once jailed, tortured, and killed.

This was a decisive moment for the United States, also. Ironically, this country, conceived in revolution, could not look with approval on revolution elsewhere, particularly near its shores. For in this modern era, no revolution could be free of Communist influence in one degree or another. Coup d'états could be tolerated, for they were always perpetrated by anti-Communist militarists who, no matter how undesirable from a moral viewpoint they might be, did not pose a threat to United States and hemispheric security. But revolutions, however justified, could too easily get out of control. And Cuba brought home this frightening truth with chilling pointedness. Therefore, when Wessin's forces started to fall back, the only reliable guarantee against a new Cuba in the area had begun, in U. S. eyes, to disappear. And so, at the moment of retreat, the Dominican people and the United States government tragically saw their most vital interests at cross-purposes.

It was not surprising that when the papal nuncio returned from a talk with Bosch in San Juan on Tuesday carrying a proposal for a cease-fire, Wessin turned it down. For it was clear that the United States would soon give him the assistance he had requested. The Embassy had started on Tuesday night feeling out, in conjunction with Wessin, likely possibilities for membership in a military junta. Wessin himself was excluded from consideration since he was the chief symbol of hated militarism. The Embassy favored lesser-known officers with reputations for moderation. But the need for civilian participation was not yet seen. After all, the rebels were on the edge of defeat. It wasn't necessary to throw them too many crumbs. When it became clear by Wednesday morning that Wessin's forces were in danger of falling apart, the establishment of a junta became urgent, even critical. For not only was one necessary to give some cohesion to the Wessin forces, but also, should the situation so require, to request U. S. military aid. It would look better if U. S. troops came at the request of some Dominican authority than without such a request.

In any event, Radio San Isidro announced the formation of a junta on Wednesday that was to be headed by Air Force Colonel Pedro Bartolomé Benoit and include an army colonel and a navy colonel. And none too soon, for as an official U. S. document stated in discussing the situation after the junta was formed:

> The situation in the city was increasingly tense and confused. Junta forces, tired and disorganized, began to crumble. Armed mobs terrorized the city, firing on homes and other buildings, including the U. S. and other Embassies.

In desperation, U. S. officials tried to use every propaganda technique to weaken the will of the rebels that the Ambassador himself had nourished the day before. Their main hope, they felt, lay in the fear of nonmilitary PRD leaders who were more politician than idealist. Breisky started to work on PRD Secretary-General Martínez Francisco, who had taken refuge in the Mexican Embassy that Wednesday morning. He telephoned him and, according to Breisky, told him that he was concerned about the fact that many PRD leaders had abandoned the revolutionary movement, leaving it to the Communists. It was high time, he said, that the PRD dissociate itself from "what was going on downtown." He then asked Martínez, a good-natured, heavyset man with a politician's instinct for compromise, if he were willing to do something to resolve the situation.

"What can I do?" he quoted the PRD leader as asking.

Breisky said he replied that he would be able to obtain for him a safe-conduct to the radio station at San Isidro so that he could appeal to party members to lay down their arms. The Embassy official said that he would personally accompany him to guarantee his safety. Martínez agreed, said Breisky.

According to Martínez, Breisky had suggested that ways of bringing about peace be discussed, but not in connection with any trip to San Isidro. He thought, Martínez claimed, that he would simply be going to the Embassy to speak with the Ambassador. Certainly, he maintained, he himself did not initiate any move to go to San Isidro as claimed later by officials in Washington.

Breisky picked him up in a car and they drove to Hotel Embajador where they took an Air Force helicopter to San Isidro Air Base. Breisky said that the PRD leader went willingly and without any reluctance. But Martínez said that he was shocked to see two Wessin men in the car, and that he didn't question Breisky about where they were going because he was afraid that they might kill him.

On arrival at San Isidro, Breisky and Martínez went into conference with junta leaders, and the group drew up three documents. One was a statement by the junta inviting the OAS to come and arrange elections. A second was an agreement between the junta and the PRD whereby the former promised free elections from which no candidates would be barred. And a third statement was prepared for radio delivery by Martínez, who was to say that he was speaking for Bosch in renouncing Bosch's aspirations, and that the people should lay down their arms.

Martínez approved all the documents, claiming later that he had been convinced that if he had refused to cooperate he would never have left San Isidro alive. He argued only about one point. The original draft of the radio statement prepared for him contained a phrase indicating that the Communists had gained control of the revolution. Martínez protested that if he said this his own partisans might kill him. It was finally agreed that the phrase should be deleted, and Martínez immediately taped the statement, which was broadcast shortly thereafter. Martínez and Breisky spent the night at the base, then returned the next morning to Santo Domingo.

What is significant about this incident is that Breisky's role in producing the three partisan documents further underscored the fact that the United States had completely committed itself to the Wessin forces even before the first American troops arrived.

But the broadcast did not have the desired effect. In fact, some rebels, instead of laying down their arms, threatened to burn down Martínez's house, although they forgave him when he persuaded them that he had been tricked into going to San Isidro.

The Embassy now pondered the question of whether to call for U. S. armed intervention. Bennett, shortly after noon, cabled Washington that the junta needed radio equipment, including walkie-talkies, critically and advised that such equipment be sent at once. Then he passed on to Washington a request radioed to him by Colonel Benoit saying that the junta could no longer guarantee the protection of foreigners. In another message, Bennett advised that it might not be necessary to send troops if the radio equipment was dispatched immediately, filling a desperate military requirement and at the same time lifting the junta's morale. Washington replied that the equipment would be sent and that it would not intervene militarily unless it looked as if the junta might lose. But at about 2 P.M. it ordered a small unit of marines to land at Haina to check on the possibilities of a large-scale landing.

A new ambassadorial message asked that intervention be considered, and another let Washington know that Benoit had confirmed in a note that the junta was unable to guarantee the

safety of foreigners, and that he wished U. S. intervention. The
note read:

> Regarding my earlier request I wish to add that American
> lives are in danger and conditions of public disorder make it
> impossible to provide adequate protection. I therefore ask you
> for temporary intervention and assistance in restoring order in
> this country.

Notably, this message mentioned nothing about the Communist threat but referred only to the protection of lives, the reason the United States was to give the world for going into the
Dominican Republic.

President Johnson later said, emphasizing this question of
motivation, that "99 percent of our reason for going in there
was to try to provide protection for these American lives and
the lives of other nationals." Yet, were American lives and the
lives of other nationals more threatened in the Dominican rebellion than in disorders, coups, and revolutions that have constantly taken place throughout the world? While a few shots
may have been heard in the vicinity of the American Embassy
in Santo Domingo, embassies, as well as other U. S. installations,
have in some countries been burned to the ground by rampaging
mobs. But Washington did not send in marines in those cases
to save American lives, or even seriously consider doing so.

This is not necessarily to question the wisdom of landing U. S.
troops in some cases for the purpose of saving lives. In fact, it
would be extremely difficult for any President to ignore an
urgent appeal from his ambassador for the dispatch of troops,
whether to save lives or to prevent a Communist takeover. And
with Cuba still a boiling political issue in Washington, President Johnson is in a particularly delicate position where the
Caribbean area is concerned. What can be questioned is the
relative importance of the humanitarian consideration in the
decision of the Administration to dispatch troops to Santo
Domingo.

Although this may have been a secondary factor, the under-
lying one appears to have been the fear of communism taking
over, if not immediately, then eventually, should a man like
Bosch return to power. And this fear was fed by what seem
to have been exaggerated Embassy reports of Communist leadership in the revolution. But Washington was reluctant to admit
this was the overriding factor apparently because other hemispheric countries, particularly the democratic ones, would certainly question the validity of the premise that there was a
genuine Communist danger, at least of sufficient scope to justify
unilateral U. S. intervention in flat defiance of the OAS Charter.
A more defensible explanation was that the United States
couldn't wait for an OAS go-ahead since lives were at stake.

Thus Mann, in his interview with Max Frankel, said that
"in view of [the] background [of Communist activity] and the
very considerable evidence of Communist influence in the
latest movement, I think we, under different circumstances, had
no lives been in danger, would have probably gone to the OAS
and presented the problem there. What made it necessary for
us to go in quickly, was, as I have said before, the urgent need
of saving lives."

At the same time, mirroring the strained effort by the Administration to cloak its decision to back a military junta—which
it felt could best thwart a possible Communist takeover—under
a façade of neutrality was Mann's reply to a question about how
the U. S. military move differed from old-fashioned "gunboat
diplomacy." Mann said in part:

"Had the United States been interested in merely the form
of legalistic procedures rather than the substance of the fundamental rights of a nation under the OAS Charter, it could have
recognized the only organized group existing at that time and
claiming to be the government (the Benoit-led junta). It could
then have responded to a request from the newly recognized
group to send in armed forces. The United States did not follow
such a course of action, because this would have amounted to

taking sides in the internal struggle. Clearly such a course of action would have been inconsistent with the principles that govern the inter-American system."

True, the United States did not officially recognize the Benoit junta. It simply helped to create it. If mere recognition of the junta would have "amounted to taking sides" and been "inconsistent with the principles that govern the inter-American system," would it not appear that involvement in its very creation would have made the United States all the more guilty of violating these principles? Moreover, the United States did in fact publicly state that it was intervening at the request of Dominican authorities, rendering unnecessary the need to recognize the junta to get its approval.

Receipt of the Benoit note set the stage for the historic decision. At 5:16 P.M., Ambassador Bennett, warning that American lives were in danger—no attack had actually been made on the U. S. Embassy up to then—requested the marines to land. President Johnson immediately met with Bundy, Rusk, McNamara, Ball, and Special Assistant Bill D. Moyers, and they agreed to the request. Someone suggested that Mann also be consulted, and Rusk and Bundy telephoned him while he was meeting with State Department Latin-American specialists. He said he would call back in a few minutes. He did, replying that he would go along with the decision despite the difficulties it would create in the hemisphere.

At 6:30 P.M., the *Boxer* received White House orders to land marines. The forces of constitutionalism that President Kennedy was to save with U. S. marines in 1961 were to be challenged by U. S. marines little more than three years later.

CHAPTER 7

Who's Behind the Trees?

At about 1 p.m. on Thursday, April 29, three helicopters flew the 22 reporters and photographers, including myself, who had been in San Juan, from the *Boxer* to the grounds of Hotel Embajador. As we landed, we saw most of the 530 or so marines who had arrived the previous evening and that morning setting up a bivouac area on the fields and golf course adjacent to the hotel. They were dressed in fatigues and armed with rifles, pistols, and mortars. About 70 of the marines were protecting the U. S. Embassy about a mile away.

As we walked from the helicopters toward the hotel past marines who were digging latrines, putting up tents, cleaning rifles, and setting up machine-gun emplacements, a clergyman accompanied by a man with a familiar face passed us and headed toward a helicopter. The man, I finally realized, was Antonio Imbert. He was obviously on the way to the *Boxer*. Later I speculated in my first story to *The Washington Post* that Imbert was apparently engaged in a mediation effort with U. S. officials.

As we entered the hotel, the lobby looked like Grand Central Station on a crowded night. Gone were the scenes I remembered from previous visits of elegantly dressed people chatting on cushioned sofas. The sofas had been turned into beds for scores

175

of refugees waiting to evacuate the country aboard U. S. military vessels. Others sat on chairs where they also slept, and children napped on the rugs. The luckier and richer refugees had obtained rooms upstairs, though it was hard indeed to find an empty bed.

We felt the initial tremor of what was to be a severe shock to most of us who had once gloried in the service and other amenities of life at the Embajador. No longer was it a mecca of dollar-backed indolence where shapely girls sunned themselves by the swimming pool, rich tourists gambled away fortunes in the casino, and international gourmets stuffed themselves with some of the finest food in the Caribbean.

True, we found ourselves occupying luxuriously furnished rooms that would have pleased the most fastidious tourist. But life here, we soon discovered, would be no bed of roses. In fact, we had to sleep on beds with sheets that had been used by previous guests, since the hotel maids were all at home behind locked doors. Sweaty as we were in the tropical heat, we wouldn't be able to shower or shave until the next morning, when the water, turned off the rest of the day, would flow for one hour. And we would have to do our own laundry.

Well, perhaps we could take a quick swim before settling down to work. Not so. The marines had installed a purifying system by the pool. "No swimming in our drinking water," a marine informed us.

So to work. We asked the hotel manager about communications. All telegraph lines had been cut, and only one telephone in the hotel worked—the one in his office. He agreed to let us use it. It was our one chance for getting through to our offices. With our deadlines drawing near, there was a scramble for the phone, and an impatient line soon formed, with those toward the end harboring a desperate look in their eyes. The first reporters in line had no chance even to write out a story. They got there first because they were prepared to ad-lib.

Hours passed, deadlines passed, but the line seemed hardly to shorten at all. The trouble was, there was only a single international telephone line open, and one had to keep ringing up to an hour or more just for the operator to answer. Then there would be perhaps a half-hour wait for the call to be put through, longer if the precarious circuit went out. And once in contact with his office, each reporter would become a pillar of greed, refusing to terminate his story until every last insignificant detail was shouted despite anguished pleas and even threats of armed assault by the others. The reporters at the end of the line, if they were able to get through at all—some waited for five or six hours—had the most complete stories, since they embraced almost every last tidbit hollered by everyone in front of them.

There were quite a few tidbits to report. Aside from the material we had gathered in our talks with military officials aboard the *Boxer* that morning, several U. S. Embassy officials and foreign diplomats we met at the hotel, some of whom were seeing their families off in the evacuation, provided us with considerable information about the developing situation.

We learned in midafternoon that the marines based on the Embassy grounds were having their first taste of combat when civilian snipers fired at them from nearby houses. There were no marine casualties, but five of the snipers were killed, three of them by Dominican troops fighting in the same area, and two others apparently by the marines. Rebels that day also fired on the embassies of El Salvador, Peru, Mexico, and Ecuador.

It soon became evident that such incidents were by no means the last-gasp, desperate actions of a beaten, disorganized civilian army as we initially thought in view of the previous day's reports that rebel remnants had only to be mopped up. The rebels, it was apparent, still had full control of most of the city after fighting that had produced up to then an estimated 1,800 casualties, including 400 dead. The Air Force, Navy, and loyalist elements of the Army had apparently been unable to subdue rebel army units and the thousands of civilians armed with rifles, machine guns, and Molotov cocktails.

The question was, who controlled the rebels? The ambassador of one Middle Eastern nation who was evacuating his wife told us that in his view the Communists were now in control. A Dominican businessman took issue: "The Reds are very militant and so are giving the impression of leading the pro-Bosch side," he said. "But the army elements still have most of the guns and they are opposed to communism."

The U. S. attitude appeared to be summed up by several radio exchanges between the Embassy and San Isidro we had picked up that morning on transistor radios while aboard the *Boxer*. The messages were being relayed to San Isidro via the aircraft carrier since normal means of communication were broken down or were unreliable.

At about 9:30 A.M., a message had come through saying:

> This is Shade Tree One [the Ambassador's radio call]. The Ambassador to Colonel Benoit . . . Do you need more? . . . Believe that with determination your plans will succeed.

Shortly afterward, another Embassy message said:

> Could you open Punta Caucedo [International Airport] for air traffic to bring in food and medicine? Uniformed marines can operate there if civilians are not there.

In still another message, Bennett wanted to know whether Benoit had sufficient supplies to deal with "the Castro forces facing you." The voice then repeated in corrected form, "the rebel forces facing you."

San Isidro, in messages to the Embassy, indicated a need for rations, batteries, and communications equipment, then reported that "a significant morale boost is evident since the arrival of rations." It further indicated that "I've got a message that the suppression attack is being initiated at 0845 local."

The Ambassador was rooting for Wessin indeed. He was convinced, he told reporters, that the Communists had completely taken over the revolution. To make this point, he said that the rebels no longer had any organized army units fighting with them, and that many troops had taken off their uniforms and gone home. Bosch, he said, was still the rebel symbol of leadership but his people were not in control. The Communists had helped to plan the revolution for at least six months. During this period, he maintained, long mimeographed leaflets signed by the 14th of June Movement had been distributed in the cities explaining how to make bombs and Molotov cocktails.

Bosch, he said, had been personally involved in the planning for a long time, but apparently did not fully comprehend the role of the Communists in the plan. The Communists, wearing Castro-style caps and beards in the marathon telecast, had taken over radio and television facilities. An employee of the United States Information Service, he said, had reported that he saw 12 men stripped to the waist being herded down the street in the downtown area, and that when they were out of sight he heard shots, apparently indicating mass murder. In another case, Bennett said, 20 sailors who had surrendered were reportedly lined up against a wall, and amid cries of *"Paredón,"* "to the wall," were shot. Reporters were told of reports that the rebels had severed heads and paraded them on pikes, and that Colonel Caamaño had personally machine-gunned Colonel Calderón, an aide to Reid Cabral.

Clearly, the Ambassador concluded, if the marines had not landed when they did the Communists might well have taken over the country. Then reporters were issued a list of 53 alleged Communists trained in Russia, China, and Cuba who were supposed to be leading the revolt.

That first evening in Santo Domingo, more than 1,000 additional marines were helicoptered ashore from naval vessels, bringing the total to about 1,700. And later in the night two battalions of the 82nd Airborne Division, about 2,500 men, started landing at San Isidro Air Base. A massive buildup of

American military power, which seemed completely out of proportion to any possible danger that might have existed, had begun, triggered by fears that had given rise to reports like the one above.

In the next several days, a number of reporters, including myself, tried to confirm the rebel atrocity reports, but were unable to do so. In fact, for a man who was supposed to have been machine-gunned, Colonel Calderón looked surprisingly healthy. He emerged from the hospital with a minor neck injury. We now had our first real doubts about the credibility of Embassy statements. True, they had only been issued as reports, but these were the kind of reports on which American policy was being based.

By the end of our first day in Santo Domingo, we were seething with nervous tension, not because of bombs or bullets, but because of the incredible communications bottleneck. There was little value in obtaining information that we couldn't transmit to our offices. We finally all got through, and, one by one, stumbled into the dining room. There was no menu. There was hardly any food. Overcoming our religious prejudices, we wolfed down what there was, mainly bagels (which had been ordered for a canceled Jewish convention) and ham. The shock was only eased by our incapacity to see clearly what we were eating in the dim candlelight that had to substitute for electric light, which had been cut off. And also the alternative—C-rations. The cost of the meal was $4.40, a round figure charged for every dinner and lunch, or excuse for one.

After dinner, tired and hungry, and with the casino and bar closed down, we made our way in the pitch-black with candles to our rooms and went to sleep on our soiled sheets to the sound of shots in the distance.

The following morning, Friday, April 30, Bert Quint of the Columbia Broadcasting System obtained a car from a local reporter—taxis, like all other public services, were not operating—and invited three other reporters, including myself, to go

with him downtown into the rebel zone. But first, we visited
the marines in the fields adjoining the hotel. Several tanks were
lined up, and nearby a number of platoon briefing sessions were
in progress. We joined one of them, and saw the sergeant trace
a diagram in the dry earth with a stick. "There's the Embassy,"
he said. "We're going as far as there."

Thus did we learn that the marines were about to move out
of the hotel area toward the American Embassy, about two
miles away, to secure an International Safety Zone embracing
most of the diplomatic missions. Fighting, it seemed, would be
inevitable. We drove toward the Embassy to see what was happening, and we soon discovered that plenty was.

The green laurel and mahogany trees that shimmered along
the steaming streets still lent a note of tropical peace and tranquillity to Santo Domingo. But in their shadows, young lovers
seeking solitude and old folks relief from the heat lingered no
more. Instead, Dominican soldiers, with rifles poised, stood or
lay behind these trees.

Who were the men behind the trees? Were they friends or
were they enemies? Within several square blocks, we were
embraced as friends by fighters of both sides. The proof was
that we stayed alive.

Neat little bright-colored houses glistened under the sun surrounded by gardens rich with full-blooming pink bougainvilleas,
red poinsettias, and other tropical flowers of every hue.

And a junta tank rumbled along outside.

Birds flew from tree to tree chirping cheerfully—interrupted
only by spurts of nearby machine-gun fire and the occasional
click of rifle locks at the foot of the trees.

Suddenly, as we threaded our way between lines of junta
troops strung out under the trees, we were stopped at rifle point.

"American reporters," one of us yelled out. "Shut up," said
another. "How do we know which side they're on?"

They turned out to be soldiers of Wessin.

"You may advance," said one soldier, lowering his rifle. We

did, for another block, and were halted again by a soldier armed
with an automatic rifle. We got out of the car to identify ourselves, when suddenly we heard a voice yelling at us from about
a block away on the street crossing ours. He was motioning to
us to get out of the way—a rebel who wanted a clear shot at the
junta soldier who had halted us.

We dashed around the corner and threw ourselves flat on
the sidewalk as an exchange of fire between the two men ripped
the air. Both missed and the rebel got away.

We continued on, and about two blocks farther stopped before a group of civilians in tattered, dirty clothes to ask where
nearby firing was coming from.

"I don't know," said one dark-skinned man after we had identified ourselves, "but I do know that we're not Communists.
Tell the American people we want nothing to do with communism. We are the people fighting against Wessin, who has killed
many of us and deprived us of food and water. Won't you
please believe us—we are the people, not Communists."

And then he advised us which street was safest to take.

We arrived at the American Embassy a few blocks away just
in time to dive in the front door as a Wessin plane screeched
down to shoot a rocket at the Wessin tank we had passed several minutes before. The aircraft had apparently mistaken the
tank as belonging to the rebels. A few more rockets were fired
before the pilot got the word.

Peace again—for about five minutes. As I stood in the Embassy garden, bullets started whizzing past. Snipers on nearby
housetops.

"The enemy's over there," cried a marine as he fired back
from behind a tree.

I dived into a patch of bougainvillea and breathed deeply of
peace.

During a lull in the shooting, I ran into the shuttered, white-
stone chancellery again. It was a seething caldron of crisis. Tie-
less, unshaven diplomats with suits rumpled from sleeping on

the floor all night and frightened, pale-faced secretaries dashed across the small reception room from one office to another laden with papers, files, and Coca-Colas ordered by their superiors. A group of marine officers in fatigues heatedly discussed the best ways to get at the snipers. The man at the reception desk hollered hoarsely into a defective emergency telephone. C-ration cans and paper cups littered the floor. And Radio San Isidro blasted forth from somewhere with a lively rendition of "The Stars and Stripes Forever."

The firing outside shortly resumed, and this time in earnest. The marines from the hotel were approaching, shooting their way forward block by block behind an awesome spearhead of tanks. From the intensity of the fire, it was clear that resistance was substantial, with snipers firing from windows and rooftops all along the way. It sounded like full-scale war.

And psychologically it was. With the support of the junta troops we had seen, the marines were simply taking over territory that had been controlled by the rebels, a job that the junta forces had been unable to do alone. No effort had been made, as far as I could determine, to contact rebel leaders about some peaceful arrangement for guaranteeing the safety of the international community. The marines, supported by the junta, just moved in, and in doing so achieved what was apparently a principal aim of the United States—to eliminate any possibility of a rebel victory, and thereby eliminate in the process, according to Administration logic, any possibility of a Communist takeover. They were, hand in hand with Trujilloite political arsonists, burning down the barn in the hope of destroying a rat.

As things worked out, the establishment of the International Safety Zone did little to appease the fears of the foreigners. For territorial control, while an effective means of bottling up the revolution, could not effectively eliminate the sniper danger. Yet, because the U. S. forces did have territorial control, they didn't bother to furnish the individual embassies with armed protection, but only guarded the perimeter of the zone.

"If the United States wanted to use the protection of foreigners as a pretext for taking over the place," one diplomat commented acidly, "the least it can do is protect foreigners."

The United States, in any event, needed this pretext to soften Latin-American reaction to the troop landings. The urgency of saving lives was certainly less disputable than the vague and difficult-to-prove charge that the Communists threatened to take over. But, as suggested by the anger of the diplomats in Santo Domingo, the Administration might have been more persuasive if it had displayed greater concern about what its Latin allies thought.

In the first place, the United States did not consult with the OAS nations before reaching the decision to send in troops. The President later explained that "we did not want to announce that they [the marines] were on their way until they landed, for obvious security reasons." But such a consideration, the Latins feel, should not have precluded discussions with the OAS on the subject. Nor were they pacified by the President's statement: "We had been consulting since the weekend with some fourteen Latin-American nations . . . we had had a meeting of the [Inter-American] Peace Committee of the OAS and we had had a meeting of the Council of the OAS. I felt it was very important that we notify all the Latin-American ambassadors forthwith. . . ."

The United States had consulted with the OAS countries, it is true, but only on the internal situation in the Dominican Republic, not on the possibility of U. S. or OAS intervention. On Tuesday, April 27, the Uruguayan Ambassador to the OAS suggested to Assistant Secretary of State Vaughn that the Peace Committee should meet to discuss the Dominican crisis. This led to a meeting of the committee that day at which the Dominican Ambassador charged that the rebels were being led by Castro Communists. The following day, April 28, the OAS Council met, and the Dominican Ambassador again spoke, saying much the same thing. That was the extent of OAS involvement in the Dominican situation before the marines landed. Nor did the OAS consider intervention at the two meetings in view of the news at that time pointing to a Wessin victory.

When, later on April 28, the Administration decided to dispatch marines, the President did not even mention the OAS in the original draft of the statement he delivered announcing the intervention after the fact. The President, on being asked at an emergency meeting with congressional leaders before the announcement why the OAS had been ignored, is said to have told Rusk, according to one version of the story: "Dean, that's a good idea; now you make certain that it's in there."

At that meeting, little emphasis was placed on the Communist issue. The Administration, though determined not to take any chances of another Cuba, apparently didn't feel it had enough evidence of Communist activity yet to underscore the danger even to American congressmen.

Rusk had, nevertheless, suggested that the President's message include a passage indicating the need to protect democratic institutions in the Dominican Republic, and thereby indirectly referring to the Communist threat. But after much discussion, including an observation by Adlai E. Stevenson, the late Ambassador to the United Nations, that an indirect charge would inflame controversy even more than a direct one, it was decided to ignore the Communist issue altogether.

Administration officials started trying to contact Latin-American ambassadors immediately after the meeting with the congressmen early in the evening, calling them at their offices, at home, and at cocktail parties. But only to inform them about what the President had done and why he had to do it. No attempt was made to call an emergency meeting of the OAS that night. U. S. officials have privately replied to criticism of this failure to do so with the pragmatic explanation that OAS procedures take too long. In other words, an emotional debate that night might have rendered quick acceleration of the U. S. intervention difficult.

By the time the OAS did meet the following morning, emotional reactions had cooled, particularly after the receipt from Latin embassies in Santo Domingo of assurances that they did indeed need armed protection. But in a deeper sense, the cooling process represented, at least on the part of some countries, not approval, but resignation tinged with disappointment and disillusionment, a bitter resignation that contained the seeds of hemispheric division.

And division would most likely be along lines parallel in ideology to those established by the United States in the Dominican Republic. In that country, almost all progressives found themselves ranged against the United States, the military, and the rightist civilians. Similarly, on a hemispheric scale, Latin-American democracies found themselves ranged against the United States and the military-rightist regimes, questioning both the violation of the nonintervention accord and the still soft-pedaled premise of Communist control.

After delegates, mainly from the democracies, had castigated the U. S. action, a majority finally agreed to send a special committee to Santo Domingo to seek peace. The OAS was not officially told of the landing of the 82nd Airborne Division until after agreement was reached. Once having established itself firmly in Santo Domingo, the United States was anxious to have its actions approved by the OAS to reduce the unilateral flavor of the intervention. But none of the liberal democracies were represented on the committee, which was composed of delegates from Argentina, Brazil, Colombia, Guatemala and Panama. Brazil and Guatemala were led by military dictatorships, Argentina was partly under military influence, Panama was controlled by a small oligarchy, and, in considerable degree, so was Colombia.

OAS efforts complemented a unilateral U. S. peacemaking attempt that was already under way when the mission arrived on May 2. When the marines first landed, there had been no diplomatic link between the United States and the rebels.

Ambassador Bennett, as a result of his Wednesday meeting with them, had burned his bridges. The rebel leaders despised him, and the feeling appeared to be mutual. Realizing this, the White House contacted former Ambassador John Bartlow Martin, who was a good friend of Bosch. According to Martin, in an article published in *Life* magazine, Bill Moyers, President Johnson's special assistant, telephoned him about midnight on Thursday at his home in Connecticut and asked him to hurry down to Washington, sending a White House plane for him. The next morning, the President asked him to go to Santo Domingo to assist Bennett "to open up contact with the rebels" and help in the establishment of a cease-fire. He arrived at San Isidro Air Base shortly before midnight on April 30, a few hours after the marines had carved out the International Safety Zone.

The next morning, after a night of heavy firing throughout the city, Martin joined in an attempt to achieve a cease-fire, at least long enough to permit the collection of dead bodies in garbage trucks. He met at the San Isidro commander's office with the papal nuncio, junta leaders, a rebel representative, Bennett, and a U. S. general. Colonel Benoit, the junta chief, Martin reported, said that he wanted a cease-fire but asked how he could agree to one after what he described as the murders and atrocities committed by the rebels. Other junta officers spoke in a similar vein. The rebel representative, for his part, charged that his people had been butchered and were hungry but would not submit to an imposed peace.

The meeting was about to break up when Martin approached Wessin, the real leader of the San Isidro generals. The two men harbored little affection for each other. At the time of the 1963 coup that ousted Bosch from office, Martin had made clear to Wessin what he thought of this action. But Martin now told the general that whatever differences they may have had in the past, they should cooperate in ending the present bloodshed. "President Johnson is deeply concerned about the senseless killing of the Dominican people," he said. "He has sent me here to try to help stop it. I ask you, General, to be the first to sign a cease-fire." After thinking it over, Wessin accompanied Martin to the office of the papal nuncio to sign. Now only Caamaño's signature was required.

The next morning, Sunday, May 2, a series of phone calls involving Martin, Caamaño, and the papal nuncio produced an agreement by Caamaño to meet the two others at his headquarters in the rebel zone later that day. When they met, Caamaño, who had been asked by Bosch to cooperate fully with Martin, said that he had already signed the cease-fire and would honor it. As Martin and the papal nuncio left, a crowd outside cheered Martin wildly, crying, "We trust you, Mr. Martin," and "We have faith in you," in a demonstration the White House envoy believed was well organized to win his sympathy.

The cease-fire actually went into effect three days later, on May 5, after mediation by the newly arrived OAS peace team.

Late in the afternoon that day, Martin and Bennett called a joint press conference. It was intended mainly, it seemed, to sweep away doubt once and for all that the Communists controlled the revolution. With the foreigners already protected, the Communist danger was no longer being soft-pedaled as the reason for the expanding American military presence. It became the official reason for this expansion. The Embassy, it appeared, was even more desirous than Washington to push the charge of "Communist control." For it was the Embassy, after all, that had sold Washington on the seriousness of this danger.

The Embassy was particularly perturbed, some U. S. sources said, because of news reports that had started to appear pointing out that some observers in Santo Domingo thought the charge of "communism" had been exaggerated.

At any rate, Martin, after two days of investigation, stated flatly at the press conference, at which scores of reporters were present, that the revolution had "fallen under the domination of Castro Communists" and "they are now in control." When

I asked him whether he thought Bosch should return, he replied that he couldn't possibly do so—as President—under the prevailing circumstances.

Martin's statement was highly significant for two reasons. First, although Embassy officials had been telling reporters privately that the revolution was Communist-controlled, this was the first time that an American official had gone on the record with so unequivocal a statement. Second, the fact that this statement was made by Martin gave the charge a special credibility since he was known as a friend of Bosch and the PRD and as a man who didn't see Communists under every bed.

Martin later told me over a hastily consumed lunch in the Embassy residence—he was busy, it seemed, 24 hours a day—that when he had arrived in the country he had had his doubts about the gravity of the Communist danger. He remembered, he said, from his ambassadorial days that the Reds had been weak, split, and incapable of taking power. But after talking with the parties concerned in the struggle and trusted independent observers, and after reading intelligence reports, he was convinced that the Communists had indeed obtained control of the rebel movement. I asked him if he could offer any concrete evidence, and he said that such evidence existed but could not be divulged.

He paused once for several moments to count drops that he squeezed with a dropper into a glass of water. Never a robust man, Martin looked much older than when I had last seen him about a year before. His thin face was more wrinkled and his frail body more bent, and his hands trembled slightly. Yet he drove himself relentlessly, ate mainly C-rations despite an ulcer condition, and slept on the floor in the Embassy residence when employees were unable to go home because of the work load.

But the physical strain of the assignment on him seemed less telling than the emotional drain. On the one hand, he appeared to have been shocked by the bitterness and hatred that racked the people whom he had once helped to guide toward tolerance and democracy. And on the other, he was deeply chagrined by what he considered indications that a basically democratic movement was controlled by Communists.

Perhaps Martin did have irrefutable intelligence information confirming such control. Nor, in considering the question of motivation, can it be ignored that he has said that he hoped his press conference charge would help to split the non-Communist revolutionaries away from the Communists. But without questioning the sincerity of his conviction, for Martin is a scrupulously honest man, it is notable that the basis for this conviction as presented in the *Life* magazine article consists mainly of impressions and assumptions rather than facts.

He offers a long list of people he personally knew to be hardcore Communists who, he writes, joined the revolt. U. S. intelligence agents saw "many of these men" at rebel headquarters, he maintains. And independently, he was told by "thoroughly trustworthy sources" that they were there. Martin may be the best judge of the reliability of his intelligence sources, but the fact is, as shall be seen later, that other information released by the United States on the basis of supposedly reliable sources turned out to be innacurate. And even if some Communists had been seen at headquarters, that does not necessarily mean they had any influence. Almost any rebel, Communist or not, could physically get into headquarters easily enough if he wanted to do so. Communists can also physically enter the State Department building in Washington if they wish, and even Dean Rusk's reception room. But what does that prove? Interestingly, Martin, while implying that the alleged presence of Communists at headquarters meant control, does not come out flatly and say so.

Martin also points to a woman he once knew as an anti-Communist idealistic leftist who, during the revolution, had apparently, in his eyes, changed, since she denounced someone who had offended her as a "counterrevolutionary deviationist"— which could be a Communist term but is not necessarily so,

since "counterrevolutionary deviationism" could refer simply
to a revolutionary rather than an ideological situation.

Martin further reports that after his first meeting with Caamaño, an aide who had accompanied him noticed a black-shirted
youth who yelled "Yankees go home" in the crowd outside.
The youth, whom the aide recognized as a Communist, was suddenly jerked out of sight by others. "He had used the wrong
script," Martin wrote. But might it not be possible that the
crowd really resented the youth for what he stood for rather
than for using the "wrong script"?

Pointing up this possibility was an incident that took place in
mid-May when a large crowd of rebels gathered at El Conde
Gate in Parque Independencia for a demonstration. The partic-
ipants, many of them fingering rifles or grenades, began crying
rythmically, "Yankees go home!" Yet if the words evoked the
impression of Communist-nourished anti-American hatred,
rebels in the crowd, when they saw U. S. reporters, good-
naturedly assured them that they were referring only to Yankee
soldiers and not to Americans as such.

However that may be, the demonstrators roared their approval when a bespectacled youth in a blue sports shirt climbed
up on the speaker's platform and shouted into the microphone
that the revolution was "our problem, not the problem of the
U. S. marines." But then the speaker yelled, gesturing wildly
with his arms, "We must join with the people of Venezuela,
with the people of Cuba!"

A frozen silence settled over the crowd. Gradually the words,
"He's a Communist," rolled like a shock wave through the park.
People at the front clutched at the speaker trying to drag him
down. But he hung on to the microphone, and even after the
wire was ripped from the base, continued to harangue the
crowd. He was finally pulled down, but somehow managed to
climb back. Before he could start talking again, however, someone fired a shot in the air and others followed suit. The crowd
scattered in all directions leaving the speaker to speak to him-

self. And it isn't likely that those who deprived him of an audience did so because he read the wrong script. It was clear that he had the wrong ideology.

This is not to say that Martin's suspicions in the cases of alleged Communist influence he cited were necessarily wrong. But these suspicions nevertheless seemed to be based on impressions and assumptions rather than facts, unless the facts were among those he was unable to divulge. And the question arises whether impressions and assumptions constituted sufficient justification for the unqualified, world-shaking announcement that the revolution was Communist-controlled.

With Martin saying publicly what the Embassy had been saying privately from the beginning, the propaganda lid was off. President Johnson, apparently convinced now that the Reds did control the revolution, said in a television address that night, May 2: ". . . What began as a popular democratic revolution committed to democracy and social justice very shortly moved and was taken over and really seized and placed in the hands of a band of Communist conspirators."

It is interesting to note that aside from the President and Martin, no other U. S. or OAS official has publicly made such a flat charge. Others have been careful to say only that the Communists threatened to take control, but not that they actually had established control. For example, some members of the OAS committee that arrived in Santo Domingo on May 2 took such a line. The chairman, Ambassador Ricardo M. Colombo of Argentina, said of Caamaño and his colleagues:

". . . They recognized that they [Communists] were their great problem. . . . They confessed to us how gradually a number of elements were being incorporated with them whom they called Communists, and that their problem was to avoid infiltration for the purpose of springing a surprise and seizing control."

Brazilian Ambassador Llamar Penna Marinho, whose government supported the U. S. position more strongly than any other Latin regime, said that one couldn't be sure that the Caamaño group was Communist, but that "in view of the real anarchy in which the country has been engulfed," any organized group might be able to take over. Therefore, he declared, the Caamaño regime "could be rapidly converted into a Communist insurrection. . . . Above all, it is seen to be heading toward becoming a government of that kind, susceptible to obtaining the support and the assistance of the great Marxist-Leninist powers."

No other committee members took as strong a view, and Caamaño himself said he had been misinterpreted. "Of course," he said, "there are some Communists trying to latch on to the movement. But the point is they have no power and are not in a position to get any." On May 10 he demanded that the OAS make an "exhaustive" investigation of "malicious propaganda" that his government "is controlled or influenced by Marxist or Castroite parties or groups." It was never made, the argument being that the Reds had already drifted into the background.

While some Administration officials thought that the President and Martin, despite their isolated stands, were right in speaking out, feeling that there was no sense quibbling over what was fact and what might be fact when the same U. S. policy would be required in either case, others felt that their statements had unnecessarily slandered a basically democratic popular movement and seriously undercut the credibility of the Administration's position.

Their black-and-white position lent increasing urgency to the problem of making publicly announced intelligence fit the accusation, rather than the other way around, as is usual under a democratic system. For the press was hounding U. S. officials in Santo Domingo and Washington for factual evidence. The facts simply had to be found—or, if necessary, created. In other words, the Administration, in a desperate effort to prove what was apparently unprovable, sank ever more deeply into a morass of McCarthyism that compounded whatever errors it may have originally made.

The sinking process had begun the first day reporters arrived

in Santo Domingo when U. S. officials said privately that the
Communists had taken control of the revolution and distributed
a list of 53 names of Reds who were supposedly running things.
On May 1, the day before the Martin and presidential announcements, the Administration had leaked a new list of 58 names,
18 of whom were supposed to have been trained in Communist
countries. On May 5, the Administration released in Washington for publication a related description of alleged Communist
activities. On the same day, U. S. officials in Santo Domingo
charged that the rebel leaders had agreed at a secret meeting
with Communist chiefs to give the Reds a "decisive voice" in a
projected constitutional government. Finally, a new list of 77
names was released unofficially in Washington in mid-June.

One of the more interesting journalistic pastimes in Santo
Domingo was to punch holes in these lists and accusations. And
it was not long before some Embassy officials were ruefully com-
menting that their release had been a "disaster," and that, in
fact, the whole Communist issue had been grossly overplayed.

To start with, it appears that the lists of 53 and 58 names had
nothing really to do with the revolution. According to one
U. S. official, they had been in CIA desk drawers long before
the revolt broke out—simply names of Communists or suspected
Communists as are gathered in every country. These very lists,
or quite similar ones, it seems, existed at the time the State Department's intelligence report, "World Strength of the Communist Party Organizations," summed up the Dominican Communist danger in 1964 as something less than overwhelming.
This report stated: "Pro-Communist influence has been found
among some university and secondary students, in a small segment of organized labor and, to a limited degree, among young
professionals." But now the lists were handed over to reporters
as "proof" that the Communists controlled the revolution. At
least that is what Embassy officials called the list of 53 when
it was distributed to us the day after the marines started landing.

Further confusing the issue was the fact that at an emergency meeting of the President with congressional leaders on the day the marines began landing, CIA Director Raborn reportedly said that one or two of the revolt leaders were Communists, and possibly as many as eight were—a far cry from 53 or 58 or 77.

Then came another discrepancy. In the list of 58 names issued in Washington, four were discovered to have been listed twice. U. S. officials promptly substituted four other names.

And what about the 53 or 58? A particularly fine research job was done by James Nelson Goodsell of the *Christian Science Monitor,* who spent some two weeks tracking down as many of the accused men as possible. He found that two of them had been in Victoria Prison, 13 miles from Santo Domingo, since several weeks before the revolt began. Six were not even in the country when it broke out and had not returned afterward. Four were captured by Dominican police and jailed within two days of the outbreak of the revolution and at least three days before release of the Embassy list. Four and perhaps six were not in Santo Domingo at the time of the revolution and had apparently been elsewhere in the country in the ensuing weeks.

One of the two imprisoned men, Jaime Capell Bello, who had traveled extensively in the Soviet Union, Communist China, and Cuba in the period from August 1961 to April 1962, entered prison on March 9 for allegedly inciting unrest. The other prisoner, Dato Pagán, who was considered one of the nation's top Communists and who also traveled in Cuba, was jailed on similar charges on April 12. When their confinement was pointed out to U. S. officials, the reply was that they still could have been giving orders from their jail cells through visitors. But again, this represented simply a possibility rather than a fact on which to build policy, and knowing the strict visiting policies of the prison, not a very good possibility at that.

When I tried to visit Victoria Prison to speak with those two men and others, I got past the high, creaking front gate of the sprawling structure, but not much farther. The khaki-uniformed warden told me in his office that I would have to obtain permission from the Chief of Police to interview prisoners. When I went to see the Chief of Police, his assistant told me I would have to get approval from the Army Chief of Staff. And when I went to see the Army Chief of Staff, I was told by an aide that he was too busy to see me.

The report describing Communist activities in the revolt also proved rather vulnerable, and on easily checkable points. U. S. officials apparently realized this, for the document was issued, in mimeographed form, in Washington, but not in Santo Domingo. At least, the Embassy didn't intend to issue it in Santo Domingo, where the facts it contained could be checked more easily. At an Embassy briefing conducted on May 5 in the press room set up on the main floor of Hotel Embajador, a State Department information officer told reporters about the document having been distributed in Washington only after we clamored for some evidence to back up the charges of Communist control.

When we insisted that we also be furnished copies of the document, he replied that this was impossible since he had only one copy. Finally, when reporters offered to type up additional copies themselves, the briefing officer reluctantly agreed. His reluctance proved understandable.

The document gave what was purported to be detailed accounts of how the Communists organized themselves for the revolt; how Communists were observed carrying weapons; how mobs sacked the headquarters of rightist political parties; how Communists set up strong points; how Communists were seen making Molotov cocktails. In other words, the report seemed to reporters to do little more than show how the Communists operated in relation to themselves. It did not show how the Communists were supposed to have led non-Communists, which they would have to have done to win control of the revolution. It seemed to have little more value than a report that showed how the Communists participated in, say, the Negro revolution in the United States. Such a document would only have significance if it could be demonstrated that the Reds participated in the policy-making machinery of the civil rights leadership.

Furthermore, the points that could most easily be checked proved in many cases to be inaccurate, casting a shadow over the credibility of the whole report. For example, Bonilla Aybar, the commentator, was supposed to have been, according to eyewitnesses, machine-gunned to death by a civilian rebel group, presumably Communists. But, in reality, he was safe in Puerto Rico. Charges that PRD leaders had quit the revolt because the Communists had taken over were vigorously denied by these leaders. Most important of all, a statement indicating that three personalities with Communist associations had been given high-level jobs in the Caamaño government proved without foundation. This discovery was particularly damaging to the report, since the "revelation," had it been accurate, would have been the first solid evidence of a link between rebel policy and the Communists.

Alfredo Conde Pausa, listed as the new Attorney General, was described as "a known sympathizer with PSPD." I visited him, and he turned out to have been a Supreme Court justice for 26 years. Breaking into tears on learning that he had been placed on the U. S. list of subversives, he said that in the last presidential election he had voted for the conservative National Civic Union, and that he had worked on the 1963 Constitution with U. S. Supreme Court Justice William O. Douglas. He said he abhorred communism.

An elderly, thin-faced man whose nephews are believed to be far leftists, Conde Pausa termed the Embassy's charges "international McCarthyism." And in any event, he added, he was not the new Attorney General, but had been offered the job of President of the Supreme Court.

Luis Homéro Lajara Burgos, charged in the U. S. document with associating with PSPD members, was listed as the new Director of Security, though he had held this job in the fleeting

Molina government but had no official position under Caamaño. He had, moreover, been the aide, as indicated earlier, who persuaded Molina in the desolation of the palace early in the revolution to go to the American Embassy and arrange for an end to the fighting. A naval officer, he was, I found, regarded even by conservative Dominicans as anti-Communist.

Lajara's son, Alejandro, is listed as the third questionable Caamaño appointee—the Deputy Director of Security under his father. A very young man, Alejandro, apparently associated with the 14th of June Movement but not regarded as a Communist by Embassy officials, had never, in any case, held an official position.

When I pointed out to one Embassy official what I had learned about these three persons, he said he agreed that they should not have been on the list.

The most far-reaching effort of all to pin the Communist stamp on the rebel regime was the charge made at another briefing in Santo Domingo, on May 5, that Caamaño had made a deal with Communist leaders at a secret meeting that was supposed to have been held the day before. The briefing officer reported that Caamaño and his supporters had agreed at the meeting to give the Communists a "decisive voice" in the government if the revolution was successful. If the revolution didn't succeed, Caamaño was supposed to have promised that he would arrange for safe-conducts for the leaders to leave the country.

When I asked the briefing officer if he regarded this information as having come from reliable sources, he replied: "I would say fairly reliable sources." After we pressed him for more details, he said he would have some the following day. And he did, issuing on May 6 a mimeographed sheet indicating the people who were supposed to have been present at the secret meeting. The list included six members of the PSPD, two members of the 14th of June Movement, and, in addition to Caamaño, five non-Communist members of the rebel command.

"Our sources for this are very reliable," the spokesman said. When it was pointed out that the day before he had said they were only "fairly reliable," he replied, "I'm now convinced that the sources are very reliable."

Meanwhile, Caamaño, Aristy, and Peña Gómez, all of whom were listed as being present at the meeting, flatly denied to me that such a meeting had taken place. "American diplomats must be nuts," Caamaño said, twirling his finger next to his head. "They have Communists on the brain."

About two weeks later, after Washington decided that the Communist threat had greatly diminished, Embassy officials said privately that the information about the meeting had apparently proved to be inaccurate.

U. S. officials in the first week of May made other charges of "communism" as well. On one occasion, to show the "Communist flavor" of the revolution, the briefing officer went so far as to complain that the rebels were always criticizing what they called the "oligarchs." He seemed unimpressed when reporters pointed out that many Latin-American democrats, and U. S. diplomats, too, have been known to criticize the "oligarchs."

Embassy intelligence officers would not comment at all on discrepancies that were constantly being found in their reports. But those in Washington argued that some errors on lists such as were distributed, put together in the middle of a revolution, did not discredit the validity of the lists. Other U. S. officials disagreed.

At least on one occasion, there seems to have been a certain amount of substance in Embassy accusations. A spokesman said that Fidelio Despradel Roque, a Communist who he said belonged to the PSPD, was an "adviser" to Caamaño. One rebel leader, while denying that Despradel—whose father, Arturo, had once headed Trujillo's Dominican Party—was an "adviser," said that he had been at rebel headquarters "once or twice" as a representative of the 14th of June Movement. He attended a meeting, for example, of the leaders of the various revolutionary factions held to discuss the replacement of Bosch as constitutional President. Despradel, like most of the others at the meeting, the rebel official said, approved of Caamaño.

But as a result of the U. S. stress on the Communist issue, Caamaño asked him not to come to his headquarters anymore.

"Why should you listen to what the Yankees say?" Despradel reportedly asked in anger.

"Just don't come anymore," Caamaño replied.

Other 14th of June leaders, namely Juan B. Mejia and Juan Miguel Román, who was killed in a rebel attack on the National Palace, had also attended meetings with rebel leaders, the rebel source told me, though many observers regard these two men as extreme nationalists rather than as Communists.

But if far leftists stopped showing up at headquarters in early May as far as could be determined, the rebels did not refuse to accept Communist military support. Captain García of the rebel command, whose job has been to coordinate the military activities of all revolutionary factions, kept in touch by telephone and messenger with leaders of the 14th of June and the MPD —the PSPD apparently ignored since it is not an action group— according to the high rebel source.

Certainly the acceptance of Communist support under any circumstances is a highly challengeable policy. But to the rebels, one didn't reject a gun in a struggle for survival. Probably there has never been a revolution, it was argued, in which the rebels have been particular who was shooting at the loyalists. And on the international plane, moreover, the United States, when it was threatened by Nazi Germany, did not hesitate to ally itself with Stalinist Russia. But, the rebels have felt, accepting help wherever it can be found is a far cry from submitting to control by those who give the help. The rebel official explained:

"In a revolution, it is too much to ask people not to accept help from any source whatsoever, regardless of the motives of the supporters. We would accept help from the devil himself.

But the fact is that the Communists have no control of the movement whatsoever. They obey us because they know that if they don't we will crush them. They are only good to us as long as they obey. And when the fighting is over, if necessary we will crush them. But now we're all Dominicans fighting not only against domestic oppressors, but against a foreign invader as well. Actually, you Americans, in your panic, have created sympathy for the Communists among some people where none existed before. Not everybody can see the ulterior motives of the Communists as well as can the constitutionalist leaders. We despise communism. But if we have been forced to accept help where we can find it, this has nothing to do with control."

The rebel political indoctrination program would appear to support this statement. Indoctrination has been left largely to the vigorously anti-Communist Revolutionary Social Christian Party, the PRD's ally, whose members, usually American-educated, have conducted lectures almost every night at the various command posts. The topics discussed, generally within the context of the Christian Democratic philosophy, include: the meaning of the revolution; constitutionalism in Latin America; the OAS and its domination by the United States; Latin-American integration; human rights; the family, the state, and society; U. S. and Soviet imperialism; and a critical study of Marxism and Communist techniques.

As a result of such courses, rebel soldiers, while not taught to love U. S. foreign policy, have been made aware of Communist aims and tactics and thus rendered more immune to Red propaganda—despite the participation of Communists in the activities of some command posts, which have usually consisted of 25 to 200 members.

Who were the "hard-core" Communists who were supposed to have won control of the rebel movement? After some difficulty, I located two of those on the list of 53, both of them lawyers, yet men of sharply contrasting character and background. I felt even before I spoke with them that it wasn't likely that I would be able to determine from a mere interview whether they were really Communists or not, much less whether they were "hard-core." Except for the top, well-known leaders, few are the Reds who will identify themselves as such, particularly before their side has won. And I had been right. Both denied they were Communists, and there was no way of knowing whether they were lying. However, Communist or not, their observations and methods of reasoning as reflected in our conversations hinted at some of the factors that had led them to be as radical and anti-American as they were—factors that might well contribute to communism far more substantially than the feared democratic tactics of Juan Bosch.

José Cassa Logrona, graying and thin-haired, looks older than his forty-eight years. Possessed of a professorial air that is accentuated by his round tortoiseshell glasses, he wears a meek expression occasionally embellished with a reluctant smile.

"You mean I'm on that list of Communists?" he asked incredulously when I referred to that fact. "It's really absurd. You couldn't find anyone more bourgeois."

And Cassa Logrona, whatever he really thinks, does appear to have at least some bourgeois instincts. He lives in a large five-room house, an old house in the rebel-controlled downtown area with high ceilings and wood panelings in the graceful Spanish-colonial style.

His den in a corner of his huge living room has the musty look of the documents section of a public library, with rows of books lining the walls almost to the ceiling. Many of the volumes are law books. Others include *The Development of Ideas in the United States* by Vernon Louis Parrington; *The Federalist: A Commentary on the United States Constitution* by Alexander Hamilton, John Jay, and James Madison; *The Rebirth of Democracy* by Henry A. Wallace; *The General Theory of the State* by Hans Kelsen; and *The French Revolution* by Alfonso de Lamartine. No books on Marxism can be seen on the shelves.

The living room walls are decorated with a painting of Christ and Spanish engravings. In a glass case are Indian relics from the Dominican Republic and Mexico and rare rocks and clay statues from Spain.

As he sat back in his chair before a large desk cluttered with paper and books, Cassa Logrona said: "I own this house and two others. I make a good living. I am not a Communist. I want a government like Bosch gave us. I want complete freedom like you Americans have."

How did he think he happened to land on the American list of Communists?

"Well," he said, "maybe it was because my political enemies told them I was a Communist."

Cassa Logrona was among the founders of the UCN. He was vice-president of the party's Santo Domingo District Committee until September 1962, shortly before the election that shot Bosch to power. He had been one of the 18 members of his committee who left the party en masse. The UCN top leadership had been under pressure to rid the party of Communists, and at least some Reds were believed in control of the Santo Domingo group.

But according to Cassa Logrona, the members quit voluntarily because the UCN had "changed its original purpose." It no longer pushed for social reform, he said, but instead began charging that all social reformers were Communists—"just as Trujillo did." The party, he maintained, never forgave him for his denunciation.

After his resignation, Cassa Logrona said, he abandoned politics and never went back to it. He is listed on the Embassy list as belonging to the PSPD, but, he maintained, he never had anything to do with that organization.

"I feel that no Dominicans, Communist or not, should be suppressed," he said, "but I personally oppose Marxist-Leninism precisely because it doesn't permit such freedom."

Cassa Lagrona said that a friend, whom he would not identify except to say that he was not a Communist, gave him one of several invitations he had received from Cuba to visit that country for the 26th of July celebration in 1963.

"Out of curiosity," Cassa Logrona said, "I decided to go. What did I have to lose? I was given a grand tour for three weeks but never attended any classes or anything like that. I only saw Fidel Castro when he spoke to the crowds."

What did he think of Cuba?

"I don't think Castro is right, and I don't want a Castro-style government here."

Cassa Logrona said he was jailed for five days in September 1963 by the Triumvirate that held power after Bosch was overthrown. And the following month he was exiled to Martinique. He claimed that he was given no explanation for this action, though he guessed that he was being accused of Communist activities by his UCN enemies on the pretext of his Cuban trip.

He said that Fiallo, the UCN presidential candidate in the 1962 election, declared over the radio that he, Cassa Logrona, was not a Communist, and that as a result he was permitted to return home after nearly two months in exile. He added that Reid Cabral had called up his wife, María, and indicated that he would do his best to bring back her husband. He had done business with Reid before and had been a friend of his, the attorney said.

"What do I want?" remarked Cassa Logrona. "I want a multi-party political system. I want social reforms. Of course I'm for the revolution. But what you should understand is that it is not a Communist revolution. It is a revolution of people who want freedom. . . . So they think I'm a Communist. What can I do? What can I do?"

Far less dispassionate in his reaction to the U. S. accusations was Juan Matos Rivera, who also lives in the downtown rebel section, but in a green-painted board shack with a tin roof and a cement floor which he shares with his mother and brother. As he sat across from me on a small, hard-cushioned sofa in his tiny living room, he extended his hands toward me, palms up, and said in a gruff, angry voice:

"Look at my hands, look. Do they look like they've been holding a gun? I heard on the radio that I was supposed to be one of the Communist leaders of this revolution. But I'm neither a Communist nor a leader."

Matos Rivera, a dark-complexioned thirty-three-year-old man with a small round face full of seething emotion, is a member of the 14th of June Movement. Although the U. S. list charges that he was trained in Cuba, he denied that he had ever been in that country.

"They have no elections in Cuba, and I believe in elections," he said. "We members of the 14th of June are nationalist and anti-imperialist. We think people must govern themselves. And Castro doesn't let his people do that. I don't like the policies of Cuba, the United States, Russia, or Britain. I'm a nationalist. I'm a poor man, but I'm proud."

His poverty was entirely believable. On the other side of a wooden partition separating the two rooms of the house was a bedroom with two backless beds covered with patched blankets. The only bright note amidst the drabness of the house was the inevitable colored portrait of Christ on the wooden wall above my chair.

"I manage to scrape out only about 80 pesos [$80] a month," Matos Rivera said. "I buy things, like bicycles, and sell them. Sometimes I help people fill out government forms. Don't laugh. I'm a lawyer, yes. But who will hire me? I am branded as a Communist."

After working his way through the University of Santo Domingo, where he was exposed to the restless leftism of his fellow students, he started working as a law consultant in Trujillo's Labor Ministry. His trouble started when, as Secretary of the Federation of Public Employees, he led a strike in July 1962 for a pay increase. The Council of State was then in power.

"Public employees," he said, "were getting as little as 15 pesos

[$15] a month. We demanded a minimum of 60 pesos, and struck for it. The government accused me of communism. It finally agreed to our demands, but three months later I was jailed and deported as a Communist without trial."

After studying at the Sorbonne in Paris and visiting several countries in western Europe—he said he visited no Communist nations—Matos Rivera returned home in March 1963 several days after Bosch took office. He got a job as law consultant in the Justice Department, but was fired after five days for demanding that Bosch reverse what he claimed was his policy of firing public employees who didn't politically agree with him.

When Bosch was overthrown, the Triumvirate government jailed him and deported him to Portugal. He returned anyway a month later—"I preferred prison to exile"—and was arrested, tried, and sentenced to three years in prison for allegedly plotting against the government. He was free on bail when the revolution broke out.

"There are some Communists in this country," he said, "but very few. They are against God. We are a party of young people who are determined to end hunger and corruption. Those who make a show of anti-communism are discredited because they are corrupt. And this includes some people in Bosch's party."

Why was he bitter toward the United States? "Because," he said, "it is never with the people. It may mean well sometimes, but it gives money to the rich in the government and the poor never see it. Your country should understand this. You should send representatives here who understand what is going on and will support the people and not the corrupt people at the top."

He repeated with passion: "Why doesn't your government understand?"

It was a question that many Dominicans less suspect asked me, too. In charging that the revolution was Communist-controlled, the United States furnished itself with an alibi for taking any steps it desired against the rebels—in the name of anti-communism. It had used the Trujillo technique on an international scale. Certainly there was a difference in motivation; Trujillo needed an excuse to wipe out his enemies, whoever they might be, while the United States needed an excuse to take measures that would eliminate even the possibility of a Communist takover. But this was a technique that could be employed to discourage, prevent, or smear any future social revolutions in Latin America, since the Communists would be certain to support all of them for their own purposes.

It was not surprising that the Latin democracies, including Venezuela, though it is itself under attack from Communist guerrillas, were aghast at the implications of the charge, which, at the most, appeared to be based on suspicion rather than facts. And even if the Administration had facts that it could not divulge, was it necessary to make the accusation if, by doing so, it felt obliged to resort to McCarthyism in order to justify it?

CHAPTER 8

Gold Braid and
Cardboard Curlers

IN THE first days of the American occupation, neither the
rebels nor the loyalists had strong political leadership. On
the rebel side, Provisional President Molina Ureña's flight into
asylum had left a critical gap; Caamaño was the accepted military leader, but he had no "constitutional" political standing.
And on the loyalist side, the three-man junta had no popular
base whatsoever, and the real strong man, Wessin, hated by the
people, was kept out of sight by the United States.

Martin was to be involved in the crystallization of strong
leadership on both sides. On Sunday, May 2, Martin wrote in
Life, he was instructed by President Johnson to fly to San Juan
to see Juan Bosch for the first talk in person with him any American official was to have, though the revolution revolved around
him. The evening before, Bosch had telephoned Martin at the
U. S. chancellery and worriedly inquired about information he
had received that the marines were attacking rebel positions so
that the junta forces could advance. Martin had replied that as
far as he knew this wasn't so, but that he would check. Bosch's
information, it seemed, was in reference to an extension by
U. S. troops of the International Safety Zone.

There had been other indirect U. S. contacts with Bosch.

Shortly after the revolution broke out, the exiled Dominican leader, ignored by Washington, had asked his friend Dr. Jaime Benítez, chancellor of the University of Puerto Rico, to keep up a flow of communications with Abe Fortas, a Washington attorney and a close friend of President Johnson. Fortas, according to Benítez, talked with both the President and Bosch in an effort to clarify for each the other's views.

Benítez cleared the Martin visit with Bosch. At about 12:30 A.M. on Monday, May 3, he called the latter to say that Martin had arrived at his house and would like to see Bosch there. Bosch went, and embarked on a two-part conversational spree with Martin that was to tragically reflect in the persons of these two men, who had long been friends, the searing bitterness and unyielding stubbornness of the confrontation between the United States and the Dominican revolution. In conflicting reports of the meetings afterward, they couldn't even agree on the time they took place—possibly, as Bosch suggested, because Martin's watch may have been on Dominican rather than Puerto Rican time.

Martin said that he had gone to see Bosch on President Johnson's instructions. Bosch, in an article he wrote for the Chicago *Daily News,* commented that this was news to him. "At no time did he tell me that he had come to see me under" White House instructions.

Martin wrote that Bosch "did not want to talk to me about events, since I had said publicly that in my judgment his party had fallen under the domination of adventurers and Castro Communists and that his country was being ripped to pieces." Bosch replied, "I cannot explain . . . why he said this. . . . I knew that Martin had said that the constitutionalist revolution had fallen under Communist control, but this was not enough to turn us into enemies. I simply said to myself that Martin was mistaken. Today, everyone in the United States knows that Martin made a bad judgment."

The two men met head on in discussing the Communist issue.

According to Bosch, "Martin was so badly informed . . . that he even told me that in parts of the city of Santo Domingo the revolutionaries had exhibited cut-off heads. As is now known, there was not one single head cut off, much less exhibited, and there was not a single firing squad in Santo Domingo in the area called the rebel zone. . . . Martin, like the majority of Americans, has no idea of what a revolution is. Revolution was and is what happened on April 24 in Santo Domingo, what we saw in Mexico between 1910 and 1920, and what happened in Venezuela in 1859 and 1912. Communists don't make this kind of revolution. Communists take power and make revolution from a position of power. In Santo Domingo, they had not taken power, nor could they take it for the simple reason that there were not enough Communists in the country to take power. In Cuba—yes, there were. Before Fidel Castro came down from the mountains, Cuba had the best directed and best organized and largest Communist party in America—something that American experts in Latin-American politics seem to ignore."

Martin maintained that Bosch had said: "Yes, it is social war. It is kill, kill, kill. . . . But I cannot accept that it is all over for my country. The only solution is a marine occupation for many, many years." Bosch said that "without any argument at all, I explained to him that what he had seen in Santo Domingo was not a Communist revolution, but instead a social revolution in the typical Latin-American style—the kind that Mexico had in 1810 and the kind others have had. . . . The truth is that when Martin insisted that in the Dominican Republic there was no way out, that everything had been destroyed, I responded that there were two ways out—either the constitutional Dominican government or a U. S. military occupation forever. But for Martin, this was not possible in my country. Benítez did not accept the position of Martin."

Of Bosch's ability to understand what was happening in his homeland, Martin wrote: "He could not believe what I said. How could he? He was in Puerto Rico, not Santo Domingo.

I would not have believed it had I not seen it." Bosch said of
Martin's ability to understand: "He explained that he had been
three days without eating or bathing, that for three nights he
had slept on the floor in the Embassy. It was evident that Martin
had been subjected to third-grade treatment for someone so
intelligent and, due to this, it was easy to confuse things and
not to understand Dominican reality."

Without criticizing Martin's performance, Benítez later said
that Martin "was almost destroyed by what he saw and experienced in Santo Domingo" and "had been reduced to a state
of physical and emotional shock."

The most important conflict revolved around the question
of rebel leadership. Martin wrote that at their first encounter
Bosch had said a meeting of the constitutional Congress had
been called for Wednesday, May 5, and that Caamaño would
take Molina Ureña from the Colombian Embassy, where he
was in asylum, to the palace to resume the provisional presidency.

Martin added: "I have seldom felt more helpless. I said, 'But
Mr. President, I'm afraid you don't understand.' He was still
dreaming of the old days. I tried to explain that a meaningful
'meeting of the Congress' was impossible in his chaotic city,
that it was extremely doubtful that Molina would accept the
presidency, and then on a map I showed him the physical im-
possibility of Caamaño's men crossing the zone line, taking
Molina out of asylum . . . and then conducting him back to the
palace—and in no man's land. Bosch shrugged: 'Then there is
no solution.' "

At a second meeting later in the day, Martin said, "Bosch
now said that the Dominican Congress would meet on Wednesday and elect either Colonel Caamaño or another colonel as
president under the 1963 constitution, to serve out the remainder of Bosch's own term—until February 27, 1967."

According to Bosch, it was in the second interview, not in
the first, that they began to talk about Molina Ureña. "I said

to Martin," he maintained, "that I had asked by telephone that the Dominican Congress hold a session in order to elect a constitutional president, since I could not return to Santo Domingo. My candidate, I explained, would be either Colonel Caamaño or Colonel Rafael Fernández Domínguez.

" 'This can't be,' he said. 'We cannot accept a military man.' Nevertheless, it happened that a few days before U. S. Ambassador W. Tapley Bennett, Jr., had chosen three colonels to form the so-called Junta de San Isidro, and the day following our interview, according to Martin, he himself helped to form the junta headed by General Antonio Imbert Barrera.

"When Martin said that the United States would not accept a military man in the presidency of the Dominican Republic, I responded that in this case Molina Ureña should be taken out of the Colombian Embassy, and restored in his post as provisional constitutional president."

Both men agreed that Bosch had said, in reply to a question from Martin, that he would not return home to "advise and assist," as Martin put it, "in rebuilding the country." "If I return," Bosch said, "I am President." Benítez later reported that Bosch twice offered to go to Santo Domingo as President but was told by Martin that "the situation was hopeless" and that Bosch "would only get himself killed." Bosch said that two days before Martin arrived for their meeting "Fortas had responded with silence to my request for a plane." He said he believed that "what Mann feared most was that I would return to my country." Administration officials privately said that they would have arranged for Bosch's safety once he had arrived in Santo Domingo.

In the end, according to Bosch, Martin agreed that, despite the difficulties, the best solution was to reinstall Molina Ureña as Provisional President. After Martin had made several telephone calls to Washington, Bosch said, the U. S. envoy reported that the "return of Molina Ureña could be arranged, but that I must send out a call to the Dominican people to give up their arms. Immediately, Martin dictated to me the points that I should deal with. The first was that the Dominican revolution had been controlled by the Communists and that, in addition, the dispatching of the marines was necessary."

Bosch continued with some passion: "Martin, a sensitive man, an American of good faith, wanted me to act like an American official—he wanted me to justify not what my people had done but instead what the government of the United States was doing. It took some work to convince him I could not do this, but finally he was convinced. I wrote the statement in which, of course, I protested the intervention, and did not mention anything about those points proposed by Martin.

"I said I knew that the Dominicans had to make sacrifices in order to liberate themselves from this intervention, and I believed that the United States also had to make sacrifices in order to correct a tremendous mistake. So I delivered to Martin a copy of the statement. I never heard anything more of it or of him."

And so it appears, if Bosch's report is accurate, that as early as May 2 or 3, only a few days after the U. S. military intervention, the United States was at least considering a return to constitutionalism under Bosch's constitution, desiring in return simply a face-saving way out of the situation, if one which Bosch could not accept. In this light, it is painful to ponder whether the constitutional question could not have been settled satisfactorily before the U. S. marines landed—with Molina Ureña serving out the remainder of Bosch's term—if only Washington had bothered to find out what was on Bosch's mind. Would the military have then accepted such a compromise? No one knows, but it is clear that Wessin was more anti-Bosch than anti-Constitution.

It is not surprising that Bosch heard nothing more about the Molina Ureña proposal. Aside from his refusal to publicly pat the United States on the back for its Dominican policy, once the troops had landed and the cry of "communism" had sounded around the world, the Administration could not very well support a rebel government without being made to look ridiculous. But at the same time, the Administration was horrified to find itself identified, especially in Latin America, with an oppressive, corrupt military organization, though this identity, it was evident to observers on the spot, was based on the facts of the situation. U. S. policy makers decided to modify their original plan for a military junta to hold power until elections could be arranged.

They began thinking in terms of a mixed military-civilian broad-based junta that might eventually entice into its fold the moderates on the rebel side, thereby isolating the Communists and other extremists within an unimportant rebel fringe group.

Martin, apparently realizing from the first that the Molina Ureña idea would never really be acceptable in Washington, did not wait long to start seeking the proper man to head a "broad-based" junta. The man who struck him as best fitting the bill was Antonio Imbert. Martin had first visited Imbert at his heavily guarded home, a few blocks from Hotel Embajador, late Saturday night, May 1, under circumstances that would have strained the nerves of a much younger man. After he had announced himself at the sentry post, the marine guard with him accidentally fired a string of shots. Martin, terrified, waited for the Imbert guards to open up with machine guns, but they didn't, and he made it into the house. But peace still evaded him. While he talked with Imbert in the light of a kerosene lamp, heavy automatic fire broke out nearby, and he and Imbert crawled on their hands and knees to another room.

Martin visited Imbert again on Monday, May 3, within hours after he returned from San Juan from his talks with Bosch. According to Martin, he went on Imbert's invitation. Imbert remarked to him, he said, that "various people, both military and civilians, had told him they could support neither the rebels nor the San Isidro crowd. They had told him that those old generals must leave the country, that Colonel Benoit's three-man military junta must be reconstituted, that only Imbert was strong enough." ֵ

By offering his candidacy in this indirect manner, Imbert was able to say later that Martin asked him to head a junta rather than the reverse. And Martin did follow up Imbert's suggestive remark with the question: "Do you want to do it?"

Imbert was modest and magnanimous. "I do it. For my country. Not for myself. Whatta hell I want to get into this mess for? I can sit here quiet."

Martin then said the United States would not support a military dictatorship and asked if Imbert could get rid of the old generals.

"I fix," Imbert replied succinctly. He added that Colonel Benoit should be a member of the junta, but that the others should be civilian technicians, not politicians.

Martin then went all-out to help Imbert form a government, inviting prominent Dominicans to Imbert's house where he tried to persuade them to join the projected junta.

Why did Martin and other U. S. officials feel that Imbert was the man? First, Martin said, he found him a "brave man, shrewd, blunt, with sources everywhere." He was a man of action, and action was needed at this critical point. Certainly he was all those things. He could hardly have participated in the assassination of Trujillo otherwise, nor survived the bloody aftermath. Furthermore, before U. S. troops arrived, when Wessin's cause looked lost, he managed to rally 300 junta troops for a takeover of the National Palace from rebel forces.

Second, Martin wanted someone with at least some claim to popularity, and Imbert was, after all, something of a national hero for his role in the assassination.

Third, he wanted someone who was not associated in the public mind with the traditional militarists, but at the same time could control them. Imbert seemed to fit the need, since he was really a civilian who had been made a general so that he could more easily be protected against the murder threats of the Trujillo family. The traditional militarists, in fact, resented him as a "pseudo general" who wanted to cut into their power and privileges. But he nevertheless had a strong following in some military circles, particularly in the national police, which he had long controlled—as reflected in the National Palace takeover.

Fourth, at a time when few potential leaders were available, Imbert let it be known that he was, as he had always been for any job under anyone's auspices that would give him power. On the fateful night of April 24, he had tried to persuade Reid Cabral to appoint him "Secretary of the Armed Forces to try to reunite them." He then suggested that he "visit the rebellious forts to explore the state of mind of the leaders." It was during that exploration that he, and two other officers, unsuccessfully offered their services to the rebels. And while the marines were still disembarking, he headed for the *Boxer,* as indicated earlier, to check with the U. S. forces on the possibilities of serving them.

Martin and the Administration were apparently aware of Imbert's shortcomings. When I was in the Dominican Republic during the Council of State era in 1962, U. S. Embassy officials under Martin, who was then Ambassador, took an optimistic view of the future—until they started discussing Imbert. "He is a man who likes power," said one diplomat typically. "No one knows what he will do. He doesn't seem to have much understanding of constitutional government. We're watching him." Pointing up this suspicion, the officers of a destroyer that visited Santo Domingo during the 1962 Cuban missile crisis invited aboard for lunch almost all important Dominican leaders, but not Imbert.

That was, however, when the United States was mainly concerned about keeping democracy alive in the Dominican Republic. Now the focus had changed. It was on keeping anti-communism alive, and democracy did not seem for the moment the best way to do it. Some of the qualities that had made U. S.

officials fearful of Imbert in the past—particularly his aggressiveness and shrewdness—made them hopeful now.

They saw nothing especially dangerous in his willingness to serve so many interests. After all, how many Dominican leaders, or, for that matter, Latin-American leaders in general, were untainted by opportunism? Considering his other qualifications, that was not an overriding vice. Nor, in any case, would Imbert be maintained in power long—just long enough to obtain a peace and to hold elections. What was important at the moment was to set up a government of action with as broad a base as possible to counter the communism that had, in the U. S. view, grabbed control of the revolution. The question is, did they disbelieve reports indicating how remarkably boundless Imbert's availability appeared to be, or did they feel that such reports, even if true, were not significant?

Born in 1920 into a moderately well-to-do Puerto Plata family, Imbert suffered from a severe case of asthma as a child and was educated mainly at home. His stepfather was an administrator for the United Fruit Company. When Trujillo purchased one United Fruit plantation, he named Antonio as administrator and came to know and trust him. Eventually, Imbert became a partner and manager in a citrus-products factory, and then an administrator of railroads. His brother, Segundo, meanwhile, was appointed by Trujillo as military commander of Puerto Plata Province, and shortly afterward, in 1948, Antonio was selected Governor, giving the favored Imbert family an unusual hold on the area.

According to Imbert's enemies, the two brothers ran the province as Trujillo ran the country, a private enterprise within a private enterprise. These foes say that before he became Governor, Antonio was directly involved in the killing of scores of Haitians during the 1937 massacre ordered by Trujillo. And they say that after he became Governor, he killed many people, including entire families, who challenged his interests. They accuse him also of having permitted workers at a local sugar refinery to be paid below the official minimum salary in exchange for a splitting of their salary differences with the administrators. But Imbert denies such charges, and none have been proved.

Imbert's future seems to have turned on an incident that occurred in 1949. Trujillo apparently expected a group of Dominican exiles, called the Movement of Luperón, to invade the country. It is not clear whether the invasion actually took place. According to persons I interviewed in Puerto Plata, who were too frightened to say much about Imbert, Trujillo faked an invasion, sending one plane over the area, in order to have an excuse for rounding up and liquidating people suspected of working with the movement. Also unclear is the role of the Imbert brothers in the plot. One version is that they infiltrated the movement in order to break it up. Another is that they actually wanted it to succeed in the hope of overthrowing Trujillo. In any case, when the dictator moved against suspected members within the country, the two brothers apparently gave him their full support, whether or not out of conviction.

According to some Puerto Platans who say they are familiar with what happened, Antonio issued an order, or at least relayed an order from Trujillo—some say he carried it out personally —for the killing of about 30 suspects. Others who concede that they are not sure of the facts maintain that only one or both of the brothers could have given the order, since no one else in the province had the authority. It is said by some that soldiers actually did the killing, and while they probably took orders from Segundo, the army commander, Antonio, as civilian Governor, may have had little power to overrule his brother. The argument is also made that the brothers may have had no choice, since to disobey Trujillo meant certain death. But then, still others ask, why should they have accepted such responsible jobs under Trujillo in the first place, knowing that they would have to be his hatchet men?

Shortly after this episode, Antonio lost his governorship and went to work as an official in a cement factory in Santo Domingo, and Segundo left the country. He eventually returned and, in 1955, was arrested and imprisoned for several years, dying mysteriously while still behind bars. The reason for his imprisonment was never made clear, though it is suspected that the dictator thought that Segundo may actually have been involved in the 1949 plot against him. Antonio thus nursed a deep bitterness toward Trujillo. His political career had been terminated by the tyrant, who may have suspected him of disloyalty as well, and his brother had died in prison. Ambition and fraternal loyalty combined to swell the courage that was to be required on that dark night in 1961 when he risked all in a gamble to remove the source of his frustration and hatred.

After emerging from hiding about six months after Trujillo's assassination, Imbert was back in politics. As a national hero, he was automatically made a member of the seven-man Council of State that was to pave the way for free elections.

'He has often been accused of having used his position on the Council, particularly his police prerogatives, to build a power base for himself—rooted in collaboration with the Communists. There have been persistent reports, for example, that Imbert distributed both arms and money to the 14th of June Movement and the Peking-oriented MPD while he was a member of the Council, and also during the regime of Reid Cabral, whom, it is charged, he hoped to oust with Communist support. He has also been accused of using his police powers to let Communists who had been exiled return to the country. Especially persistent is the report that Imbert arranged for Maximo López Molina, head of the MPD, to hide in the home of a friend in mid-1962 when the Council decided to arrest him.

Certainly Imbert made no secret of his sympathetic attitude toward the June 14th Movement while he was a member of the Council. As indicated earlier, he did not hesitate to reveal this sympathy to me, nor were Embassy officials unaware of it. One of them told me at the time that it appeared Imbert might be trying to use the party as a springboard to power. And however communistic the 14th of June might or might not be, U. S. officials made it clear that they considered it Communist-dominated.

In fact, even today American diplomats say that they have heard many rumors of flirtations between Imbert and the Communists since Council days, maintaining simply that they don't know whether any of them are true. But despite the volume of such reports, they nevertheless backed Imbert to form a government that was to be a bastion against communism.

Undeniably, there was a certain logic to this, from the viewpoint of both Imbert and the United States. To Imbert, who risked his life to kill Trujillo, it was only fair that he replace Trujillo and enjoy some of the fruits of power that the dictator had denied him. To the United States, Imbert, as the assassin of Trujillo, had purged himself of the Trujilloite odor, but at the same time had some of the "practical" qualities necessary to bring order and unity—the kind of qualities that in the 1920's Americans had seen in Trujillo himself when they trained him in the manipulation of force. Even if Imbert had supplied the Communists with arms and money, he did it strictly for opportunistic, not for ideological, reasons. He could be trusted to hold in check the Communists he may have helped. Certainly he wasn't as dangerous as Bosch, who may not have given the Communists arms and money, but who let them demonstrate freely in the streets in the name of democracy.

The United States later saw its mistake. "Imbert may not have been the perfect man," one American official in Santo Domingo told me in what possibly was the understatement of the crisis, "but it isn't easy to find fully qualified people at a moment's notice during a chaotic revolutionary situation." And it is probably true that U. S. officials did sincerely regret their decision. Certainly they didn't want another Trujillo taking over the Dominican Republic.

But what their choice of Imbert reflected was the inability

of many U. S. diplomats, particularly at a time of crisis, to shake
off completely the disastrous and discredited axioms of the past,
the axioms that held that it was simpler and safer to maintain
purchasable, controllable rightist strongmen in power in Latin
America than to fool around with democratic regimes that
might be less dependably pro-American, and therefore more susceptible to Communist penetration.

The remnants of such thinking are particularly difficult to
shake off in the Caribbean, which had always been more or
less an American lake, and where one recent rebellion—in Cuba
—turned out to be a catastrophe. The fact that it took a Batista
to pave the way for a Castro was apparently too subtle a lesson
in cause and effect for many U. S. officials to consider at a time
when force was the order of the day.

And so Martin and Imbert worked to hammer out a junta.
As Martin put it in *Life:* "Imbert proposed names, his friends
proposed names, I proposed names, and nearly everybody whose
name was proposed in turn proposed other names, for few were
willing to accept responsibility." Finally, after many failures, a
Government of National Reconstruction was formed consisting
of Imbert, Benoit, and three civilians—Alejandro Zeller Cocco,
an economist; Carlos Grisolía Poloney, a lawyer; and Julio D.
Postigo, a bookstore owner and publisher who was a friend of
Bosch. He told me that he wanted to "contribute to peace."

The new junta was announced several days after the installation of Caamaño as constitutional President. With both sides
now led by two indisputable leaders, U. S. officials started pushing for a meeting between the two men with a view, apparently,
to amalgamate their forces under Imbert or some mutually
acceptable third figure, at least until a free election could be
held. Imbert seemed willing, but Caamaño insisted on a constitutional solution.

The way had been paved for Caamaño's ascension to the
rebel presidency on Tuesday night, May 4, when the constitutional Congress met secretly in rebel territory and, on the advice

of Bosch, elected him by a vote of 49 to 7. The seven negative ballots were cast for two other candidates of Bosch's party. Fifteen of 27 Senators and 41 of 74 Deputies were present for the election. The following morning, Caamaño was sworn in at a ceremony in a park square attended by several thousand people.

It was clear from a glance at the exuberant faces of the spectators jammed together, most of them raggedly dressed and many carrying rifles, that the rebels felt this was a stunning victory for them. True, their hero Bosch had stepped down as President, but to them that was of secondary importance. Bosch had himself taught them to regard him, or for that matter, any national leader, with less awe than the Constitution that governed his behavior. The rebels were not fighting for a man, however much they might have liked and respected him, but for an idea—the idea that their only permanent guarantee of freedom and human rights lay in the Constitution. Bosch had taught them that, and they had learned more easily than most people because they had suffered more under arbitrary rule. And so now they shouted their loyalty to Caamaño, whom most of them hardly knew. They didn't have to know him. He was their constitutional President.

In a conversation I had with Bosch several days later in the home of a friend of his in San Juan, Bosch said that Caamaño, as President, would fill the constitutional political vacuum. He seemed to feel that one of the worst blows to the constitutional cause had been the flight of Molina Ureña into asylum, since he had been, as leader of the House of Deputies, the legal successor to Bosch. (Juan Casanova Garrido, the Senate President, who preceded Molina in the line of succession, was, as noted earlier, caught and sent into exile after Bosch's overthrow.) And the Constitution did not extend the line of succession any further, simply providing that Congress select someone. Furthermore, Bosch was aware that some people were challenging the constitutionality of Caamaño's choice since the Constitution

said that the President had to be a citizen possessed of all his
civil rights, and members of the armed forces were not, being
unable to vote. The rationalized reply was that Caamaño was
no longer really a member of the armed forces as such, since
he was fighting them. He was now simply an armed civilian
with the honorary title of Colonel.

Bosch pointed out another interesting legal point. He had
publicly announced his resignation to pave the way for Caamaño's selection, but if he returned to the Dominican Republic
he would still be President, since the Constitution provided that
a President can resign only in person before Congress. Would
he eventually return then and reclaim the presidency? He
would only go back, if he went at all, Bosch replied obtusely,
at Caamaño's invitation. "I would never try to take the presidency away from Caamaño," he said. "He's the one who's
risking his life for the Constitution."

After the swearing-in ceremony, Caamaño held a press conference in his shabby military headquarters, sitting at one end
of a long table beside Aristy, who was his interpreter, political
adviser, and Secretary of Government in his new cabinet. The
two men quietly discussed each question put to Caamaño by
a reporter, then the colonel would speak in Spanish, and Aristy
would follow with a translation in English in a slow, deliberate,
authoritative voice. The most notable remark was: "We will
not tolerate a dictatorship of either the right or the left."

It was obvious that Aristy, as he leaned over and whispered
into Caamaño's ear time and again, was coaching the colonel
on some of his answers. Indeed, on other occasions when Caamaño spoke with me, Aristy, if he was present or happened to
come by, would sometimes correct his boss, particularly on
points of fact. Once Caamaño started speaking about the importance of the "1962 Constitution." "He means the 1963 Constitution," Aristy cut in. Sometimes after Caamaño offered me
information on the record, Aristy would put it off the record.

Such close public supervision over Caamaño's contacts with

the press and also with diplomats led to many reports that Aristy was the real rebel leader and that Caamaño was something of a front. Other reports, including those of Martin, suggested the possibility, based on his reluctance to make decisions on his own, that he was not a "free agent," but took orders from the Communists. One U. S. Embassy official said that he suspected that Aristy "might be a deep-cover Communist."

Other observers, however, including some representing the OAS, saw nothing sinister in the Caamaño-Aristy relationship. Caamaño was a military man who, though intelligent, knew little about politics. He had not joined the rebel movement as a politician, but as a soldier. But suddenly, because of the political vacuum and the need for a strong individual to fill it, he was thrust into political leadership. He needed advice and coaching on how to commit himself on political issues from experienced politicians.

Some of his advisers were leaders of Bosch's PRD party. A PRD liaison official occupied an office at his headquarters, and one PRD leader, Peña Gómez, even slept in a bedroom there. On one occasion, I saw and spoke with as many as eight PRD officials at the headquarters. Among the PRD people whom I often observed were senators and deputies, and I also noted some UCN congressmen as well. Whether Communists were among the people at the headquarters I couldn't be sure.

But Aristy was the man Caamaño appeared to listen to most closely, and it can at least be said for him that he had joined the constitutionalist movement, as indicated earlier, as soon as Bosch had been overthrown. Whether Caamaño was taking orders from Aristy is a matter of speculation, though the likelihood is not very great.

It is known that on some occasions when Caamaño had a definite view he ignored the advice of Aristy or other advisers. In negotiations with the OAS on the withdrawal of most junta troops from the National Palace, Aristy said the rebels would not agree to a proposal for a retreat by rebel forces from the immediate area. Caamaño, however, after being convinced that such a retreat was logical, agreed despite Aristy's opposition. And as he learned the political ropes, many people who dealt with him noted that he was becoming less dependent on Aristy and other people around him for advice. But, of course, he was not a completely free agent. Like every leader, he had to take into account the wishes of his followers. Not being a completely free agent, however, did not necessarily mean that he was a prisoner of the Communists or any other person or group, as was sometimes charged.

Be that as it may, Aristy seemed to be top adviser, and for political shrewdness and drive, Caamaño could not have picked a more effective adviser, as his turbulent career clearly shows. Born in 1933, as was Caamaño, Aristy, who comes from a wealthy, well-known family, claims to have run into trouble with Trujillo in his teens. While still in high school, he says, he joined in a demonstration against the dictator. The high school was closed, and Trujillo sent for him and other demonstrators to try to persuade them that he was really an enlightened leader after all. A short time later, he and some cousins and friends tried to take over a police post in his native town of Azua, and ended up in jail for 20 days.

Aristy attributes the lightness of the punishment to the fact that two other cousins were in Trujillo's government—one as Labor Secretary, and another as Chief Justice. But at the age of seventeen, he was exiled to Puerto Rico by the dictator. He spent the next nine years studying political science and economics in the United States, Latin America, and Europe. He also worked for a while as a stockbroker in New York and Washington. In Washington, he met a valuable contact—Robert (Bobby) Baker, the now-famous congressional aide—whose help he solicited, Aristy says, in trying to get the support of U. S. congressmen for anti-Trujillo measures.

When Trujillo was assassinated in 1961, Aristy returned as the head of a small strongly nationalist group called the National Revolutionary Front. This group agitated against Ramfis Trujillo, who had taken over power, with Aristy shouting to crowds to end Trujilloism. Enemies of Aristy dispute that he really opposed Ramfis, claiming that he had been a secret Trujillo agent abroad and that Ramfis had actually brought him back to use him for his own political purposes, that is, to offer the impression that there was really democracy in the Dominican Republic. This charge, however, is denied by Aristy and has not been proved.

After one demonstration in September 1961, Aristy's followers fought with police at Duarte Bridge for over four hours. Two persons were killed and 87 wounded. His group then moved to his headquarters in town, and he boomed over a loudspeaker to a crowd of thousands that "freedom has never conquered without blood. We shall finish off Trujillo's soldiers." The police destroyed the headquarters, and Aristy was forced to leave the country for two months, returning in November after the Trujillo family had fled.

Aristy immediately began to rebuild a political base. He organized in the south a "private social organization" called the Southern Socio-Economic Union, which he claims was a nonpolitical group he set up to improve economic and social conditions in the area. Political enemies, however, including Rafael Bonnelly, charged that the group was far-leftist, an accusation denied by Aristy. In any event, the organization had become so influential that Bonnelly later offered him a job in the Council of State government. He turned down the first offer, the position of Secretary of Recuperation, which dealt with the disposition of the Trujillo properties, because the Council wouldn't meet his conditions. But he finally agreed to be Undersecretary of Agriculture. He resigned soon afterward, he says, when he felt that Council members were involved in corrupt practices within his ministry.

After the election of Bosch, Aristy, who had made many contacts with businessmen during his stay in the United States,

brought some of them to the Dominican Republic in the hope
of getting them to invest there. He says that the arrangement
was that he would share in any joint enterprises that might be
set up. One wealthy friend, an oil man from Indiana, he says,
lent him $200,000 to set up a joint tractor business.

When Bosch was thrown out, Aristy maintains, "I was angry.
After returning from nine years in exile, I appreciated democracy under Bosch. I decided to fight to get him back." It was
then that he became involved in a plot with dissident Army
officers.

After his original plot failed and he refused to leave the
country as advised by the Triumverate government, he joined
a new political party formed by Amiama Tio, Imbert's surviving partner in the assassination of Trujillo. "They needed an
experienced politician with a big following," he explains. Although the party was basically rightist, Aristy wrote a "liberal"
charter, and in such a way, he says, that the rightist leaders
could not control the party. After a struggle over the charter
at the party convention, Aristy won out.

On April 17, 1965, several days before the revolution broke,
Aristy charged at a national party convention that Reid Cabral
intended to hold on to power. He shouted that there must be
a return to constitutionalism.

"I was the first person to say so openly," Aristy says. "And
the day the revolution started, I joined Caamaño and the military group carrying out the revolt."

Is Aristy an opportunist, or perhaps a secret Communist, as
some American officials suspect? No one knows what is in a
man's mind. He may well be an opportunist in the narrow
political sense, as most politicians, not excluding Latin Americans, are, having moved from party to party. But whether he
is an opportunist in the larger sense where principle is concerned is less certain. Would such an opportunist have strug-
gled so doggedly for what looked at the time like a lost cause,

or would he have tried to curry the favor of those with power? As for his possibly being a secret Communist, so could almost any Dominican politician. If one must judge tentatively on the basis of the evidence at hand, there is none that has linked him with far-leftist causes.

Caamaño and Aristy differ in many respects. One is basically a simple, patriotic soldier, if possessed of an intense, explosive character. The other is a complex personality, an "operator," with personal ambition and a hungry ego. But the two men appear to be linked by a common compulsion to rebellion. And whatever their side interests may be, they seem to believe in the rebellion that they have led for restoration of constitutional government.

One of the most remarkable aspects of covering the crisis in Santo Domingo, a city of 460,000 people, was the process of moving from one zone to the next with seemingly nothing in common between them. Junta headquarters was located in the Congressional Palace, a gaudily luxurious building at the Fair Grounds, the site of a lavish fair held by Trujillo in the late 1950's. It was the favorite destination of our taxi drivers, who implored us to visit the U. S. military post exchange just across the street and buy them items unobtainable elsewhere. I spent considerable time roaming through the PX, past rifle-bearing marines and soldiers in full battle dress, looking for men's shirts and women's underwear (for the cabbies' wives) amid the luxury of Parisian perfumes, Swiss watches, and brocaded silks.

Inside the palace, well, it looked like a palace—broad winding staircases, marble pillars, polished floors. And the people we saw looked polished, too. Military guards cradling sub-machine guns in their arms wore neat, khaki uniforms, and ties, and were close-shaven. Civilian administrators rushing through the corridors and hangers-on slouching in chairs looked like Madison Avenue types, with their pressed, well-cut suits, starched collars, and shiny pointed shoes. General Imbert, when he showed himself, wore a perfect-fitting tan uniform complete with a blinding array of ribbons and yards of gold braid.

The atmosphere spoke elegantly of the makeup of Imbert's civilian following. He represented the upper classes. Yet, only because these classes had no choice. The rebels, in their eyes, were still Communist riffraff out to destroy them. But they had no love for the armed forces that supported Imbert, either, nor for Imbert as an individual. The bitterness that the UCN, to which most of them belonged, had displayed in the 1962 electoral campaign toward the armed forces has not been dissipated despite the need to collaborate with them in the struggle against the lower-class rebels. The military leaders were still the Trujillo-trained generals and colonels who had protected the Trujillo family's economic monopoly for so many years. They were still corrupt and power-hungry, making millions on the blacket market at the expense of civilian businessmen.

Imbert, they well realized, was entirely dependent on these generals and colonels for his political existence. But aside from that, they distrusted him. Not because he was said to play around with the Communists. A good conservative could deal with the Communists for tactical purposes and not lose anything. But they saw Imbert as a power-hungry man with the ambitions of a Trujillo. He wasn't the kind of person one could safely collaborate with in economic matters. And many saw him as no less corrupt than the real militarists.

"I don't know why the Americans picked Imbert to run the government when there are so many good civilians they could have picked from," a business executive commented to me over beer on the veranda of Hotel Embajador.

Nevertheless, such Dominicans were by no means about to abandon Imbert. To them, Imbert represented "democracy" just as the rebels represented "communism." In other words, almost any government right of center, except for the Trujilloite extreme, was regarded as democratic, since it represented the status quo, and almost any regime with a program of social reform, meaning nearly any group left of center, was "Communist," because it threatened their economic and political power.

"This is a struggle between democracy and communism," said one upper-class housewife I met in San Francisco de Macorís, typically. Then, she frankly explained what she meant. "This is really a class war, you know. Bosch started it by stirring up one class against the other. The armed forces need a good cleaning out, but they're only running things on a transitory basis. Eventually there will be elections."

"Very soon?"

"I hope not," she replied. "Of course, I believe in elections. But the fact that a man like Bosch can be elected shows that the people are not ready for such responsibility. We'll just have to have democracy without elections for a while."

Similarly, Reid Cabral, after his ouster from power, advised against holding elections soon in view of the "Communist" influence.

It was always a shock to move from the world of the status quo to the other world, the rebel world, the world of Caamaño, Aristy, and—Diego Guerra. Dressed in a green and brown speckled sports shirt and khaki trousers cut off at the thighs, Diego Guerra sat in a rocking chair and barked orders to one of his lieutenants who was standing by the small table he used as a desk.

"Go out and tell that sniper to stop shooting at the helicopter. He's scaring hell out of the OAS people."

Guerra, civilian assistant to Colonel Manuel Montás Arache, a strong anti-Communist who had commanded the elite "frogmen" commandos and, as rebel Minister of Defense, now ran military operations in Santo Domingo, was referring to a U. S. marine helicopter hovering nearby as members of the OAS peace team discussed cease-fire terms with rebel leaders a few blocks away.

Shortly, the sniper fire ended.

"You see," said Guerra, "we're pretty much in control of the situation here."

Guerra, a powerfully built man with a shock of black hair and a round, handsome face, was one of thousands of civilians-turned-soldier supporting Bosch. Owner of an auto parts supply firm, Guerra voted in the 1962 election for the UCN. Why, then, did he now support the left-of-center pro-Bosch movement?

"As a businessman I have one outlook," he replied, "but as a Dominican citizen and patriot I have another. I joined the Bosch forces because he was elected the constitutional President. Either we have democracy or we don't."

A young, unshaven aide dressed in a khaki shirt and blue jeans interrupted. "We are fighting now but we hate to fight. And the only way to guarantee peace in the future is to have constitutional government. We don't want any more coups or de facto governments."

In the rebel-held areas I visited, Bosch's name was not as visually evident as the word "constitution." PRESERVE THE CONSTITUTION, FIGHT FOR THE CONSTITUTION, DIE FOR THE CONSTITUTION, screamed the slogans scrawled in all colors on walls, telephone booths, cars, and sidewalks.

Reporters, if they were willing to risk it, had little difficulty entering rebel-held areas, where the poor and the lower middle class live. At the log-barricaded entrances to the rebel section, mere verbal identification was sufficient to get by the rifle-carrying guard. Immediately, the city took on the look—and smell—of siege. In the center of almost every intersection, uncollected garbage was piled high. Sometimes it was burned; sometimes not.

Jeeps and small trucks loaded with soldiers and rifle-bearing civilians, and screaming the painted word PUEBLO, meaning "the people," on their hoods, sped along the narrow streets between lines of old, gaily colored colonial houses with balconies and large shuttered windows from which sullen-faced women peered as if searching for the sleepy, peaceful world they had known.

In the first weeks of the revolt, at least, the shops were all shut, and dirty, rubbish-strewn sidewalks were frequented mainly by young men dressed in varying combinations of military and civilian clothing—virtually all of them armed. When I got out of my car to take some pictures, people suddenly materialized from nowhere.

"We will never give up," they yelled time and again.

That is the spirit that seemed to propel Diego Guerra. His headquarters was located in a long, narrow street-floor bakery that temporarily had gone out of business. Along the cement wall and concrete floor were stacked dozens of rifles, gas masks, Red Cross flags (which the enemy charged were used by rebels to carry arms), and wooden stools for visitors. Sacks of flour were stored in a corner, a reminder of the days of normalcy. At the rear, two women were preparing a lunch of beans and rice over a small stove.

Guerra called in four young prisoners his forces had captured. They were armed with rifles. "They want to fight with us and we trust them," he said as several shots in the distance rang out. "We trust the people. That's the difference between us and our enemies."

If the contrast between the two Dominican headquarters was startling, so was that between two Americans who attached themselves to the respective causes, each with the public relations job of trying to convince reporters that the cause he was supporting was right and just. Working for Imbert was Francisco Cardona, a slim, dour-expressioned, pompadoured Puerto Rican public relations expert with a serious, sincere, highly persuasive manner. He fully lived up to the clotheshorse standards set by his superiors. I never saw him with an unpressed suit or without a tie, even in the Hotel Embajador where he lived and where sports shirts were the rule. And he was efficient, too. He

held a press conference almost every day, announcing each one
in advance on a notice pinned up in the lobby of the hotel.
He also came up with some good public relations ideas.
Several times he invited the press to attend Imbert rallies in
distant towns, promising them tours of historical sites and free
lunches. Usually, however, he found few takers as the reporters
suspected that the intention was to shanghai them so that they
would not be around to report on some attack or other operation
that Imbert might have had in mind. He suffered his greatest
embarrassment when Imbert's police at International Airport
refused to permit several arriving reporters to leave the airport,
making them continue on to the next stop. It was all a big
mistake, he assured us. Actually, Imbert loved reporters. He
needed them to tell the truth about what was going on.

Often I would observe Cardona sitting alone in the hotel
restaurant looking in his lonely way out on the veranda, his
chin resting on his hand, his eyes peering off into the distance,
his face expressionless. He would seem oblivious to the noise
and conversation around him, looking up only occasionally
when he saw a reporter he knew to smile an unhappy smile.
No one could tell whether he liked his job, but certainly it was
clear that it was a difficult one.

His counterpart on the rebel side was William Bailes, an ad-
venturous thirty-four-year-old Miami airline pilot with a sturdy,
short build and uncut wavy brown hair that usually tumbled
into his quizzical blue eyes. He invariably wore old baggy trousers, a misfitting sports coat, and a shirt open at the neck. He
looked like a beachcomber. In his closet-sized office at Caamaño's
headquarters, he spoke to reporters with the enthusiasm of a
young lawyer going all-out to convince the jury that his client
was right.

In one effort to gain reportorial sympathy he had a baby who
had been killed in a junta strafing raid brought to headquarters,
and suggested that reporters see for themselves the horrors being
committed by the enemy. Several of us showed no inclination

to do so, having viewed enough corpses, and we explained that we believed him when he said the baby had been killed. He, and the Dominicans around him, seemed hurt and even angry that we would not bother to see for ourselves.

Why was Bill Bailes working for the rebels? Because, he said, "I happen to believe in their cause. My wife calls me an idealist, a crusader. Well, maybe I am. But I've got to fight for what I think is right. All that stuff about communism is hogwash. If Communists were running this thing, I wouldn't be here. I simply want to help make this place safe for capitalism."

And Bailes' background would indicate that he at least has a nose for business. After spending four years in the Navy, he went to work as a hydraulics technician for the West Virginia Air National Guard, learning to fly, meanwhile, under the G.I. Bill of Rights. Once getting his commercial pilot's license, he joined Eastern Airlines in 1957 as a co-pilot, taking odd jobs as a piano player between flights. In 1958, he went into the construction business, then became chief pilot of a small airline company in the British West Indies.

In 1962, he set up a small airline in the Dominican Republic for a Miami Beach lawyer. He liked the country and decided to stay, getting a job as assistant manager of the national Dominicana Airlines under the Bosch regime. Meanwhile, he opened up a travel agency with a Dominican partner. He quit the airline job when Bosch was ousted, went to Miami, and became general manager of the Miami Aviation Corporation. When the revolution broke out, he headed for Santo Domingo again, this time to help the rebels, leaving his wife and seven children in Miami.

"What I'm trying to do," Bailes told me, "is to help spread the kind of government we have in the States to this country. A lot of the people at the Embassy don't like me, but that's too bad."

One evening Bailes took two other reporters and me to the home of his travel agency partner to spend the night so that we could learn how it felt to sleep in the middle of a firing range. Valentín Menaldo's house was located in Ciudad Nueva only two blocks from an American marine checkpoint leading to the International Security Zone. Almost nightly, rebel snipers in the area and the marines had exchanged heavy fire, with many of the bullets whizzing past Valentín's white, Spanish-colonial house.

Our visit was on a rather untypical night. I was awakened only five times by bursts of machine-gun fire nearby. Valentín, though he had been unable to accommodate us with a saturation bombardment, was a gracious host, as was his wife, María. The previous evening he had managed to obtain a valuable bottle of rum from a friend to celebrate our visit. And dinner, which consisted of salad and rice, had been deliciously prepared. We ate by candlelight since bullets had cut electric wires. So immersed in conversation were we that we hardly noticed when shots rang out down the block, though once Valentín, without missing a phrase, walked to the open door and shut it, as if seeking to stop stray bullets with a slab of wood.

A short, stocky Negro, Valentín was a rebel through and through. He spoke angrily about what he described as American intervention on the side of the militarists. He spoke lovingly about what the 1963 Constitution meant to him—freedom, dignity, eventual prosperity. He spoke hopefully about the chances of a constitutional victory.

"What about communism?" I asked.

"What about it?" he replied. "Could I ever have achieved what I have under communism?"

Certainly Valentín had achieved a lot. Two years before, he earned $15 a month as a clerk. He, his wife, and his little girl lived in a tiny wooden house with a tin roof. Then, with the help of Bill Bailes, he opened the travel agency, and, before the revolution, was earning about $600 a month. He lives in a comfortable home.

When the revolt broke out, Valentín went around picking

up the guns of policemen who had been shot on the street and redistributing the arms to rebel civilians. He participated in the bitter fighting against the Wessin forces when they were trying to move tanks across Duarte Bridge, and delivered messages from one rebel command headquarters to another.

"I learned what it felt like to be free under Juan Bosch," Valentín said. "I want the security of freedom for my child and for my business."

After dinner that evening of arrival, in a burst of courage we stood by the front door and gazed upon a dead city revealed dimly only by pale moonlight. An evening curfew imposed by the rebel command banned the appearance of anyone on the streets of the area. But in the distance under a palm tree in Parque Enriquillo, which was adjacent to Valentín's house, we saw the shadows of several people, youths who had defied the curfew. Two rebel policemen were leading them away. The youths could be heard arguing—then complete silence again, until several shots pierced the thick night air.

At bedtime, I suggested that I sleep on the sofa in the living room, but Valentín vetoed the idea. That part of the house was too exposed to gunfire, he said. He insisted that two of us sleep in his bed, and another on a cot that he set up in the small kitchen. He, his wife, and little girl, he said, would sleep on the floor. They were used to it from poorer days, he explained. Bill, who temporarily lived with the family, slept on a wooden chest.

We finally agreed after considerable argument, sleeping soundly between machine-gun bursts that seemed to explode right over our heads. Valentín slept soundly, too, a tommy gun at his side.

Dawn broke silently. The deserted streets were littered with rubbish scattered by the wind from pyramids heaped against the curbs. A woman wearing hair curlers made of cardboard toilet-paper rolls pushed open a panel of her large green door and poked her head out. From around a nearby corner came

another sign of human life—a man in ragged clothes carrying
a large basket. The woman bought several hard rolls from him
and then closed the panel. Other doors creaked open along the
narrow street of colorful wooden houses, and from them
emerged several women dressed in formless cotton dresses,
sandals, and kerchiefs around the head, carrying buckets to
the garbage piles.

Valentín said to me apologetically as he opened his door.
"I'm sorry the night was so quiet. It usually isn't, you know."

CHAPTER 9

The Babies Didn't Cry

UNITED STATES officials vehemently claimed from the first moment the marines landed that American troops were "neutral" in the civil war. In practice, however, neutrality was a myth and could not help being so.

For one thing, Washington had made a policy decision even before the troop landings that the Embassy should push for the establishment of a military junta. This decision automatically precluded neutrality since it coincided with the aim of the Wessin-Imbert forces but clashed with that of the rebels.

For another thing, one of the stated purposes of the landings was to prevent what Washington considered the Communist-controlled or dominated rebel movement from taking over the country. Could the United States logically be neutral between such a movement and an anti-Communism opposition group?

The United States remained neutral, it seems, only in the sense that, while it helped the junta keep the revolution under control, it did not want to leave the country, at least permanently, in the hands of the militarists, but favored a coalition of moderate leaders.

Actually, the very fact that U. S. troops took over territory controlled by the rebels was a violation of neutralism. For such moves obviously were to the junta's advantage. This was particularly true of the establishment by U. S. forces on May 2 of a corridor running through rebel lines to the Ozama River to secure communications between the International Safety Zone and San Isidro Air Base. The corridor divided the rebel forces in two, compacting a part in the one square mile of Ciudad Nueva.

Nor did military commanders necessarily tell their troops what military public information officers told reporters at the daily news conferences at Hotel Embajador. As far as many commanders were concerned, the rebel movement itself, not just the leadership, was Communist. It was simpler to fight a war that way, and it often seemed that in the military's eyes the United States was involved in a war.

At least one gathered this from the May 7 issue of the mimeographed newsletter, *U. S. Land Forces News,* which described itself as "an authorized daily publication," though "views and opinions expressed are not necessarily those of the Department of the Army." On the front page of the issue, a message from Lt. General Bruce Palmer, commander of U. S. forces in the Dominican Republic, to his troops referred to "the revolution ... between the Communists and the government of the Dominican Republic. ..." Yet the Administration had never claimed that one side was composed only of Communists, nor had it officially recognized either force as a government.

General Palmer also congratulated "each of you for your extremely fine combat performance. ... Continue to fight as well as you have. ..." This advice appeared to indicate that the troops had come to "fight" rather than to maintain peace, again contrary to the stated policy of the Administration.

When I asked the general about these statements, he declared that they simply reflected what President Johnson had said. Later, when he was asked about them at a press conference attended by Undersecretary of Defense Cyrus K. Vance, he denied, with obvious discomfort, ever having made such statements. Embassy officials were highly embarrassed by the "message to the troops," which they said did not reflect U. S. policy. They would try, they said, to improve the coordination of military and diplomatic information programs.

But U. S. troops understandably remained under the clear impression that the junta troops were their friends and the rebel troops Communist enemies. Typical of the sentiments of many U. S. servicemen was the remark of one paratroop lieutenant who said he couldn't understand why the United States doesn't "starve those commies out," referring to the rebel-controlled section of the city.

American officials attributed this attitude to the fact that it was the rebels who were sniping at the U. S. troops, and that naturally a soldier regards as the enemy someone who shoots at him. The rebels replied that the attitude of the United States when it intervened in the Dominican Republic, one of hostility toward them and of friendship toward the junta forces—as expressed so succinctly in General Palmer's message to his troops —could hardly have produced a warm greeting from their side.

Nevertheless, with the marines and paratroopers exposed to sniper fire from almost any window or rooftop, their discipline in holding fire until the last moment was admirable, and their edginess was understandable, even if sometimes frightening, for American civilians as well as Dominicans. Troops halted and searched pedestrians and cars moving in and out of the International Safety Zone with nervous devotion. It was particularly rattling during the first weeks of the revolution when one approached the Hotel Embajador at night. Headlights had to be turned out as the approach was made, and the driver, as he barely crawled along in the darkness, knew it was time to stop for identification only when a voice from nowhere quietly said, "Halt."

At one checkpoint, my car had been given clearance by a marine, but another, who didn't know it, stuck his pistol into the vehicle as I started to drive off, and might have pulled the trigger if I hadn't slammed on the brakes.

I was luckier than two of my colleagues, reporter Al Burt and photographer Douglas Kennedy of the Miami *Herald.* One day they were waiting in a taxi at a checkpoint to be passed through when their driver, panicked by the sight of a marine pointing a sub-machine gun at him, put his car in reverse in an effort to turn around. The marines panicked themselves and opened up on the taxi, seriously wounding the two newsmen, who were immediately flown to the *Boxer* for life-saving operations.

The shooting of Burt, a short, highly able, quietly aggressive reporter, had a particularly chilling effect on me since he and I together had barely escaped from a similar situation two years previously in Port-au-Prince, Haiti. At that time, a conflict had broken out between the Bosch regime, which was then in power in the Dominican Republic, and the iron-fisted Haitian government of President François Duvalier, with Bosch threatening to attack. The Kennedy Administration, meanwhile, sent warships offshore and tried to pressure Duvalier out of power.

With tension rising in Port-au-Prince, Burt and I, in a rented car, were reconnoitering the city one night when suddenly our headlights held in their glow the image of a Haitian militiaman aiming a rifle directly at us. Burt, who was driving, slammed on the brakes and we came to a dead stop, but the militiaman continued to aim at us, without saying a word. In desperation, we decided to move backward slowly in the hope that he wouldn't shoot—even though the gears of the car were defective and we were never quite sure whether the car would go forward or backward. Knowing that a lurch forward could be fatal, we held our breaths as Burt slowly depressed the accelerator. To our indescribable relief, we edged backward. Finally, we turned around and headed back toward our hotel.

We lost our way, however, and blundered into the most sensitive area of all—the palace grounds, where Duvalier sat waiting for Dominican bombs to fall. Suddenly, millions of volts of light beat down upon us from searchlights located in the palace, atop the palace, and elsewhere in the area. In the blinding glare, we saw flashing caricatures of humanity on all sides waving rifles, urging us on, yelling "Halt." We stopped and got out of the car, and were immediately surrounded by scores of Duvalier's militiamen and Ton Ton Macoutes, his so-called "bogeymen" who are reputed for the delight they take in torturing and hacking to pieces suspected enemies of the dictator.

They began pushing us around, poking us with rifles, brandishing machetes, and searching us. They were in an ugly mood, and I envisioned myself nailed to a wall as had been the fate of some of Duvalier's victims. Suddenly Burt pulled a card out of his wallet and waved it at our captors. "President Duvalier gave me this," he yelled. On one side of the card was a calendar, on the other side a photograph of Duvalier. "We are honorary members of the Ton Ton Macoute."

The men lowered their rifles and machetes, and studied the photo. While they looked, I prayed. Then, instead of being pushed, we were being slapped—on the back. "They are with us," one of them cried. And we were suddenly heroes. We were guided back to our hotel by a whole convoy of militia trucks. Burt had probably saved our lives. And so it was ironic and somehow deeply foreboding that he should finally be shot under similar circumstances—by U. S. marines.

Popular resentment toward the United States because of its "unneutral" stand was only eased by two elements of American policy that did reflect genuine neutrality—Peace Corps activities and food distribution. Most of the 108 Peace Corps members, in an incredible display of courage, remained among the poor in Santo Domingo's rebel zone and in other towns and villages throughout the country, as did those mentioned earlier in the book, despite rebel anti-American bitterness and the physical danger involved.

Peace Corps nurses, in the true Florence Nightingale tradition, worked night and day in the rebel hospitals in the midst

of bloodshed and bombing helping Dominican doctors to operate on hundreds of wounded, sometimes on the floor and often
in the glare of candles which they held when kerosene for the
lamps that substituted for electricity ran out. They participated
in surgery done without medicine, anesthetics, or oxygen,
quietly enduring the screams of agony.

They ignored the taunts of rebels who cried "Go home
Yankee," as well as those of U. S. troops who called them "Com-
mie lovers." The rebels couldn't understand why they stayed
despite the insults and the anti-Americanism. "It is very
strange," said a young rebel to a Peace Corps nurse after she
had treated his wound. "You care for us so we can go out and
shoot your people."

The situation became so dangerous that Robert Satin, the
youthful Peace Corps director in the country, ordered the girls
to leave the hospitals. Miss Virginia Pearson, twenty-five, of
Portsmouth, Virginia, a dark-haired, vivacious registered nurse,
recalled:

"We said we wanted to stay. We went to another hospital
and finally the Peace Corps said, 'All right, stay.' We were gone
only about half an hour, and when we came back the doctors
kissed us and the four nuns kissed us and patients got up and
embraced us."

Pausing for a moment to hold back tears, she added: "These
are our people."

Other Peace Corps volunteers whose efforts to get the people
electric power, water, and sewerage service were interrupted
by the war, sullenly remained in Hotel Embajador waiting to
return to their work.

"There are people in my barrios who love me, who would
die for me," explained Roberta Warren, twenty-five, of Win-
dom, Minnesota.

Peace Corps Director Satin himself is the one U. S. official
the rebels fully trust. A good-looking, dark-haired young man
who could invariably be recognized by the broad-brimmed

straw hat that he wore, he sometimes even attended news conferences at Caamaño's headquarters. Once, when he went there, he happened to see two captured marines leaning against a wall in the courtyard and persuaded rebel leaders to let them go.

The U. S. distribution of food to all hungry people was another major factor in keeping alive the image of an Uncle Sam who could be generous and humanitarian.

"I hate to see Yankee soldiers in my country," a housewife told me as she waited in an endless line of women queued up on a sidewalk in Santo Domingo to be ladled out some rice and beans by U. S. troops in full battle dress. "But Americans do have a big heart."

Even before the revolution, the United States distributed through various relief agencies about five million pounds of free food a month, valued at $350,000, to the Dominicans, made available under the PL-480 surplus food program. With the economy ravaged by the revolt, the amount of food contributed tripled. Thus, more than $1 million worth of U. S. food was distributed to more than two million people—the population is only 3.5 million—in the month of May.

This sudden massive influx of food, mainly rice and oil, but also powdered milk, beans, cornmeal, and flour, strained distribution facilities almost to the point of chaos in some cases, though this situation gradually improved. In no city was the strain greater than in San Francisco de Macorís, a northern town of 40,000 people, most of them, according to American residents, frustrated and embittered by the failure of the revolution to restore the 1963 Constitution that they felt was their only guarantee of freedom and prosperity.

Actually, trouble there began a few days after the outbreak of the revolution before the U. S. emergency food relief program got under way. Food was being distributed at four places—a Roman Catholic Church, a CARE warehouse, and two schools, when gangs of hoodlums, called "tigers," pushed aside the people waiting to be served and carried off virtually the whole food supply. These gangs had seized some food in previous months, but never before so brazenly and on such a scale. About mid-May, while food was again being distributed at the CARE warehouse, a new riot erupted when mobs showed up. In the melee, one woman was killed and another injured. At the same time, the priest of the Catholic church became so frightened that he refused to receive a truckload of oil that was delivered to him for distribution shortly afterward.

Similar incidents occurred in other towns. In Baní, on the southeast coast, for example, a gang made away with a whole truckload of food as a priest was about to distribute it. When a second truck arrived, "tigers" attacked it but it was able to speed off to the next town, its load intact.

This situation, however, began to improve when the U. S. Embassy in Santo Domingo on May 19 sent three- or four-man food teams to nine central provincial towns, including San Francisco de Macorís, to organize effective mass distribution systems. With the local charity groups in a state of shock and disorder, the team in San Francisco formed, as did other teams elsewhere, a committee of leading citizens to help them in their task. With the aid of this committee, a census of the most needy families was taken that indicated a need for feeding about 5,000 people.

Truckloads of food were then distributed on a door-to-door basis in accordance with the specified list. This new system was not entirely successful, since "tigers" clambered on the trucks as they made their way down the block. However, when the situation started to get out of hand, the truck began heading for another section of town.

"It's hard to finish a whole block at a time," an American distribution official in San Francisco said.

Even so, large numbers of policemen started guarding food distribution sites throughout the country, and some accompanied the trucks; though, when the crowds got too large, they were reluctant to prevent vandalism.

The vandals were not generally regarded as hungry people stealing food to keep alive, but disgruntled young men who were taking advantage of the revolutionary atmosphere to profit financially from the food influx. About 10 percent of American food contributions were being sold by Dominicans who received such food free, U. S. sources told me. But most of this amount, they added, was sold by people who obtained the food legitimately, the raiding mobs having gotten away with only a minute proportion of the total food contribution.

"Their main effect has been," one U. S. official said, "to disrupt the food distribution system in some areas."

Such officials actually did not seem overly perturbed by the sale of some food by Dominican recipients, arguing that with little money in circulation, food, to a limited extent, could serve as a useful instrument of exchange. The extension of the food distribution program to areas distant from the main centers, which started in June, it was hoped, would reduce gang onslaughts on food shipments arriving in these centers. For it was believed that many of the raiders came from outlying villages and might stay there if food were distributed to them in a normal manner.

In any event, with the Dominican economy picking up, the ration system based on censuses of needy families was instituted throughout the country, reducing the number of people receiving free food to about 500,000. In Santo Domingo, U. S. troops, in June, were no longer ladling out food on the streets, but at central distribution points. But whatever the problems of the U. S. food program, it was a major factor in making the presence of American troops bearable, if not, to some extent, desirable, despite a general distaste for the U. S. attitude toward the revolution.

Aside from the question of "Communist control," the principal point of conflict between reporters and U. S. officials lay in the issue of "neutrality." At the news conferences, military information specialists constantly proclaimed the United States neutral. Just as constant were questions put by reporters who had seen with their own eyes instances of collaboration between these troops and junta soldiers.

We pointed out, for example, that at almost any checkpoint in the International Safety Zone U. S. troops and junta troops could be seen searching people and cars jointly. In fact, there was one jointly manned checkpoint in front of the hotel. Yet a military spokesman stated, "As far as I know there is no such situation." Finally, after we insisted he check further, he told us the following day that the junta "soldiers" we saw were in reality policemen who dressed in soldiers' uniforms so that rebel snipers would be less likely to shoot at them in view of the rebels' presumed special hatred for policemen.

Reporters then went to various checkpoints, got into conversations with the "policemen," and asked them about their military status and who their boss was. In every case, it appeared, the "policeman" would say that he was in the Army and that his boss was Wessin. When I asked one what his mission was, he replied: "To help the Americans make sure that no Communists come through here."

U. S. officials, moreover, insisted for two days that they didn't have any information about reports that U. S. troops had taken rebel prisoners and turned them over to the junta forces. One major said he hadn't been able to find out. Apparently nobody would tell him that the 82nd Airborne Division had done exactly that. This fact came out only after the most bitter questioning.

It was also denied that armed junta forces were being permitted to cross the International Safety Zone whereas the rebels were not. Undersecretary Vance, at a press conference, was particularly adamant about this. When a television reporter said that his crew had shot film of trucks loaded with armed junta soldiers crossing into the zone, the reply was that there may have been isolated instances of this, but that such permission had been granted against orders. But to many reporters, including myself, observance of such crossings had been commonplace.

U. S. spokesmen had an especially bad time after they had assured reporters that the United States had no intention of widening the military corridor across the city. When paratroopers, having missed the news conference, went ahead and occupied dozens of new blocks anyway, an Army major sheepishly announced, as if the assurances had never been made, that the extension had taken place.

Furthermore, he said in answer to a question, the United States, in occupying the new area by force, did not violate the cease-fire agreement that had been signed between the junta and rebel forces since the United States had not been a signatory. But did the rebels violate the agreement when they shot at the U. S. troops? Yes, officials said. They had signed the agreement.

If U. S. troops had, in fact, acted in a neutral manner, if their disposition had been decided by negotiation rather than by force, if collaboration with either side had been avoided, the U. S. occupation would probably have been greeted with a minimum of resentment. Even some rebels were at first glad to see the arrival of the troops, figuring that they represented a guarantee against an ultimate victory by the militarists. But the United States' open collaboration with the junta troops overnight turned untold thousands of Dominicans who had been friendly to the United States into bitter foes of this country. For the United States had clearly identified itself, however reluctantly, with the hated military forces. It had become, in the eyes of many people, their enemy.

This bitterness was most dramatically exhibited whenever U. S. troops would accidentally enter the rebel zone. Some of them were not just taken prisoner. They were shot down. One unhappy story I wrote started like this:

"Cha-cha music emanated gaily from a distant shuttered window, carried by a gentle morning breeze. A child's laughter drifted from another window. And in an alley, a U. S. marine lay dead, his lips frozen in a faint smile."

This marine was one of seven who, in two vehicles, had blundered into rebel territory from the International Safety Zone. A volley of fire greeting them killed three and wounded two. The remaining two were captured unhurt.

I had just arrived in the rebel zone when I saw more than a dozen men darting across an adjacent street firing as they ran. I drew up to the curb and asked a rebel soldier guarding a corner what was happening.

"We've got some gringos," the soldier replied grimly.

It suddenly struck me that I was a "gringo," and it was only with reluctance that I continued on toward the scene of the shooting.

When I arrived there, the tragedy had reached its climax, symbolized by an abandoned jeep in the middle of the narrow street outside the telephone exchange building. Several bullet holes marred the windshield, and all the tires were flat. Several rebels, noting that I was a reporter, called me over to an alley about 20 yards away. And there in the alley, in front of the marines' second vehicle, a quarter-ton truck, lay the body of the smiling marine, his face yellow except for the bloodstain on one cheek where a bullet had apparently entered.

About twenty spectators, most of them armed with rifles and dressed in a combination of military and civilian garments, gazed silently at the corpse, as if trying to comprehend the meaning of this stranger's death.

I then drove to the hospital, a few blocks away, where the other marine casualties had been taken in a rebel truck. I was met at the entrance by a rifle-bearing rebel in fatigues who led me up one flight of stairs to a small room, and I was ushered in by a nun dressed in white. A marine in full uniform, his face smudged with dirt, lay on an operating table, blood on the sole of one foot and on the back of his head.

"He isn't too badly injured," the nun said. "A bullet grazed his head and another broke a bone in his leg, but he'll be all right."

The marine, who had just been given a shot of morphine to relieve his pain, opened his brown eyes slightly, stared blankly at me for a moment, and breathed out hesitantly, "I feel terrible. Do something for me, will you?"

I reassured him that he would be all right, and followed the nun into an adjoining room where another wounded marine lay on an operating table, also in full uniform. But his fatigue shirt had been pulled up and as he lay on his side writhing and moaning in pain, bullet holes in his stomach and back were clearly visible, the missile having passed through his body.

A doctor in a white smock entered and said, "This one is seriously wounded."

"Are you going to operate?" I asked.

"He said he doesn't want me to," the doctor replied sympathetically. "He wants to wait until he gets to the American hospital. To operate on him without his permission we'd have to have approval from the American authorities."

"Can the operation wait?"

"I think so," he said.

Later, I heard, the marine had died during an operation on the *Boxer*.

The doctor then led me down to the ground floor into a room where a dead marine lay on a table. His clothes were ripped open and the area around his stomach was stained with blood. In an adjoining room lay another body, dressed in fatigue trousers and a grease-smeared T-shirt. The face had been nearly shot away.

"This is a Dominican," the doctor said, though later, hospital authorities identified this dead man as a marine.

When I walked outside, dazed from the experience of seeing high politics reduced to torn bodies and maddening moans, two hospital ambulances had pulled up and the two wounded men, carried on stretchers, were placed in them while a crowd gathered around the vehicles.

I then went to rebel headquarters nearby. It could be distinguished by the knots of people gathered on the sidewalk and street outside, many of them simply waiting to get a glimpse of Caamaño when he sometimes stepped out on the balcony of the old Spanish-style structure. An armed guard let me in, and I walked up a flight of creaking stairs to his office where dozens of rebel soldiers and leaders were milling around.

In an adjoining room, I could see—and hear—through open shutters the two marines who had been captured unhurt. They sat sullenly side by side in chairs while rebel officials questioned them. One wore glasses and looked scholarly. The other looked as big and tough as a prizefighter. They had taken the wrong turn, they explained, when asked why they had entered the rebel zone.

"You're lying," said the interrogator.

The marines then would give only their names, ranks, and serial numbers.

"I believe they are telling the truth," Caamaño said to me as he came out of the room, apparently contradicting the interrogator.

Would the U. S. forces now try to clean up the rebel area as a result of the incident?

"I don't think so. They'd have to kill thousands of people to do it," Caamaño said as the strains of cha-cha music still persisted in the distance.

Actually, according to Martin in his *Life* article, "pressures began to mount for us to take the city." Generating these pressures, he wrote, were rebel efforts to use the cease-fire to move snipers and agitators into the northern part of the city and into the interior, and to stir up the people with inflammatory radio programs and mass meetings.

On Tuesday, May 11, Martin and the papal nuncio went to see Caamaño at his office at the rebel leader's request. The two visitors tried to persuade Caamaño that he should meet with Imbert to discuss a peace arrangement. Imbert, they pointed out, had indicated his willingness to meet with him. But Caamaño argued that he would only agree to such a meeting if Imbert removed General Wessin and two other officers from command.

According to Martin, Caamaño said: "Imbert is not a free agent with those two there. . . . Imbert is not the enemy." Aristy, who was present, agreed with this view.

But after much discussion, accord was reached on an Imbert-Caamaño meeting if Imbert agreed to meet at one of three places: on the International Safety Zone line, just inside the rebel area, or in a public square deeper inside the rebel area. Caamaño said, however, that he would have to consult his advisers and that Aristy would have to come along. He promised to call the nuncio at 3 P.M. to say whether he could agree to the meeting.

Martin then went to see Imbert, who said he would meet with Caamaño either on the zone line or just inside the rebel area. But just before 3 P.M., Caamaño called the nuncio and said there would be no meeting. He charged that "troops of Wessin," with U. S. support, had killed one rebel and wounded others in an attack inside the rebel zone. Then another rebel official called Martin and said that U. S. troops across the river were shooting indiscriminately at rebels on the other side. He threatened that the rebels would destroy that night the U. S.-controlled flour mill on the American-held side of the river.

According to Martin, the suspicion grew that the rebels did not want to talk, and that "the Communists behind" Caamaño were creating incidents in order to prevent the talks. "Pressures were mounting on every side for U. S. forces to smash the rebel stronghold—take the city and get it over with."

On Thursday, May 13, another jeepload of marines blundered into the rebel zone and into a barrage of fire that killed two of them. Within an hour after this incident, Caamaño and his

aides, including Aristy, arrived at their headquarters in the
Capello Building on Calle Conde, and stormed into the building with enraged expressions. Aristy, as he entered, saw me
outside, and with a gesture invited me to join them.

Upstairs in a large office, I witnessed a scene tense with drama
and prospective disaster. With his aides, most of them armed
with rifles, gathered around him, Caamaño telephoned Martin
at the U. S. Embassy.

"Señor Martin, Señor Martin, is this you?" he screamed in
English as he stood by a desk, telephone in hand, his brown eyes
aflame and the muscles in his round face taut and twitching.
"Señor Martin, listen to me carefully. If your troops don't stop
attacking our territory immediately we will attack with all our
strength."

After a brief pause, he said: "What, you don't understand?"
He swore under his breath and began shouting in Spanish.

"I said we will attack, attack, attack. Do you understand,
Señor Martin, we will attack you with everything we have unless you stop attacking us immediately."

Caamaño slammed the butt of his tommy gun on the desk
and threw down the telephone receiver, which hung for several
moments by its short cord, while aides urged, "Calm, Colonel,
calm."

The rebel chief put the receiver to his ear and started speaking again, in Spanish, this time in a more controlled voice.
"No," he said, "you withdraw your troops first. We'll discuss
the situation later. I'm only trying to defend the honor of my
country."

Then, his rage rising again, he gave the receiver to rebel
Foreign Minister Jottin Cury and stormed out of the room with
several of his aides. Cury said over the phone in broken English:
"Señor Martin, the President has gone to join his troops. He
means what he says."

The Foreign Minister, in turn, handed the receiver to a rebel

official who spoke better English and repeated the substance
of what Caamaño had said. The official then hung up.

"Well, the fat's in the fire now," commented an English-
speaking rebel aide.

And so it appeared to be. A few minutes later, about noon,
rebel-controlled Radio Santo Domingo reiterated the warning
that I had heard Caamaño give in person. A half hour later,
the radio station went off the air, and reports circulated that
Air Force planes of Wessin had bombed it.

This didn't sound illogical. Rebel control of Radio Santo
Domingo, or RSD as it is called, was certainly a vital element
in keeping the rebellious spirit alive, not only in the capital
but throughout the country. So vital, in fact, that U. S. technicians tried to jam it. It was the bitter, and sometimes hyster-
ical, voice of the revolution. And some observers felt that if
Communists did have influential positions in the revolt, they
were probably scriptwriters for radio and TV, though RSD
repeatedly denied that the struggle was controlled by Communists. Some typical comments heard over RSD were:

". . . Yankees came to rape, kill, and wound the Dominican
people, not to establish peace."

". . . The American invasion with its atrocities is a nice example of prehistoric bestiality."

The most violent treatment was reserved for Ambassador
Bennett, who was called a "liar," "maniac," "fiend," and even
more often, a "traitor" to his country. This was consistent with
rebel efforts to keep the line open to Washington, if not to
the American Embassy. President Johnson, the argument went,
was not really at fault. He had been "fooled" and "misled" by
Bennett. Despite the viciousness of some of the broadcasts, this
argument did not seem to fit into the Communist propaganda
pattern which seldom pictures the President in so generous a
light.

From the RCA telegraph office in the heart of the rebel zone
where I had been preparing a story, I went in a taxi with two

other correspondents—Louis Uchitelle of the Associated Press and Hal Hendrix of the Scripps-Howard Newspapers—to the station, about a mile away.

As we approached, shots rang out, seemingly from every direction. We got out of our car at a corner about 100 yards from the station just as an Imbert P-51 dived down in the direction of the station building. A barrage of fire was heard, but apparently emanating from rebel rifles aimed at the plane. However, the aircraft dropped no bombs, nor did it appear to do any strafing.

From our vantage point, we could see no damage inflicted on the building. The towering antenna was intact, and not even a window was broken. We made our way to the entrance of the station, guided by several armed rebels we met, and found the station director, Luis Acosta Tejeda, sprawled on a chair beside a desk in the large reception hall.

"Wessin's planes strafed us three times," he said excitedly, his dark glasses giving him a sinister look as he spoke. "They killed a child near here and wounded the mother. Those animals."

He said that a power line had been cut, apparently explaining why the station went off the air.

At that moment, a rebel soldier dashed in and reported that three truckloads of men—he didn't make it clear whether they were U. S. or Imbert troops—were approaching, and that a battle was apparently about to start. My two colleagues and I ran out in the street toward our waiting taxi, hoping to get away before the station came under attack.

But heavy fire nearby made us think twice, particularly when rebels hiding behind the porch walls of houses along the street motioned to us wildly to take cover. We darted into the courtyard of a building just across the street from the station, and lay nervously behind a low wall, while rifle and machine-gun fire seemed to be aimed directly at us.

Quiet suddenly prevailed, and we saw a rebel crawling across the street toward us. "Get out of there," he yelled. "Come into the station or you'll be killed."

Instead, we crawled into an open room of the building adjacent to the station, and, cringing in corners, waited out new spurts of fire, interspersed with periods of complete silence that gave the scene a sense of "High Noon" tension.

Finally, when we saw women and children, raggedly dressed and utterly unconcerned, come out of nearby buildings into which they had lunged when the firing had begun in earnest, we too emerged from our shelter and walked as calmly as possible to our taxi—still unaware of who had been shooting at whom.

The driver, who had been hiding in a gas station behind a sign reading in Spanish, "Put a tiger in your tank!" greeted us at the car with a casual "Where to now?"

When we got back to the RCA office, we learned that a remarkable thing had happened. The planes that had strafed Radio Santo Domingo had apparently shot in the direction of the American Embassy on their approach to the station. Reports indicated that Ambassador Bennett and his staff had dived under office desks as the planes came over. U. S. marines nearby had fired at the planes and, we learned later, shot one of them down. It never was made clear whether the strafing was simply an accident.

May 13 thus, in a sense, represented a turning point in the crisis. Rebel anti-American hysteria had, on the one hand, reached a peak. And an indication that Imbert, too, was beginning to grow irritated with the Americans was seen by some observers as implicit in the "accident." Simultaneously, for the first time, U. S. troops had fired on junta forces, with the United States protesting the plane attack to the OAS.

The following day, I went to the Embassy, arriving just as a tropical storm sent sheets of water bursting upon the city. As I ran into the chancellery entranceway, I was halted and pushed back into the downpour by a marine guard with a

cruelly immobile face. "Sorry," he said, "but no visitors can
come in anymore, including reporters."

"But I'm soaking," I protested. "At least let me into the
reception room."

"I have my orders," said the marine stubbornly.

I shook my dripping finger at him. "Look here, I'm not just
a reporter. I'm an American citizen. And this is my Embassy.
I insist on being protected. That's my constitutional right. [I
wasn't quite sure that it was.] Now please let me in."

The marine seemed slightly shaken by the forcefulness of my
argument. He asked: "What do you want to be protected from?"

I couldn't think of anything at the moment, except the driving rain, but I added authoritatively: "Never mind. I insist on
speaking with an Embassy officer."

Flustered, the marine finally went inside, and I heard him
tell someone that a reporter was demanding entry. A voice replied: "Hah, a reporter, eh? You mean he's standing out there
in this hurricane?"

"Yes, sir."

"Well, I hope he drowns," said the voice with a note of satisfaction, and, it is to be hoped, a touch of humor, however
distorted. It added: "If he tries to get in here, you have my
permission to shoot him. We've got enough trouble without
those reporters hanging around."

The man who spoke was not exaggerating about the trouble
besetting U. S. officials. At the root of this trouble, it seemed,
was the increasing anti-Americanism in the country, even
among, ironically enough, the junta followers. Indicatively,
many Dominicans of both sides had, as one of them put it, been
"tickled" by the plane incident.

"You know," remarked a rebel official wryly, "that attack
really hurt us. Heaven knows how many people have shifted
their support to Imbert because of it."

Adding to this embarrassment, and perhaps the root of it,
was an earlier display of impudence by Imbert, who didn't seem

to appreciate all the efforts the United States had made to establish him in office—and the strings it tried to attach to its support. The United States had hoped to appease the rebels and set the stage for an Imbert-Caamaño agreement by getting Imbert to rid the armed forces of the most corrupt generals, as well as of Wessin himself, the center of popular hatred.

Wessin had apparently agreed to cooperate. Or at least the Embassy thought so. For Bennett managed to obtain a letter from him saying that a number of generals should go, and that, if it would help, he would step down, too. On his list of those who should go were two Imbert appointees and a colonel close to the junta leader. Imbert agreed, after balking, to expel the colonel, but would not give in on the other two. In all, he lured five generals and a naval commander to the naval base, reportedly gave them $1,000 each, and placed them aboard a departing Dominican warship. Bennett then went to San Isidro, and Wessin apparently confirmed his offer to resign. A U. S. spokesman told the press that he understood that Wessin had quit.

The next day, May 11, I discovered that this announcement had been slightly exaggerated. Driving to San Isidro with only a faint hope of seeing Wessin—he seldom spoke to reporters—another reporter and I found that a telephone call from the sentry to his office was all that was needed to clear the way for an interview. Receiving us with an uncertain smile on his swarthy, sphinxlike face, he asked us to sit down in a chair in front of his small but cluttered desk, and flatly denied the reports that he had resigned or intended to resign. He further said that he had never told U. S. officials or anyone else that he intended to resign. He said he had written a letter to Bennett, but that he had not indicated in it such an intention.

"I haven't resigned, nor will I resign, while the danger of communism in the Dominican Republic remains," he said forcefully in a low, staccato voice, while a score of uniformed officers standing around his desk nodded in agreement. "I will remain in my position as long as the Dominican people want me to stay."

Wessin, who often replied to questions only after prompting from an adviser, as in the case of Caamaño, appeared anxious to publicize his denial of the Embassy statement, replying in short clipped answers while nervously tearing a cigarette carton into tiny bits. He obviously hadn't appreciated the U. S. pressure on him to get out.

Significantly, Wessin said that he had held "cordial conversations" with Imbert and other members of the junta the previous evening—after reports of Wessin's resignation had circulated. This contradicted assurances offered to reporters by Imbert that morning that he had not conferred with Wessin since the crisis started. Imbert, seeking popular support, was doing his best to remove the Wessin aura from his regime. But he had apparently advised Wessin to renege on his reported offer to resign, perhaps to let the Embassy know who was boss. One U. S. official privately suggested to me that Imbert may have been trying to bolster the junta's bargaining power in its dealings with the United States. Perhaps coincidentally, the plane incident occurred two days later. The United States, it seemed, couldn't trust any longer even those Dominicans it had embraced as friends.

With the rebels at the boiling point and the loyalists apparently untrustworthy, the United States started to reconsider its Dominican policy. And the process of reconsideration seems to have been accelerated by the growing realization, fostered by the press, that U. S. policy had deeply antagonized a substantial segment of Dominican, and Latin-American, public opinion. It was probably fostered further by a decision of the United Nations to send a special representative to the country in response to a rebel request. The feeling in Washington was that the United States would have to move toward genuine neutrality.

Martin perhaps set the stage for this redirection of policy

when he took the edge off Caamaño's rage by telephoning him shortly after the rebel leader had issued his threat of all-out attack. Martin had checked with General Palmer about Caamaño's charge that U. S. forces had attacked the rebels, and was told that the Americans had that morning moved out and stopped the fire of rebels who had been shooting at them, but that they had returned to their positions.

Martin told this to Caamaño over the phone, and a mild argument ensued about who broke the cease-fire. Finally, Caamaño said that he would ask the OAS to investigate. Martin said he would, too. And temperatures went down.

It is not clear whether any further conversations between Caamaño and American officials, possibly concerning U. S. intentions, took place that day, but the rebel chief was now apparently persuaded for the first time that the United States might be moving toward real neutralism at last. The conciliatory telephone call, plus the U. S. protest to the OAS over the junta plane incident, seem to have had a drastic effect. For when I saw Caamaño and Aristy the next morning, May 14, their belligerence appeared to have dissolved completely.

"We are optimistic," Caamaño told me with a smile after completing a television interview in his office. "The United States seems to be getting more neutral."

And I had never seen Aristy in better humor. "I think everything is going to be all right," he said, grinning and putting his arm around my shoulder in a way he had with people he wanted to influence.

Caamaño then hinted—for the first time—that the rebels might be agreeable to a peace under which he would resign to make way for another President to be selected by constitutional means. He said he did not necessarily plan to resign, but that he would not hesitate to step down if he considered such a move would be in the interest of his country and if his successor were chosen constitutionally. He added that he was "not happy" as President because of the tremendous work load the job entailed.

It was clear that Caamaño and Aristy were not thinking in terms of a deal with Imbert, as the Embassy had been urging. He would agree, said Caamaño, only to give Imbert an "army job" if he were willing to cooperate with the constitutional government.

In an article indicating this apparently new rebel attitude, I wrote that "presumably the choice of a new president would be governed by the need of satisfying the United States that he would not permit the Communists to gain control of the government."

Undoubtedly adding to the optimism that such a government might now be possible was the expected arrival of a United Nations representative. The OAS, the rebels were convinced, was under too much pressure from the United States to be able to deal fairly with them. Moreover, they felt, as most democratic countries would not cooperate with the OAS operation in the Dominican Republic, only countries tending to look favorably on military or oligarchal regimes were in judgment on the crisis. When the UN representative arrived, the OAS peace team left in a huff, protesting the world body's interference.

As rumors flew that a period of conciliation between the United States and rebels was in prospect, a reporter inquired at a press conference on May 16 about a report that White House Adviser McGeorge Bundy and other high U. S. officials had arrived in, or were on their way to, Santo Domingo. A State Department spokesman flatly denied the report. The following day, however, news leaked out that the report had indeed been true. Bundy had come, together with Undersecretary Vance, Undersecretary Thomas C. Mann, and Assistant Secretary Vaughn. And they had come on a remarkable mission—to explore the possibilities of establishing a government under the 1963 Constitution and getting Imbert, whom they had lifted to power about a week before, to resign and support such a regime.

The United States, it appeared, had completely reversed its policy. No longer did one hear in the Embassy—when reporters could get in—that the Communists controlled the rebel movement. The Communists, under pressure, had withdrawn from overt activity, reporters were now told. It was now safe to negotiate with the cleansed constitutionalist leadership.

Negotiations had, in fact, started in Puerto Rico where the American team apparently stopped off on the way to Santo Domingo to see Bosch and Antonio Guzmán, who had been Bosch's Secretary of Agriculture. The idea was to support Guzmán as Caamaño's presidential successor under the 1963 Constitution. Guzmán was generally considered by Dominicans to be a moderate who was liked by both the lower and upper classes. Bosch gave the proposition his blessing. Guzmán, according to the Bundy plan, would fill out Bosch's constitutional term, and then elections would be held in late 1966 as prescribed by the Constitution.

A U. S. Air Force plane brought Bosch's personal emissary, Colonel Fernández Domínguez, from San Juan to Santo Domingo to convey Bosch's attitude in detail to the Caamaño government. On his first trip to Santo Domingo since the revolution that he had planned broke out, he told other rebel leaders at headquarters: "I've come to share your fate." Then discarding his traditional-style officer's hat, he said: "Get me a constitutionalist hat [a French-style, bucket-shaped hat with a peak]. The old Army is finished."

Fernández, who had been named the rebel Secretary of Interior, then gave Caamaño details of the Guzmán plan, and Caamaño, after consulting with PRD leaders, told U. S. officials, informants said, that Guzmán would be acceptable.

But hardly had relations between the United States and the rebels started to thaw when a tragedy occurred that threatened to destroy the developing entente. At about 11 P.M. on May 20, I was awakened by a telephone call from PRD Secretary-General Martínez Francisco. Almost hysterically, he screamed: "The Americans have killed him. They've killed him—Colonel Fernández Domínguez. Oh my God, he was such a good man. But they've killed him. And Washington can speak of neutral-ism..." For a moment I thought he would break into tears.

Fernández Domínguez had been killed that evening together with four other rebel leaders as they stole up to the junta-controlled National Palace, leading an attack on it. Officer friends of Fernández who had commanded the junta soldiers guarding it had agreed in advance to support the attack, but junta leaders, apparently hearing of the plan, had changed the guard the day before, and an unexpected battle had developed.

No one denied that U. S. troops had shot them. But the rebels claimed the shooting had been unprovoked and intended to protect the junta forces, while U. S. officials said that the rebels had fired at U. S. troops, wounding three, and that these troops simply returned the fire. What apparently happened was that some rebel fire intended for junta targets in the palace area swept U. S.-controlled territory two blocks away.

Whatever happened, Fernández Domínguez, a known supporter of democracy—U. S. officials agreed to that—was dead, and so, it appeared for the moment, were the chances for genuine U. S.-rebel conciliation. In fact, Caamaño, on hearing of the tragedy, immediately canceled a meeting that had been scheduled with members of the Bundy mission, though such a meeting was held later when tempers had cooled.

Even so, the Bundy mission, on arriving in Santo Domingo, lost little time visiting Imbert in an attempt to persuade him to resign. Imbert flatly refused. "You Americans were the first to say Caamaño was controlled by the Communists," he said, "and now you want me to join with the Communists."

Imbert, who had attained his position after years of plotting, planning, and even gambling with his own life, now went all-out to meet U. S. pressures to knock him down. He held pro-Imbert and anti-American rallies in various cities. He sent hordes of women armed with signs reading DOWN WITH COMMUNISM to the American Embassy to protest U. S. efforts to deal with the rebels.

To broaden his political support, he called a meeting of conservative anti-Bosch political parties and proposed the establishment of a provisional legislative council in which leading political, business, professional, and labor groups would be represented. In a memorandum issued to the party leaders present he described the proposed structure as a "corporate form," which recalled to some observers the "corporate state" of Italian dictator Benito Mussolini. The memorandum said the project had a precedent in the structure of the former Cuban government of Fulgencia Batista.

The party leaders, an Imbert spokesman told a news conference, were so impatient to defeat the rebels that they offered to provide armed civilians to fight them if Imbert's regular forces were unable to do so.

These regular forces didn't seem to need much aid. Imbert's ace hand in building up his bargaining power was to launch a major offensive in the northern part of the city which rebel armed civilians had been infiltrating for some days, many of them crossing the corridor that separated the area from Ciudad Nueva via underground sewers so that they could smuggle guns. The area, which had been controlled by neither side, became the scene of a grotesque little war. If he won it, Imbert felt, his hand would be strengthened in his dealings with the United States.

Bitter building-by-building, block-by-block fighting went on in this section while U. S. forces stood on the sidelines and watched. Unofficially, U. S. sources appeared to approve a junta victory in the area, since it would serve to produce a military "impasse." This was not taking sides, they reasoned, since the United States would guarantee the security of the main rebel stronghold of Ciudad Nueva, refusing to permit junta troops to cross the U. S.-controlled corridor to get there.

Officially, U. S. officials explained that the American troops, to intervene in the north, would have to get involved in the actual fighting, and that it was considered inadvisable for them to shoot at Dominicans except in self-defense. Furthermore, they argued, the U. S. troops could only involve themselves if they entered the no man's land between the two sides, becoming targets for both, or from behind the lines of one side, making it appear to the other side that the troops were helping the enemy.

Unpublicized was the fact that Bundy, who seemed to have a better grasp of the forces at work in the Dominican Republic than any other high American official, proposed that a new corridor extending northward from Ciudad Nueva be opened to cut off Imbert's troops, but that Washington rejected the idea.

Certainly it was true that getting caught in no man's land was not a pleasant prospect. Three other correspondents—Leslie H. Whitten of Hearst Newspapers, Lee Winfrey of the *Miami Herald,* and Leon Daniel of United Press International—and I discovered this the hard way. Accompanied by a rebel guide, we started our adventure at rebel headquarters in Ciudad Nueva, where we hired a Cadillac taxi to take us to war. The car took us through several American checkpoints where paratroopers searched people and their vehicles, including our own, for weapons. We then headed for a rear rebel headquarters located about one mile east of the area where fighting was in progress. Slovenly dressed civilians with rifles, sub-machine guns, and bazookas clustered on the sidewalks and streets, and twice we were suddenly stopped by nervous-looking rebels with their weapons pointed at us and asked for identification. Once, even the assurances of our rebel guide, who had a pass from Caamaño's headquarters, only sufficed to satisfy a guard when we had explained in detail who we were. We had to drive slowly in order to make sure we would stop in time in case anyone cried for us to halt. The driver slammed on his brakes at one corner after seeing in his mirror someone raise his rifle to his eye, apparently just as the rebel was about to pull the trigger. We had somehow failed to hear his order to stop.

At our destination we met Captain Sylvio Arzeno, a friendly

man with a small moustache and a round face who was in charge
of that headquarters. He took us into a small bungalow of a
friend next door to the headquarters building, and advised us
not to advance any farther toward the fighting zone. However,
he offered to provide us with a jeep escort if we were determined to take the risk. We decided to do so, and, after we had
taped the word PRENSA on our windshield, the captain saw us
off with a smile and a quiet "Good luck."

We sped toward the front lines behind the escort jeep at
about 50 miles an hour. One of the occupants of the jeep was
armed with a sub-machine gun, another with an automatic rifle,
and two others with standard rifles. They fired bursts of bullets
into the air at every intersection to scare possible snipers into
hiding. The street was virtually deserted, except for a few
armed rebels. Our intention was to advance to a position just
behind the rebel line, where we could be afforded some protection, but the taxi went all the way into no man's land, turning
down a cross street about two blocks beyond the rebel line. We
turned again and advanced still farther toward the northern
edge of National Cemetery, where Imbert troops were dug in.
To our speechless dismay, it seemed that we were going to drive
right into the junta line. A barrage of fire broke out, and we
swerved into the driveway of the small, dingy Union Hotel
about a half block from the cemetery.

At the entrance, we leaped out of the car and took refuge
on a winding stairway leading to the second story of the abandoned pink and blue structure. Finally, while machine-gun bullets pecked away at the rear wall of the hotel, we crept to a
yellow, cinder-block house next door where we found a group
of terrified civilians.

Fourteen people, including five children, two of whom were
five-months-old twins, were in the house. The adults—the oldest
was a fifty-five-year-old grandmother—greeted us calmly under
the circumstances, though one of the women began crying. They
represented five families from the same block who had gathered

in this house when fighting broke out two days before. They were the only people still left on this block of colorfully painted, shuttered houses, mostly made of wood.

The babies didn't cry. They only stared blankly as they clung naked like little monkeys to the women. Even as machine-gun bullets raked the area, they were quiet, too weak to cry, too hungry to care. As I gazed at one of them, sharing a moment of terror with him, the whole war seemed suddenly to dwindle down to the question of why that baby didn't cry; how sane men, of whatever side, could permit, even create, conditions that would deprive that child of the will or the strength to cry; how men could shoot at that child; how U. S. troops sent to save lives could help some of these men aim their guns, figuratively, at the child so that they wouldn't fire into the American-controlled zone; how other G.I.s could sit bivouacked on a grassy field hardly 1,000 yards away detachedly watching the child being shot at. Why were men so cruel to that baby? I wondered. Why did they stop him from crying?

"Food, by tomorrow we shall have no food," a woman sobbed, bringing me back to reality but not out of the nightmare. She explained that all the merchants in the area had fled. Aside from some bananas we saw cooking in a blackened pot on a small wood stove, there remained, she said, only a day's supply of rice, beans, and sugar. Another woman, patting the hunger-swollen belly of a baby in her arms, added, "There is no milk for the children, only water."

As the firing grew in intensity, Leon Daniel put his arm around the grandmother as she sobbed, "How sad, how sad." During a lull in the shooting I herded the whole group into the patio and started taking family pictures, forgetting for a moment that this was no picnic. I soon came down to earth, literally, when a mortar shell seemed to burst almost upon us. Everybody scrambled hysterically into the house, and I cowered behind a refrigerator. The grandmother had left one sandal behind in her rush, but a teen-aged granddaughter ran out to pick it up, and she gently replaced it on the older woman's foot.

In the comfortably furnished middle-class house, which belonged to a Chinese family that had temporarily abandoned it, most of the new and much poorer inhabitants slept on the hardwood floor of the small living room, embracing each other with every deafening mortar-shell burst. Photographs on the wall of a Chinese family posing smilingly lent an incongruous note to the scene. The way things turned out, the junta forces soon overran the area, and the families moved back into their homes.

As the shooting and shelling grew worse, we exchanged pathetic farewells with the group and, one by one, crawled along the wall to where our taxi was parked in the driveway next door. Behind the jeep, we zoomed northward into rebel territory, about two blocks ahead. We turned wildly to the left to get out of the north-south line of fire, but as we passed a crowd of armed civilians standing outside a green wooden house that served as a forward command post, firing in the area became so heavy that the driver leaped out of the car in search of cover before the vehicle could come to a halt. So there we were, for one surrealistic moment, in a driverless Cadillac taxi floating through a spray of bullets. Before we could react, a rebel standing nearby jumped into the front seat and slammed on the brakes just before the car jammed into the halted jeep in front of us. I later denied scurrilous rumors spread by jealous competitors that I leaned over and turned off the taxi meter when the cabbie left us on our own.

We joined the rebel fighters, who were dressed in every tattered variety of civilian clothes, outside the house for several moments. They were angry, frustrated, but, it seemed, utterly determined men. "We are not Communists," one of them said typically. "Why must we suffer like this because the Yankees don't want us to have a constitutional government? Why must our families go hungry?"

As we returned to the taxi and started off again toward the

rear, they looked at us almost pleadingly—as if we had magic answers that could somehow spell an end to their suffering.

We had none. The fighting continued for several more days as junta troops methodically cleaned out block by block. One of the last rebel strongholds to fall was Radio Santo Domingo, the voice of the revolution, which had been so effective an element in rallying national support for the rebel cause. The struggle was bitter. In one case, junta soldiers disarmed four men, three of them brothers, ordered them to lie down on the street, and machine-gunned them. Finally, rebel resistance collapsed.

Paradoxically, at the very time U. S. negotiators seemed to be taking a friendly line toward the rebels, U. S. troops were being accused, not only of standing by while the killing went on, but of helping the junta crush the rebels in the north. I saw two jeeploads of Americans parked in front of junta military headquarters at the Transportation Center during the fighting. And other reporters saw several paratroopers enter Radio Santo Domingo after it was captured, and kick in doors looking for snipers.

U. S. officials claimed that these Americans were simply liaison troops whose job it was to make sure that junta forces aimed their weapons so as not to fire into the U. S.-controlled corridor. But rebel sympathizers were by no means appeased by this argument, even if it were true. To make sure that junta troops fired more accurately at the rebel forces was hardly their definition of neutrality.

The apparent contradiction in U. S. policy began to spawn rumors that Washington was simply trying to give the impression that it was sympathetic to the rebels in order to mute world criticism of the support it had openly given Imbert and his fellow militarists previously. With Imbert winning the military battle, these rumors suggested, the United States could eventually drop its diplomatic support of the rebel politicians on the prextext that Imbert "unfortunately" had physical control of the country.

This was certainly the hope of Imbert and the militarists who supported him. His tough, scarred face beamed at one interview I had with him at the Congressional Palace just after the most influential military leaders, including Wessin, had agreed at a meeting to support Imbert solidly against attempts by the United States to get him to step down.

"I'm not goin' step down and let the Communists take over," he said in a hesitant Marlon Brando manner. "And you should realize that this is a fight between communism and democracy. I'm gonna stay as head of government. But hell, I'd see Caamaño if he wanted see me. He's an old friend of mine."

As if to make the point that if Caamaño didn't listen to reason, he might be sorry, Imbert, playing with one of the buttons of his immaculate tan uniform, added after a pause: "The military situation's going very well."

An Imbert aide later said that Imbert was "disappointed with the American attitude." He added that his regime "could function without U. S. support if necessary. Your country changes its mind so quickly. We are simply defending the principles of the United States." In any case, he said, as soon as the northern area was mopped up, the junta intended to take over Ciudad Nueva by force. What of the U. S.-controlled corridor separating the junta troops from that area? Well, he replied, a naval and air attack could probably do the trick.

When I asked Imbert's American press spokesman, Francisco Cardona, what Imbert would do if the United States used force to stop him from taking over more rebel territory, he went so far as to say:

"Rebel snipers have been shooting at American troops and causing a lot of damage. We're much stronger and could cause a lot more damage."

But if the United States was willing to see the rebels with whom it was negotiating defeated in the northern zone, it was determined to keep faith with them to the extent of protecting Ciudad Nueva from a junta attack. Ambassador Adlai Stevenson made this clear when he told the United Nations that the United States would not permit such an assault. To back up these words, the marines symbolically turned half of their howitzers, all of which had been aimed toward Ciudad Nueva, toward junta positions, to the utter confusion of troops who had thought they knew who the "good guys" and the "bad guys" were.

Also, U. S. forces twice prevented Air Force fighter planes from taking off from San Isidro Air Base. U. S. staff cars, trucks, and fire engines rushed in the path of P-51 Mustangs as they were about to take off, apparently to bomb rebel targets. U. S. military craft also kept an eye on junta warships. UN and OAS representatives, meanwhile, pressured Imbert to agree to a cease-fire. He did, for 24 hours, so that the dead and wounded could be removed from the war-torn northern area. He then agreed to "abstain from renewing any attack unless it is provoked."

The rebels now found themselves in a safer but extremely painful position. They had been winning the war when the landings took place; enemy resistance seemed to be crumbling. But with U. S. forces now standing by, apparently ready to step in if the rebels made too much headway, the 1,500 junta troops had regained their morale and confidence and found little difficulty advancing against a small rebel force of about 300 armed civilians who were largely cut off from their main stronghold.

It was now rebel morale that dropped. The rebels realized that they could no longer use their military might as a bargaining factor with the United States. It was Imbert who now could. Worst of all, from the psychological point of view, the rebels saw themselves dependent on the hated American troops for protection against the junta forces, rather than the other way around as had been the case when the U. S. troops first came.

Adding to the rebel agony was the humiliating need to negotiate every cabinet position in the projected Guzmán government with the Americans. The United States first came up with a handpicked five-man "constitutional" junta that it wanted the rebels to accept. In addition to Guzmán, it would include four other moderates. But the rebels turned down the proposal.

Guzmán is understood to have argued that the other four men were all related to each other, and that it was hardly practical to have a "family government." He also said that one candidate, Milton Messina, an economic expert who worked for the Inter-American Development Bank in Washington, would be unacceptable to the people since he had been Secretary of Industry and Commerce and Governor of the Central Bank under Trujillo. Furthermore, Messina was an uncle of Donald Reid Cabral, and Guzmán was uncertain where his loyalty might lie in view of Reid's ouster by the rebels. New names were then considered and discarded endlessly.

During the negotiations, President Johnson, it was learned, secretly sent a team of FBI agents to the Dominican Republic, apparently to check on the backgrounds of candidates being considered for government posts. It was not clear whether this dispatch of FBI agents, whose job of rooting out subversion had previously been confined to the United States, meant the President had doubts about reports submitted by the CIA, which normally conducts such investigations abroad. But their presence added salt to the wounds of many Dominicans, who felt that this was approaching the ultimate in foreign interference in their affairs.

Guzmán himself was not free from personal humiliation. Some of his associates received telephone calls from U. S. Embassy officials inquiring about his family background. They were particularly interested in information about his "brother-in-law," who was reported to have Communist connections. Those questioned indicated to the officials that they must be referring to the brother-in-law of another "Guzmán," a very common name in the Dominican Republic.

Guzmán was then charged by a U. S. newspaper, apparently on the basis of a tip from an American friend of Reid Cabral, with involvement in a financial scandal. It was stated that he was a director of a Dominican agricultural bank, Banco Agrícola, accused of irregularities. An audit showed that the bank's assets had been overstated by $75 million and that thousands of notes and $1 million in mortgage collateral were missing. Guzmán flatly denied to me that he had in any way been dishonest, and this denial was backed up by the local manager of the New York accounting firm of Ernst & Ernst, which had done the audit. The manager said that Guzmán's job in no way gave him influence or access to the bank's funds without the knowledge of many highly respected officials and representatives of international organizations.

Despite such difficulties, Guzmán appeared to be optimistic that he would in the end be the head of a constitutional government. He had promised the Americans that he would not publicize the negotiations and therefore kept away from reporters, who for many days did not know where to find him. However, I had been tipped off where he was staying about a day after word filtered out that he was being considered for the presidency. I went to the designated house, knocked on the door, and was confronted by two men. I introduced myself and asked to see Guzmán.

"He's not here," a short, good-looking man with wavy gray hair said.

"When will he be back?" I asked.

"I don't know," the same man replied.

I then asked this man if I could have his name so that I would know whom to ask for if I returned.

"Antonio Guzmán," he said, suddenly breaking into a smile as he realized he had given himself away.

In a quiet, dignified manner, he explained that he was unable to speak with reporters, but he did say that he was "hopeful" that a political solution to the crisis might be reached soon.

"Things are going well," he commented, adding that U. S. officials were fully cooperating in the effort to find a solution.

But he looked like a troubled man. And indeed, few were the rebels who weren't troubled. Their distress was bitterly revealed one day at a press conference in Caamaño's office when they openly assumed two seemingly conflicting attitudes toward the United States.

Caamaño reported on a "friendly" meeting he had held the previous day with Bundy and Vance at the white stone Music Conservatory in a no man's land between the junta and rebel lines. He smiled when he described how he and the Americans arrived only to find the doors locked and nobody in possession of the key. Finally, a window had to be broken, and the two distinguished visitors, standing on chairs, climbed through it.

Turning serious, Caamaño said he told the Americans that the rebels had five basic demands: return to the 1963 Constitution, a guarantee that elected government officials would return to office, constitutional control of the armed forces, a cabinet composed of democratic civilians, and departure of occupational forces as soon as pssible. Bundy, Caamaño added, indicated that he would discuss these problems in Washington.

After the news conference, the rebel leader told me that the present U. S. "neutral" attitude was gratifying and contrasted sharply with the previously antagonistic American stand toward the constitutionalists.

Yet, at the same conference, the text of a cablegram sent by the constitutional parliament to the parliaments of 38 countries was read, acridly accusing the United States of trying to impose "solutions openly contrary to the democratic interests of the Dominican people. . . . It is no longer a secret for anyone in the Dominican Republic that the government of the U.S.A., through the employment of dilatory obstructionist tactics which could well be termed coercive, has been strongly pressuring organizations and individuals."

After the text of the cable was read, Anível Campagna, President of the Senate, an elderly, gray-haired man who was sitting next to Caamaño, got up and offered an impassioned explanation for the cable. Pointing out that he was not a "Boschist," but a member of the National Civic Union, he said with a trembling voice that the United States had humiliated the country. The U. S. forces, he charged, had been responsible for the "massacre" in the northern part of the city, for it did not act to stop it. The United States was also responsible, he said, for what he described as the terror in the interior, where people, he maintained, were being killed and imprisoned. Again the United States closed its eyes, he charged. Caamaño sat listening impassively, refusing to comment on the cable or the Senator's remarks.

The juxtaposed "friendly" and bitterly antagonistic attitudes exhibited at that meeting reflected the reality of the relationship between the United States and the rebel regime. On the one hand, the United States appeared to be interested in backing a constitutional rather than a military government—a significant victory for the constitutionalists who only some days before had been the "bad guys" in U. S. eyes. On the other hand, in order to win this U. S. support, the constitutionalists had to swallow their pride and, in large measure, agree to American-imposed conditions.

In this context, the parliamentary cable appeared to serve a necessary political purpose. It was designed apparently to convince the world in advance of a possible announcement of a constitutional government that the rebels would never consider forming a regime according to U. S. requirements. In fact, Caamaño himself said at the news conference that only Dominicans would have a say in the formation of a new government, though it was clear that this was not possible under existing circumstances.

The United States, for its part, was trying to give the impression that it was not interfering in Dominican politics by publicly denying, like the rebels, all reports implying that a new government was being worked out through compromise.

But the large dose of pride that the constitutionalists had to swallow did not appear to bode well for future U. S.-Dominican relations. Whatever the political motivation of the parliamentary cable, it obviously reflected a deep-seated hostility toward the United States for its efforts to dictate rebel policy.

Moreover, it was clear, the projected Guzmán government would be, once in power, regarded even by its supporters as an American-made regime, a fact that could well reduce its ability to govern effectively. Indeed, it was pointed out, what could stop the new president from making changes in his cabinet without consulting the United States, which would find it difficult to involve itself in the overthrow of an established constitutional regime?

Finally, after a week of talks, the Bundy mission and rebel leaders reached a tentative agreement, subject to approval by President Johnson, on the composition of a new government that would be installed under the 1963 Constitution. In addition to Guzmán, the projected cabinet would include five PRD members, two conservative independents, and one member of the Imbert junta—Julio Postigo, who had been a friend of Bosch.

Rebel leaders were jubilant, despite doubts that the proposed government could ever be really independent. But the fact was that tentative agreement on a cabinet by no means meant that all was over but the shouting. In the first place, the United States imposed other conditions. It insisted that the projected government would have to deport the more than 50 "hard-core" Communists on the American list and outlaw the 14th of June Movement. Rebel leaders refused. They argued that a basic tenet of the 1963 Constitution was that deportation could only be done through legal process. And they balked at outlawing the 14th of June Movement, since, they said, it was basically a nationalist rather than a Communist movement.

Furthermore, though Bundy himself flew back to Washington to advocate establishment of the Guzmán government, which he had taken such pains to help form, it was not at all clear that other powerful forces in Washington would be as favorably disposed. Some congressmen and Administration officials started asking why the United States was suddenly trying to place in power the Boschist forces which had been described as Communist-controlled only days before, and trying to remove from power a junta that the United States had helped to set up only days before. After sending in tens of thousands of troops to prevent a rebel victory, they asked, did it make sense to hand victory on a platter to the rebels now? Nor did the refusal of the rebels to accept the conditions on how to deal with the Communists lend weight to the arguments of those who said that communism was no longer influential in the constitutional movement. Indeed, one U. S. official in Santo Domingo said the rebels still would not face up to Communist elements, which, he maintained, were still around their headquarters, though Dean Rusk himself had said the Reds had receded into the background. Some U. S. officials wanted Aristy, whom they thought could be a Communist, removed from any position of power or influence.

But perhaps the basic criticism concerned the 1963 Constitution itself, which, critics charged, protected Communists—much, others pointed out, as does the U. S. Constitution—and contained questionable leftist concepts.

And coming on top of the Communist issue, the charge of dishonesty directed against Guzmán did not help the rebel cause, however documented the denials and fervent the claims of U. S. officials that they had no information indicating Guzmán was ever involved in questionable practices.

Ironically, rebel charges that had been publicly made by parliamentary elements that the United States had been pressuring the Dominicans to accept a particular kind of government further added to Washington's doubts about the Guzman formula. Some State Department officials are understood to have argued that the United States would be leaving itself open to more such accusations if it went ahead with the scheme.

Finally, since the Imbert junta physically controlled almost the whole country, and since Imbert had refused to accept the projected government, the United States would have to put enormous pressure on him—and on the armed forces that backed him—in an effort to force the regime down their throats. A cut-off of funds to Imbert could possibly have a serious effect on the political alignment of the armed forces. The military leaders, whatever their own sentiments, might find it difficult controlling units of hungry men, who depend on the United States for their salaries.

However, some U. S. officials calculated that the morale of Imbert's troops was so high after the north Santo Domingo victory that they might well remain loyal to the junta even if they received no pay. They could always subsist, it was argued, on the food and medicines distributed by the OAS to any Dominicans, without discrimination, who might be in need.

In any case, the exertion of such pressure on Imbert was not regarded as a sensible idea. There was no telling in what explosive way he and the armed forces might react. And such action might not look very well to the congressmen and other influential people in Washington who were opposed to a regime based on the 1963 Constitution regardless.

The Guzmán formula, it was clear, was far from over the hill.

CHAPTER 10

Blood on a Sunday Dress

A s THE crisis in Santo Domingo settled into what seemed to be an American-controlled political stalemate, with little new fighting possible in view of the U. S. buffer corridor separating the two forces, life started to edge ever so slowly toward a semblance of normality.

Some shops began to reopen in both the rebel and international zones, though few people, particularly in the poorer rebel area, could be seen in any but the grocery stores, which were well stocked with food of every variety. With the economic life of the city at a standstill for weeks, not many Dominicans had money for anything but the most dire necessities.

Living conditions in the hotel also improved. The hotel maids started coming regularly and made our beds. At first we found it strange sleeping on clean, crisp sheets. The lights went on, though there were frequent power failures. Sometimes when there was light only in the corridors, dozens of people could be seen sitting against the walls reading, talking, playing cards, or typing a story. The hotel laundry service started working, though the power failures made it difficult to gauge when one's clothes would be returned. On one occasion, my roommate, Jeremiah O'Leary, Jr., of the *Washington Star*, grew desperate when he found himself out of shirts. Noting that many Chinese Dominican residents were living in the hotel to assure their families' safety, he angrily remarked that there were "hundreds of Chinese around and I can't get one shirt washed."

The hotel switchboard had also begun operating again, but it would sometimes take up to an hour just to get an outside line. To reach the long-distance operator might take another hour or two. Installation of Telex machines in the press room finally gave us another outlet for our stories, though copy piled up so heavily that a reporter often had to wait three or four hours to get in contact with his office.

Such conditions, though better than they had been when we first arrived, tended to lead one to the edge of nervous prostration, and beyond. On one occasion, a fellow reporter told me in the press room that he had heard that an agreement on a new government had been reached. About twenty minutes later, I met the same reporter in another part of the hotel, without realizing that it was the same one, and asked him: "Did you hear anything about the U. S. agreeing to a new government?"

"Yes, I did," he replied blandly.

"Well, maybe it's true," I said. "That's two of you who've told me that."

Particularly pleasing to the reporters was the opening of an Italian restaurant that catered to people who had passes permitting them to be on the street after curfew. After subsisting on C-rations and expensive, poorly prepared meals at the hotel, we began gorging ourselves nightly on first-rate Italian food, if at even higher prices than those charged at the hotel. The problem was to get transportation to the restaurant, for few taxi drivers were available after curfew. Although they could accompany us without getting into trouble, many were afraid of snipers and nervous marines. Also, they could not drive to their homes afterward, but had to sleep on sofas in the hotel lobby. On some occasions, as many as eight reporters crowded into a single Volkswagen, a feat which was particularly difficult after we had stuffed ourselves with Italian delicacies.

On returning to the hotel, too tired to work, we sought recreation. But there was none. The casino and bar were closed down—though the bar eventually reopened for a few hours nightly—as were all cabarets and bars in this city which had always been a favorite of reporters seeking nocturnal pleasure. But the reporters learned to improvise. In fact, even in the early days of the crisis, the hotel, then lightless, was alive with the drunken cries of maladjusted reporters who had had the foresight to bring with them the magical medicines they required to see them through their assignments. Strangers carrying candles in the dark sometimes wandered into the nearest open-doored room where a party might be in progress, poured a drink, and left without anyone knowing, or caring, about the intrusion.

As time went on, the improvisation varied. One enterprising photographer with an imaginative sense of values risked his life passing through armed checkpoints with three young ladies he met in the rebel zone. He established them in a room on the fifth floor, publicized their availability, and collected 20 percent of their take. Did he make much money? Yes, he reported, but he was plowing back all his profits.

Furthermore, he soon found himself in competition with an American businessman who was bringing in better-looking girls and offering special morning rates—"feel relaxed before you start dodging bullets."

The photographer finally shut up shop after an episode in which he mixed business with too much pleasure. He and one of his protégées were partying with a group of his friends, including a clergyman. As the evening progressed, gaiety and good fellowship prevailed increasingly until the happy clergyman arose and offered to marry off the photographer to his business associate. The young couple agreed, and the clergyman performed the nuptials. Then, instead of kissing the bride, as tradition required, the guests offered her a more intimate token of their affection—on the house.

The next morning, the photographer was highly disturbed, uncertain wehther he was really married to the girl or not. He was particularly concerned about what his original wife would say if she discovered that she was part of a harem. Finally, when he learned that the ceremony was not legally binding, he sighed with relief and sent the girl packing. But she had her revenge— retroactively. The photographer and most of his friends who had shared his joy that fateful evening found themselves visiting the doctor several days later.

Actually, there were few moments when the newsmen could escape the depressing story we were covering. In one case, a policeman chased a suspected rebel sympathizer down the hotel corridors, finally catching him and dragging him off to police headquarters past whole units of bivouacked marines. Another time, a woman ran hysterically into the press room and implored reporters to "do something" about the apprehension of her husband, who had been taken from his place of work under arrest.

What these incidents meant was that, while the rebels waited hopefully for what they thought would be confirmation of the Guzmán formula in Washington, the Imbert regime tightened its grip on the country to further strengthen its bargaining power with the United States. It intensified efforts to round up enemies of the regime, using the police, which, unlike the armed forces, could "legally" carry—and use—guns in the International Safety Zone, to do it. The U. S. forces did little to clamp down on such police action, even though it took place right in their midst. The argument offered was that the United States had no right to prevent what police authorities claimed were legitimate arrests of suspected criminals. As a result, the police went wild.

One American citizen, Andrés Gilbert García of Puerto Rico, was among the victims. I met him the day he was released from

Victoria Prison where he had been brutally beaten during a 15-day stay in a cell crowded with people accused of being Communists. He described his experience to me as we sat on a bench in the U. S. Embassy garden shortly after arriving there to ask for help in getting back his clothes and money, which, he said, were taken from him by Imbert police.

Slim and dark, García had come directly from prison, where, he said, more than 5,000 prisoners were being held under "bestial" conditions. He had a two-weeks' growth of beard and wore no shoes, which he said had been taken from him. His checkered red shirt was spotted with blood from cuts on his scalp resulting, he said, from beatings with rifle butts and clubs.

García, a twenty-nine-year-old maker of riding saddles, arrived in Santo Domingo from Puerto Rico on April 24, just before the revolution broke out, to deliver some racehorses for someone. Unable to leave when the fighting started, he roomed with a Dominican family. About two weeks before I met him, police rapped on the door of the house, and threatened to shoot if it was not opened at once.

García said he and five other men came out with their hands over their heads. He protested that he was an American citizen, showing his tourist card and birth certificate, but one of the soldiers guarding the men simply said, prodding him with a tommy gun: "You dirty Communist." García said the men were led outside and piled into a truck, which then stopped at a nearby factory to load on dozens more men and women who worked there. "We were crowded in like pigs," he asserted.

They were taken to the baseball stadium, which was being used for prisoner processing. Guards took all valuables from them, García said. He added that he had surrendered his shoes, $30.40 he had in his pocket, and his identification papers. They then continued on to Victoria Prison. As they jumped from the truck, soldiers struck them with rifle butts and guided them through two lines of other soldiers, who systematically beat them with butts and clubs. When the prisoners had gone through the double lines, all the soldiers crowded around beating them until a major appeared and ordered them to stop. One man, García said, died later from the wounds inflicted.

García was put in a six-by-eight-foot cell with ten other prisoners. They could only lie down crushed aaginst each other. Five days later, he was transferred to a larger cell—about 25 by 100 feet—but it contained some 220 people, some of whom had to sleep standing up leaning against a wall. For breakfast and dinner prisoners were given a half slice of stale bread and a small cup of chocolate milk. Lunch consisted usually of rice and beans or herring, which was usually half-cooked and spoiled.

"I had such a pain every night that I could hardly stand it," García said.

Finally, International Red Cross representatives were permitted to visit the prison, and García told them his story. They obtained his release. As he was leaving the prison, an Imbert official interrogated him for the first time. "Are you a supporter of Fidel Castro or Juan Bosch?" the official asked. García replied, "I'm an American citizen and have nothing to do with Dominican politics." He then walked out. But thousands of others remained behind, and many would probably die in prison.

The situation was hardly better in the interior where the Army was free to do what it wanted and there were no U. S., OAS, or UN officials around all the time to exert a moderating influence. On a trip to the northern part of the country, two other reporters—Georgie Anne Geyer of the Chicago *Daily News* and Robert Boyd of the Miami *Herald*—and I found that the areas we visited appeared to have fallen in large degree under arbitrary police rule.

"It's as if Trujillo were back," one housewife in the Atlantic coast town of Puerto Plata said.

What proportion of the people in the northern region opposed the junta regime and favored the rebels was not clear, although talks with scores of Dominicans and the estimates of many Americans in the area pointed to a very large percentage. But what was clear was that among those who did oppose Imbert, who militarily controlled the interior, fear in varying measure was a constant companion. Arbitrary arrest in many towns was common. And in San Francisco de Macorís, two people had been killed and three wounded the day before when police fired into a group of peaceful demonstrators.

A civilian official in one town explained when asked why people had been arrested: "The police got used to arresting people under Trujillo, and they were getting restless. I don't approve but what can anybody do?"

United Nations officials in Santo Domingo were aware of this situation and reported it to UN headquarters. And the Human Rights Commission of the OAS used its influence to ease the police rule. Indeed, if fear in the Dominican interior was still relatively low-key, the reason appeared to lie, at least partly, in the widespread hope that the two organizations would help them.

"We want international observers sent here," said a lawyer in Puerta Plata. "The UN, the OAS, and the U.S.A. have all sent people to this country. But why don't they help us?"

In some cases, Dominicans were living in outright terror. We visited a man in one town who was hiding from the police in the bedroom of a friend's house. His lower lip trembling, he pleaded with us to inform U. S. representatives of his whereabouts so that they could come for him. "They will kill me if they find me," he said in a quiet voice agonizingly contained.

On returning to Santo Domingo we informed both UN and OAS officials of the man's plight, and they said they would try to bring him to the capital with a laissez-passez.

The tension appeared to be greatest in San Francisco de Macorís when we visited there after the shootings. Blood smears on the floor and almost a dozen bullet holes in the interior walls of Santa Ana Church attested to the violence that erupted when

police fired into a crowd, and followed fleeing people into the
church still firing.

"I thought the police were just trying to intimidate us," said
a wounded youth in his hospital bed. "When they started firing
I dashed into the church, but they came in and shot me in the
leg."

Other Dominicans who claimed to have been present said
that policemen, when they weren't firing, struck people, including women, with their rifle butts as they were on their knees
in prayer. A butcher was killed as he was leaving his tiny, board-
walled shop across the street from the church. Below a bullet
hole in the wall, flies swirled around chunks of meat still left
on a table. Another man was killed in a nearby house when a
bullet struck him as he was about to enter a shower.

A machine gun set up in front of the local police station and
roving jeeploads of policemen reminded the populace that they
had better not shout again, "Viva the Constitution," the slogan
of the demonstrators. An indeterminable number of people
were under arrest. A few weeks later, a mob attacked the police
station and took it over for a while until they were overpowered
in a new bloodbath.

In Puerto Plata, about 200 people—lawyers, doctors, businessmen, secretaries—were jailed for two weeks, but almost all were
released two days before we arrived after word falsely spread,
Dominicans said, that OAS representatives were on their way
to the town. Antonio "Cuchi" Imbert, son of the junta leader,
who comes from this town, personally participated in house-to-
house arrests, some released prisoners said. Cuchi was a captain
in the police force.

"I was dragged out of my house by the police," one prisoner,
an intense, dark-complexioned man, said. "At the jail, I was
thrown into a cell about twenty by ten feet with some hundred
other people. The only ones with beds were the common criminals. Political prisoners had to sleep on the cement floor."

When we asked the man for his name, he replied: "You give me a hundred men with guns and I'll give you my name."

One woman, a teacher, told how she had been put in a cell with two murderesses. Other released prisoners said that beatings by the guards had been common. All maintained that they had been given no reason for their arrest.

An indication of the widespread indignation engendered by such police action lay in a strike by all of the 450 students at the local high school in protest against the arrest of two teachers. In a sympathy move, students from a Catholic high school delivered gifts to the imprisoned teachers.

Terror also extended to murder in some parts of the country. An official at rebel headquarters told a group of correspondents, including myself, that eight bodies had been found dead along the Yuna River on the road from Victoria Prison. Some days later, Caamaño accused Imbert of executing 56 people in the vicinity. UN and OAS officials went to have a look, and at a stud farm once owned by Rhadames Trujillo, the second son of the dictator, were led by farmers to the graves of some bodies. The farmers had buried them. UN representative Major General I. J. Rikhye reported that "evidence is sufficient to say that killings took place here and that the bodies were cremated here." Ward Just of *Newsweek* magazine, who went along with the investigators, saw a mound of freshly turned earth nearby, started digging, and found another body, that of a youth.

In mid-July, the OAS issued a report by three criminologists indicating that the bodies of 17 persons who died under mysterious circumstances were found in areas controlled by Imbert. "Strong indications exist," said the report, "that the arrests, movement of prisoners, and the executions may be attributed to police and military elements."

Trujillo, it seemed, had indeed come back.

And so, while Imbert consolidated his position throughout the country, Caamaño stewed in anger, frustration, and disillusionment in his empire of a few square blocks, gradually realiz-

ing that the hopes that had soared when Bundy returned to
Washington had been rooted in sand. He and his followers
bitterly attacked a statement by Secretary of State Rusk referring to the desirability of a strong OAS influence in the country.
They argued that this statement ran directly counter to a remark made by President Johnson several days before calling
for a constitutional government—though not specifically desig-
nating the 1963 Constitution.

A new wave of tension rolled across the city as the rebels
feared that the United States was reverting to something approaching a pro-Imbert position, and might permit the loyalists
to attack Cuidad Nueva after all. They dug sandbag-protected
trenches in park squares and distributed about 10,000 Molotov
cocktails. They began, for the first time, to search cars at checkpoints with meticulous care, looking for arms. In fact, it became
difficult to drive three blocks in the rebel zone without being
asked for identification.

Tension was high indeed one day after loyalist troops in the
National Palace, which was in a no man's land between the
International Safety Zone and the rebel zone, shot a girl of
fourteen as she was crossing the street a short distance away.
Several rebels took four reporters, including myself, to the hospital to see the body. It was the same hospital where I had gone
to see the wounded and dead marines about three weeks before.
And the girl lay on the same table where one of the dead
marines had lain.

A colored girl with small, sensitive features, she was wearing
a blue silk Sunday dress. Her scalp was blotted with blood where
the bullet had entered, and her hands were clasped stiffly in
front of her. Otherwise, she gave the impression of being peacefully asleep, in dreamy repose, a sweetly innocent child who
couldn't possibly have been caught up in the violence, hatred,
and misery of the adult world around her. But there she lay—
dead. And in the eyes of those who silently crowded around—
rebel officials, relatives, hospital attendants—I saw, with a sense

of horror, the controlled despair of people overly familiar with death and suffering and the logic of bloodstains on a silk Sunday dress. But I also saw the brightness of an emerging strength, the strength given to people in the throes of desperation, to those who do not fear death because they have lived like dead men.

When I asked one guard who searched my car with particular devotion who and how he expected the rebels to fight, considering that the rebel zone was sealed off he replied with a surly, tense expression: "I don't know, but if we don't get a good answer from the Yankees soon, we're just going to fight."

But the rebels did not get a "good answer." The Guzmán formula, it soon became clear, was no longer being considered in Washington. Instead, the United States decided to start all over again, this time using the OAS as the instrument for peacemaking in order to reduce as much as possible, at least on the surface, the unilateral nature of the outside interference in Dominican affairs. The OAS had been represented in Santo Domingo almost uninterruptedly after the arrival of the five-man peace team on May 2, but had accomplished little. For one thing, the rebels were convinced that the group was simply taking orders from the United States, particularly as no large democratic countries were represented on it, and did little to cooperate with it. For another, the team did show surprisingly little initiative in pushing for a real cease-fire, particularly after Imbert's forces started advancing in the northern part of the city.

When the UN then decided to send a representative at the rebels' request, the team picked up its marbles and indignantly went home, convinced that its efforts to make peace were being undercut by that organization. But Secretary-General José Mora soon returned alone with greater powers than the five-man team had had. Prodded by the "competitive" activities of the UN, Mora, who had never been reputed for aggressiveness in dealing with problems, contributed materially to keeping tempers cool, though he did not have too much of a substantial nature to do while the Bundy mission was negotiating on its own.

A heavyset Uruguayan with jowls and long slicked-back hair who had never been seen in Washington without a neatly starched shirt and a perfectly pressed suit, Mora seemed suddenly to discard the trappings of dignity in a determined effort at at least keep the peace, running constantly from the office of Imbert to that of Caamaño to that of the papal nuncio. He worked through the night, appearing at dinner, unimaginably, with an open shirt. He refused to be ruffled, no matter what went wrong. He was even able to recover with remarkable speed from a minor humiliation he suffered when he told a news conference that, among his accomplishments, he had helped to get the city's electrical network working again. Hardly had he spoken when the hotel suffered a power failure and the lights went out.

One of his major achievements, registered with the help of his extremely able adviser, Arturo Morales Carrión, who had helped to establish democracy in the Dominican Republic after Trujillo's death, was getting both sides to accept an arrangement for neutralizing the National Palace. Imbert agreed to remove several hundred men from the palace, leaving only a token force of 25, Caamaño agreed to move his forces from the vicinity, and both sides approved the stationing of Brazilian troops on the palace grounds.

Mora's efforts finally antagonized both sides. Tipped off that Imbert, who was short of revenue, planned to remove the funds stocked in the Central Bank in the International Safety Zone, the Secretary-General called for U. S. troops to be sent to the bank on the night that Imbert was to move. When Imbert soldiers arrived to make the withdrawal, they found the U. S. troops there. The funds remained in the bank.

Simultaneously, Mora irked the rebels by announcing that the OAS would meet, with U. S. funds, the May salaries of all government employees, regardless of which government they worked for. Imbert, for whose regime the bulk of such employees worked, readily agreed to accept the money. But Caamaño angrily refused. He maintained that such payment would only serve to prolong the life of the Imbert regime. Furthermore, he pointed out, payroll checks were signed by the junta finance minister. He would no longer deal with Mora, he announced, venting his fury on an individual apparently so that he could make the rebel point without breaking his links with the United States and the OAS as an organization.

With the United States now in need of a new negotiating team and with Mora boycotted by the rebels, Washington decided to kill two birds with one stone. Ellsworth Bunker, who was both the U. S. Ambassador to the OAS and the chairman of the OAS Council, was just the man to go to Santo Domingo. Together with two other OAS Ambassadors, Illmar Penna Marinho of Brazil and Ramón Clairmont Duenas of El Salvador, he went, representing the interests of both the United States and the OAS.

For two weeks the team negotiated with both sides unsuccessfully. And then, on June 15, the inevitable explosion in Ciudad Nueva came. A fire fight broke out on that morning between rebel sharpshooters and U. S. troops, who now belonged to the OAS Inter-American Peace Force, which ballooned into one of the biggest battles of the crisis. The Peace Force commander, Brazilian General Hugo Panasco Alvim, charged that the rebels had started the firing, and that OAS troops only acted after the most extreme provocation.

The rebels had a different story. According to Pedro Casals Victoria, who had tried to organize the Santiago revolt and was later captured and placed in a junta prison for a few weeks, a junta official had told him during his confinement—two days before the battle—that U. S. troops planned to provoke an incident which would give them the opportunity to attack in force. The official, he said, indicated the placement and caliber of the mortars that were to be used in the assault. Casals asserted that he informed his sister of the plan when she visited him in prison, and that she relayed the information to a high rebel official.

"I advised our command to denounce the plan before it could be implemented," Casals said, "but nobody took it seriously."

However the battle started, paratroopers blasted their way four blocks in Ciudad Nueva while U. S. guns across the Ozama River fired in the vicinity of Caamaño's headquarters, destroying and setting buildings afire. A truce was finally reached in the evening with the OAS forces, but shells apparently fired by Imbert troops continued to explode in the area for several more hours. When calm finally settled on the tortured city, four Americans and 67 Dominicans were dead, and 36 OAS soldiers and 265 rebels were wounded.

Caamaño accused U. S. troops of committing "an act of genocide without precedent in our country," charging that "it was a form of pressure by the OAS to force us to accept an undignified solution" to the civil war. U. S. officials did not deny that they hoped the incident would render the rebels more amenable to a "reasonable" settlement.

In any event, shortly thereafter the OAS group proposed a plan calling for the return of all army regulars to the armed forces and "irregulars" to civilian life; formation of a neutral provisional government headed by Héctor García Godoy, who had been Foreign Minister and Ambassador to Great Britain in the Bosch regime; collection by the temporary government of all arms in the hands of civilians; and elections in nine months. All this would be done under the supervision of the Inter-American Peace Force. With some conditions, both Caamaño and Imbert seemed interested. The constitutionalists, in danger of being destroyed altogether, had finally indicated that they would give up their struggle for restoration of the 1963 Constitution, in the hope that in a genuinely free election, Bosch or some other democrat would win anyway. Their principal condition was that Wessin and several other top junta officers be dismissed. They privately warned that if this condition were not met, they might, in fact, release a tape recording they claimed to have of telephone conversations in which two U. S. military attachés allegedly asked the junta leaders to bomb the rebels, early in the revolution.

The OAS made some concessions to the rebels, and its peace plan was finally approved at the end of August. The way was thus cleared for the installation of García Godoy as Provisional President in September. Under a gentleman's agreement García Godoy promised, with the OAS team's knowledge, to oust the traditionalists officers when he took office.

Meanwhile, Joaquín Balaguer, Trujillo's old puppet president, returned from exile in early July. Imbert had granted him a 72-hour visa so that he could see his dying mother. But no one insisted that he leave. Certainly not the United States, which saw him as a possible answer to its troubles. He was popular despite his Trujilloist background because of his demagoguery following the dictator's death. He could perhaps beat Bosch or whatever other candidate the PRD put up. But even the State Department was reluctant to deal with him directly. It used a Washington lobbyist, I. Irving Davidson, one of whose clients is Haitian dictator François Duvalier, to speak with him shortly before the Dominican politican left for his homeland.

Balaguer had fled his country after the Kennedy Administration had helped to thwart a military coup against the fledgling Dominican democracy. Now the Johnson Administration apparently saw him as its best hope for a new Dominican democracy. And thus had the wheel turned full circle.

CHAPTER 11

The Core of a Dilemma

THE United States role in the Dominican crisis pointed up the dilemma in which Washington finds itself entrapped in Latin America. The Johnson Administration has been accused, particularly since its Dominican intervention, of reverting to the days of "gunboat diplomacy" when force was commonly used to impose the will of the United States on the Latin-American countries. On the surface, this might seem true. Marines were, after all, sent into the Dominican Republic in 1965 just as they were sent into hemispheric countries, including the Dominican Republic, in the days of Theodore Roosevelt.

But there is a big difference. In the past, the marines, and other instruments of force, were used primarily for the purpose of furthering U. S. economic and strategic interests. Washington, in fact, rationalized that it had a moral right to do this, since where U. S. capital went local living standards rose. It did not seem to occur to U. S. leaders that this big-stick policy of casual intervention was a form of colonialism alien to the U. S. tradition. Nor did they appear to realize, especially before President Franklin D. Roosevelt instituted far-reaching social reforms in the United States itself, that the economic advantages of U. S. "imperialism" benefited only the ruling classes to the exclusion of the suppressed lower classes.

A gradual change in the U. S. attitude began on a substantial basis with F.D.R.'s Good Neighbor policy, with the accent on nonintervention by the United States in the internal affairs of its Latin-American neighbors. This process crystallized into a truly revolutionary shift in thinking with the inauguration of President Kennedy's Alliance for Progress, which was intended to foster large-scale social and economic development within a democratic framework.

In a sense, the Alliance was a negation of the Good Neighbor policy. For whereas the latter gave the United States an excuse to recognize and accept any rightist or militarist who might come to power in a Latin-American country, since the United States was bound not to interfere, the Alliance, in calling for democratic reforms, gave the United States an excuse to exert pressure for the establishment of democratic regimes. And this excuse, as indicated earlier, was used to the maximum degree when Kennedy sent warships to the Dominican Republic in 1962 to save the country for democracy. In other words, he reintroduced the policy of intervention, but in the service of the people rather than of the dictators as had been the case in the pre-F.D.R. decades.

How does the Dominican intervention differ from the "gunboat diplomacy" of those decades? The guiding purpose of the latter was basically colonial in nature, but this was not true of the former. The Johnson Administration sent troops to Santo Domingo as the result of a genuine fear, whether justified or not, that a second Cuba was about to materialize. These troops were sent with the greatest reluctance and not with the casualness that characterized "big stick" thinking. Collaboration with rightist, nondemocratic forces was pursued as a temporary tactical need in the face of an emergency, not as a matter of policy.

The Johnson Administration is still basically committed to the principles of the Alliance for Progress as espoused by President Kennedy, and the Dominican adventure appears to have been an individual diversion from the main track of policy.

But the fact that this diversion was considered necessary is the core of the American dilemma. On the one hand, Washington wants to promote democratic development as an essential alternative to Castro communism among the oppressed masses. But on the other, it fears such development, particularly in the less-developed countries, since inexperienced democratic regimes, it feels, in many cases subconsciously, will prove less resistant to Communist infiltration than the rightist military regimes with which U. S. diplomats have for so long dealt. It was true that many of these regimes often cozied up to the Communists for their own tactical ends, but there was always a residual confidence that the militarists, with their penchant for the use of force when necessary, would know how to handle the Reds.

Thus, conditioned by the diplomat's ingrained reluctance to gamble on unknown quantities—and democracy, particularly in the Caribbean area, is largely an unknown quantity—U. S. officials, when they see the slightest danger of a Communist advance, veer almost reflexively toward the strongman rather than the democrat for suppression of the threat.

And they are encouraged to do so, in most cases, by the natural tendency of the democrats to assume a more independent and nationalistic attitude than the dictators who, lacking popular support, must often depend on U. S. backing to stay in power. Juan Bosch told me in a mood of bitter reflection:

"Washington is not satisfied with a government that is friendly and cooperative. It wants a government that it can control completely. But it cannot control a democratic government completely, because such a government is responsible to the people, not to any foreign power."

U. S. distrust of democracy is bound to be most pronounced of all during a popular revolution. Since Communists are certain to participate for their own purposes and since they are usually the best-organized street fighters, the chances of a Red takeover are correspondingly greater. Yet part of the U. S.

dilemma is that revolutions take place only against undemocratic governments, since violence is usually the only substitute
for elections in the establishment of a popular regime. Therefore, the United States, by supporting unconstitutional governments, however reluctantly, for the purpose of averting communism, may be actually promoting the conditions which
sooner or later will produce revolution and give the Communists
their best opportunity for a power grab.

Even the fact that Castro took over not from a democratic
regime but from a military dictatorship has not been sufficient
to bring home this point to many U. S. officials. On the contrary, Castro's victory appears to have frightened U. S. policy
makers into growing reluctance to trust democracy. As Bosch,
referring to Castro's public declaration in December 1961 pro-
claiming himself a Marxist-Leninst, wrote recently:

> With this declaration Fidel Castro, who had been the leader
> of a fervently popular democratic revolution, engraved in red
> one single word, "Communist," on every attempt to make a dem-
> ocratic revolution for a long time to come. It is hazardous to say
> whether he did so consciously or unconsciously, but there can
> be no doubt that by doing so he rendered an incalculable service
> to the cause of world communism, since after his declaration it
> became virtually and even totally impossible to make a demo-
> cratic revolution in this part of the world, and without a demo-
> cratic revolution in Latin America there is no way out. The
> Latin-American revolution, which is inevitable even if it takes
> 15, 20, or 25 years, should not be Communist, but the fear of the
> democratic revolution will make it sooner or later fall into the
> pattern of a Communist revolution.

The lesson was clear enough in the Dominican Republic.
When the de facto Reid Cabral government fell, the United
States, fearful of Communist infiltration, decided not to support
the return of Bosch, thereby encouraging the military to resist
his return. This resistance, in turn, set off the revolution, which
sparked the Communists to life. The landing of U. S. troops

followed. Critics of the Administration's actions say that all this might have been avoided if Washington had helped to set up a constitutional barrier against communism. If the United States had tried so hard to keep Bosch in power a year and a half before, apparently unfearful that he would lead the country to communism, why, they ask, was his return suddenly regarded with fear? Was it consistent of the United States, which has so often publicized its desire for constitutional governments, to refuse to back the constitutional leader, and, in fact, to support the very forces it had so castigated for throwing him out? Was it, in the last analysis, for the United States to judge who would be best for the Dominican people after they had made a free choice of their own?

It is not enough, argue these critics, for the United States to desire democratic government. It should also promote it in active opposition to the rightist-military regimes. It must realize that the sole genuinely effective barrier to communism is constitutionalism, together with social reform that will make democracy more than window dressing; that the Communists shouldn't be given the power to destroy the credibility of democratic movements by simply attaching themselves to it; that people enjoying the benefits of political freedom and social equality turn a deaf ear toward communism since they already have what the Communists promise but never give; and that the political stability achieved under military rule is a temporary illusion that could eventually burst with the buildup of social revolutionary pressures, and possibly produce the very communism that the strongmen are supposed to suppress, as Cuba so tragically illustrated.

Some Administration officials hold that the United States cannot always afford to gamble on an ineffectual democratic government. Other observers agree that it is, of course, a gamble to support democracy whether or not the United States happens to like the electoral choice, but that in the end, to support an unconstitutional regime with no popular mandate is, in Latin America, a much greater gamble.

President Kennedy appears to have felt that way, and that is why he so strongly supported Dominican democracy, though even he would not go all the way, hoping to have his constitutional cake and eat it, too. He supported not only Bosch, but also the Trujilloite armed forces as a factor of stability, though it was clear that Bosch could never have real power as long as the militarists remained unpurged.

Basically, the Latin-American philosophies of the Kennedy and Johnson Administrations are the same. Both have envisaged the Alliance for Progress as an instrument to foster economic, social, and political reforms in Latin America. But their differences lie in their methods of pursuing this end. President Kennedy gave the Alliance an idealistic, revolutionary tone through the exertion of powerful unilateral pressures on reluctant governments for reforms by speaking directly to the Latin people of their right to such benefits, and by using diplomatic and economic leverage on these regimes.

At first, President Kennedy applied his antidictator policy rigidly, as illustrated by the dispatch of warships to Dominican waters in 1961. Also, when a military junta overturned democracy in Peru in 1962, he publicly denounced the coup in the harshest terms he was ever to use after such an event, and cut off diplomatic and economic relations for several months. But as new coups occurred, he eased up on his reaction, feeling that his tactics in Peru had not worked. In reality, they had worked. They frightened the military into holding free elections within a year, and, even more important from a long-range point of view, helped to persuade Latin Americans that, whether or not the United States actually succeeded in forcing dictatorships out of power, it was finally on the side of the people.

In general, however, the Kennedy Administration was tough on Latin-American governments that came into power through the use of force. At the same time, President Kennedy emphasized in public and in private to militarists that coups would bring immediate and strong U. S. "sanctions"—suspension of diplomatic ties and economic aid.

Gradually, this warning-and-action policy began to yield fruit. The Argentine as well as the Peruvian junta restored constitutional rule, and others promised to hold elections within two years.

The Johnson Administration has not invalidated this approach but has greatly diluted it. President Johnson and Thomas C. Mann, the principal designer of his Latin-American policies, are more conservative tacticians than were President Kennedy and his top advisers on Latin America. They started in where the previous policy makers left off in moving toward greater "pragmatism," or diplomatic conservatism, in the handling of democratic development. They have been less willing to take a chance on new approaches to the Communist problem. Their attitude has been geared not to the "punishing" of dictators and coup perpetrators, but to the more cautious approach of trying to guide juntas back toward democracy once a coup has occurred —if democracy can be trusted in the country in question.

Thus, the Johnson Administration, while keeping public pronouncements to a minimum after democratic setbacks, in a sharp tone-down of the Kennedy attitude of indignation, has tended to deal in a conventional way with all Latin-American governments, except Cuba, of course. While affirming the need for democracy, it has pragmatically indicated the desirability of maintaining good relations with all non-Communist governments, whether democratic or not.

This policy of "pragmatism," it was felt, could ease the way toward both democratic development and possible collaboration with the military in the event of a Communist threat. What happened was that the Johnson Administration reduced the stress that President Kennedy had placed on democracy and increased the stress on the Kennedy tactic of dealing with the traditional militarists. As a result, it appears, when a Communist threat was thought to have emerged in the Dominican Republic, the Johnson Administration, unlike its predecessor, was conditioned to look not to the democrats, but to the militarists for the answer. It ignored Bosch and embraced Wessin.

An integral part of this "pragmatic" policy has been, naturally enough, to assign "pragmatic," that is, traditional-style, ambassadors to most Latin-American countries. Diplomats like Bennett would probably be just right for developed countries with basically middle-class cultures. They would have no social problem, nor would they have to deal with many social problems. But in the underdeveloped world, particularly in Latin America, which has a special background and psychological relationship with the United States, such men can only damage American efforts to build bridges to them.

It is not necessarily their fault. According to some people who know Bennett, for example, he really wanted to get to know the people. But he simply didn't have the training or the temperament to succeed. Except for ceremonial purposes, it simply wasn't in character for him to visit the villages, speak with the people, and and strike up warm friendships with leaders of political parties with a lower-class base. He wouldn't know how to dress for the occasion or what to say to a poor farmer or worker. On the other hand, he felt perfectly at home with the upper classes, not necessarily the aristocrats, but with the upper-middle-class businessmen, professional men, and politicians. Inevitably, they molded his thinking.

Yet the lower classes must be dealt with if the United States is really to foster democracy in Latin America, for the simple reason that democracy is based on the consent of the majority, and the vast majority of people are members of the lower classes.

President Kennedy, realizing this, made every attempt to give the Alliance for Progress, which is dedicated mainly to the social and economic development of those classes, a grass-roots flavor, in his policies, his speeches, and the kind of men he sent to Latin America, men like Murat W. Williams, former Ambassador to El Salvador, Ben S. Stephansky, former Ambassador to Bolivia,

and yes, John Bartlow Martin, who disappointed most Dominicans in the civil war, but who, like the others, was an ambassador
to the people and not just to the government. They were men
who helped to change the image of the United States in Latin
America during the Kennedy era, and who were at least partly
responsible for the late President's incredible popularity in virtually every Latin-American nation. They were men whom the
Communists couldn't easily fight. Understandably, the Reds and
the oligarchs have one thing in common: they both prefer traditional-style American diplomats.

Typically, Bennett, in supporting Wessin so strongly from the
very beginning, was working against the declared policy of his
government, which is to foster democracy. He, and his supporters in Washington, ignored the most fundamental of all
political facts in Latin America, and particularly in the Dominican Republic—that the power of the traditional militarists must
be eliminated, certainly not enhanced, if democracy is to have
a real chance to flourish. And, as a corollary, that young, constitutionally minded officers like Colonel Fernández Domínguez,
who have learned their democracy in the United States, are the
real military hope for halting the advance of communism, just
as the democratic politicians are the political hope. Such realization must be the kernel of any solution to the U. S. dilemma.

Closely related to the Johnson Administration's "pragmatic"
attitude toward democracy is its policy in the realm of social
reform. Actually, social reform does not pose nearly the problem in the Dominican Republic that it does in many Latin-
American countries, since the Trujillo family owned most of the
land and controlled most of the big industrial enterprises in
the country. The Dominican problem is mainly one of proper
administration and redistribution of this wealth, not of getting
entrenched oligarchs to share what they have with the people.
This, in fact, is probably one reason why the political aspects
of reform are relatively more important to the Dominican
people than to most other Latin Americans. In some Latin-

American countries the exploited people think primarily of just ending feudalism, which is keeping them in virtual slavery.

But the Administration's treatment of the social problem does help to throw light in some degree on what has happened in Santo Domingo. The Latin-American policy makers in Washington strongly favor social reform just as they favor political democracy. But they do not appear to regard social change in the sense of peaceful revolution, as President Kennedy did. In one of his most stirring addresses, the late President called on Latin-American countries in March 1961, when he first proposed the Alliance for Progress, to join with the United States in "a vast cooperative effort, unparalleled in magnitude and nobility of purpose, to satisfy the basic needs of the American people for homes, work and land, health and schools."

A year later, on the first anniversary of the Alliance, he said in another speech: "... We must not forget that our Alliance for Progress is more than a doctrine of development—a blueprint of economic advance. . . . It says that in our hemisphere no society is free until all its people have an equal opportunity to share the fruits of their own land and their own labor. And it says that material progress is meaningless without individual freedom and political liberty."

While the Johnson Administration subscribes to the basic tenets of this Kennedy philosophy, it has thought more in terms of evolution than peaceful revolution, in respect to both speed and spirit. It views progress in Latin America as a rolling motion in which, as Mann has said, political, social, and economic advances are registered together, each of these factors being dependent on the others. Typically, U. S. officials have told me that immediate large-scale redistribution of land could be interpreted by foreign investors as an invasion of property rights and might discourage needed foreign investment.

The theory attributed to the Johnson Administration is that prosperous, anti-Communist Latin-American societies can best be achieved by giving middle-class development priority over lower-class advancement. Such thinking is perceived not only in the seemingly growing U. S. disinterest in such structural reforms as land redistribution, but also, for example, in the expenditure of most housing and educational aid funds for the apparent purpose of building up the middle class. Of nearly $400 million committed by the United States to housing loans under the Alliance by the end of 1964, almost all was to go for houses—the average costing almost $3000—intended for the upper one-fourth income strata of Latin America, though this situation began to improve in 1965. As for education, the U. S. allocation of about $55 million yearly, or less than six percent of America's Alliance contribution, is about equal to the sum expended on the U. S. military aid program in the area.

Whatever the merits of the theory of middle-class priority, it would seem to have little appeal for the vastly underprivileged lower strata of Latin Americans who would be expected to wait patiently, while ignoring Communist blandishments, until justice finally seeps down to them. Freedom from feudalism, they feel, is more urgent than long-term economic development.

Supporters of the Kennedy formula, including many social reform experts for the OAS and the Inter-American Development Bank, seem to back the thesis that social progress must proceed at a swifter rate than economic development. As Arturo Morales Carrión, Special Adviser to the OAS Secretary-General, put it: "Economic development is, of course, an urgent need. But it must of necessity take a relatively long time. Social change cannot wait because the people will not wait." In other words, it is argued, economic development, if social reforms are not rapidly forthcoming, could come within a Communist context, just as social reforms, if democracy is not forthcoming, could also come within this context.

The Administration's distrust in hemispheric democracy reflects a lack of understanding not only of the basic forces at work in Latin America, but of the unique problem posed by that area in relation to other underdeveloped regions. President Kennedy did seem to have appreciated this distinction. He thus emphasized the need for democracy in Latin America, but, in general, did not do so in the Afro-Asian world. A coup in Thailand or in Afghanistan, for example, elicited no White House statements about the importance of constitutionality.

The difference lies basically in the social and cultural backgrounds of Latin America on the one hand, and the Afro-Asian world on the other. The Afro-Asian nations settled their most important social problems when they ousted the European colonialists who had both exploited and helped them for many decades. These colonialists had, in a sense, played the role of the upper ruling class of society. Their physical departure left in charge, in most cases, indigenous nationalists with at least some roots in the people. Many of these nationalist leaders have become dictators, and many are corrupt, but they have also displayed varying degrees of social consciousness. If they haven't given their people political freedom—and in many cases, the Afro-Asians are too underdeveloped to understand the modern state, much less democracy, which, in general, is completely alien to their clan, tribal, and village cultures—they have given them a feeling of being equal with their fellows, and they have instituted many social reforms, often too many in relation to the available resources. Democracy in some of these countries, therefore, is not necessarily an essential prerequisite for social and economic progress, and in some cases is not even desired by the people.

The contrary is true, however, in Latin America. For one thing, it is not as easy there to throw out exploiting colonialists. They are not foreigners, but part of the country; built-in colonialists whose Spanish ancestors (Portuguese in the case of Brazil) ruled the continent with an iron hand. These ancestors left a legacy of feudal authoritarianism with those sons who decided not to return to Spain and Portugal when the Latin-American nations won independence. That legacy is today at the root of the region's troubles. As reflected in the case of the

Dominican Republic, the independent oligarchies that developed allied themselves with ambitious middle-class military officers who discovered that profitable business opportunities, social prestige, and important privileges could flow from such arrangements.

Thus, no Ataturks have ruled in Latin America. The dictators there have seldom had roots in the people, nor any inclination to promote social reform, or even economic progress beyond that which has been beneficial to themselves and their relatives and friends. Under these circumstances, real social and economic advances can only be made if the people have a direct say in the government. And this means, in the Latin-American context, either democracy or the twisted equality of communism.

Democracy, if given the opportunity, would have a particularly good chance, since most Latin Americans, unlike most Afro-Asians, have a basic understanding of modern political systems because of their higher educational levels, their Western-oriented culture, their proximity to the biggest democracy in the world—and above all, their particularly agonizing experience with oppressive dictatorships.

The tendency of the Johnson Administration, however, to apply uniform solutions to the Communist problem in all threatened or supposedly threatened countries could be seen in the common approaches it has taken in Viet-Nam and the Dominican Republic, though the situations in those two countries are in no way comparable.

In Viet-Nam, the struggle is that of a minority of Communists supported by outside Communist forces to impose communism on the majority of people by force as a prelude to the conquest, by military or subversive means, of all Asia. As I wrote in *Subversion of the Innocents* in 1962, "if the United States permits South Viet-Nam to fall, even through the latter's own weaknesses—and as a last resort the United States may have to dispatch fighting troops to prevent such a disaster—it might just as well abandon all Southeast Asia to the Communists."

The troops have had to go into Viet-Nam in force, and they may have to stay there until such time, whenever that may be, as the Red Chinese and North Vietnamese are prepared to agree to meaningful negotiations that will ensure the independence of the non-Communist Asian nations.

But the troops who were sent into the Dominican Republic basically confronted not the Communists, whose cause was immeasurably helped by the anti-rebel character of their mission, but the Dominican majority which wants democracy and rejects communism, regardless of Red efforts to exploit the situation. By doing this, the United States not only unnecessarily antagonized people who were among the best friends it had, but it placed in question, by casting doubts on the Administration's judgment and credibility, the wisdom of its action in Viet-Nam.

Certainly the Dominican experience was a serious diplomatic and moral setback in the relationship between the United States and Latin America, which had so improved over the last few decades, and particularly in the last few years. But it need not be a permanent reversal. President Johnson, whose great breadth of vision and humanity is so clearly mirrored in his program for a Great Society at home, can still reach the hearts of Latin Americans if he makes an earnest effort to explore what is in their hearts.

The fact that many American officials privately admit, some with a sense of regret bordering on shame, that the United States blundered reflects the likelihood that this country will think twice before making such blunders in a similar situation next time. And for all the anger and resentment of the Latin-American democrats, most of them appear to realize that the Dominican episode was not a return to the bitter past, but an unfortunate digression from the road leading to a brighter future. The Administration, it can be hoped, will demonstrate that it was nothing more.